OAKWOOD REMINISCENCES SERIES

DERBY DAYS

Memories of a Midland Railwayman

by
John Weston

THE OAKWOOD PRESS

British Library Cataloguing in Publication Data
A Record for this book is available from the British Library
ISBN 978 0 85361 724 2

Typeset by Oakwood Graphics.
Repro by PKmediaworks, Cranborne, Dorset.
Printed by Berforts Information Press Ltd, Eynsham, Oxford.

Acknowledgements

I wish to thank:

Colin Garratt (the railway photographer) for recommending Oakwood Press to me.
Michael Arkle (the inspirational former Head Teacher of our village school). He did much of the typing of my handwritten first draft.
Steve Andrews (a former journalist, and local resident) who initially advised me about writing techniques.
James Lindsay (Railway Chaplain) for his interest and encouragement.
My sister, Ida Wright, for the family photographs.
Neighbour Mick Shaw for local photographs.
The *Derby Evening Telegraph* for publishing letters and short stories I have written over the years.
All other friends and neighbours who have read through and listened to my stories, for their constructive criticism.
My daughter, Helen Devaney, for helping me to bring the whole book together, so that it was suitable for submission to the publishers.
The Oakwood Press, for realising the ambition to get this into print.

Front cover: Midland Compound 4-4-0 No. 1000 departs from Derby on 13th August, 1959 on its first run after being refurbished and painted in Midland Railway livery. I am leaning out of the cab with Reg Haynes, running inspector. The BBC sent a camera crew along to film for its 'Blue Peter' programme. *R.J. Buckley*

Title page: Ex-LMS Stanier '8F' class 2-8-0 No. 48167 passes Derby North Junction signal box with a freight train *circa* 1963. *P.J. Lynch/Kidderminster Railway Museum*

Rear cover: The Railway Clearing House junction diagram for Derby, 1913.

Published by The Oakwood Press (Usk), P.O. Box 13, Usk, Mon., NP15 1YS.
E-mail: sales@oakwoodpress.co.uk
Website: www.oakwoodpress.co.uk

Contents

LMS-built Compound 4-4-0 No. 41077 arrives at Trent with a Derby-St Pancras relief passenger train in August 1953. The Compounds worked heavy passenger trains all over the system.
J.F. Henton

Johnson 0-6-0 '2F' class 0-6-0 No. 58246 and Fowler '4F' class 0-6-0 No. 43978 at Derby No. 4 shed on 17th February, 1957. We worked the class '2' engines tender-first from Shirland colliery, and suffered because the small cab roof offered no protection from the weather. Note the stores window (from where we collected cleaning materials) is just visible in the left of the picture.
A.N.H. Glover/Kidderminster Railway Museum

Introduction

I began writing my personal history over 20 years ago. I have often thought about what shape my introduction should take. One man, one book, which no-one else could write.

As a railwayman working in the Midlands, based at Derby motive power depot, my story is of the working practices of a very high standard, those of the Midland Railway, at the great railway town which was the headquarters of that company. If you want to know exactly what that means, I would recommend that you also read *Derby and the Midland Railway* by Peter Billson and published by Breedon Books. A great historical survey of where and how it all began.

My total railway service encompassed 44 years, starting in September 1937. My first nine months were pure hard graft, black wax and elbow grease. Coming in towards the end of a 3½ year period of recruitment by the railway, I would always be at the back end of the line of promotion, cleaner to fireman to driver. All subject to passing the strict medical and eyesight examinations, and being able to stand up to the disciplined life of a footplateman.

Starting as engine cleaner, if you can cope with the hazards of working on a steam locomotive, all the rigours of shift-working, one day you will reach another position – fireman. You will spend a varying number of years at that grade, working with men who will be anything from 20 to 40 years older than you. Engine drivers, many of whom will have shared your experiences. Just a few will treat you harshly, or will have standards that you will not wish to copy.

You will work with some drivers for just one day, particularly if you are a passed cleaner, the 'Maid of all Work'. Later, as a fireman, you will work with the same driver for six months, or even a calendar year. Many of them will be experienced and highly competent enginemen, which is what you will aspire to be one day yourself: able to work any class of train over any section of the line. One day you will make out a route card, deciding where that line will be. Some men prefer to work on local trips, shed or shunting duties. Some others will be forced into this kind of work due to medical or eyesight problems.

At a big locomotive depot, which Derby No. 4 shed certainly was, the young engine cleaners recruited in the Autumn of 1937 had a hard and slow journey on their path to becoming a driver. Some fell out along the way, but most of us who came back to No. 4 shed after a period of redundancy stuck it out right through to retirement.

A long journey, but what a journey. One that spanned the years when the steam engine was the king of the road, to the days when it was shunted into the breaker's yard. To be replaced by the more efficient, but less loved diesel traction.

I have read a number of books by other enginemen. Some of them had interesting experiences as firemen, but never became drivers. And there is even one by a man who started on exactly the same day as I did. Not at Derby, but at a small depot near Walsall. It is a good read.

Of the thousands of enginemen who served their time at Derby No. 4 shed in the steam era, only one has ever written in detail of all the highs and lows, of a journey through his life. Of a time that can never be repeated. For me it has been a privilege to make this very personal, very special journey. I hope that you will follow it through with me.

White House Farm, Tonge, where my sister and I were born and brought up. I remember the laburnum tree in the front garden with beautiful plumes of yellow flowers in the early summer. The old Methodist chapel, which I remember as being across the road, has been demolished and replaced by houses since I was a child. *Author's Collection*

One of our four fields. We called it the 'Big Field' being over five acres, the others were around three acres. This photograph was taken some time after I had left home to work on the railway, when my sister Ida and her family were working the farm, we never used a baler for haymaking when I helped with the harvest. When I was young this field still bore the evidence of 'strip working' from much earlier times. Tonge had been quite a big village at one time, and there may have been as many as 20 families dependent on crops grown in this field. *Author's Collection*

Chapter One

Living off the Land

In 1919, the victorious powers of Europe were carving up the great empires - and making such a mess of it that war broke out again 20 years later. In the same year, an event of rather less significance to them - but much more to me - took place in the tiny village of Tonge on the Leicestershire/Derbyshire border.

Like most of us, I date my earliest memories from the age of three or thereabouts. And I first began to take it all in during the Christmas of 1922.

There's magic in the air. Young John Albert Weston, a bit over three years old, just beginning to look about, secure in the knowledge that Santa Claus would be coming to my house. I had his personal assurance of that.

At the side of our kitchen fireplace, in the angle between the chimney-breast and the door to the front room, was a cupboard with three triangular shelves, on which stood all the things we used at mealtimes.

Two or three weeks before Christmas, my father, sitting by the fireside with me on his knee, called on Santa Claus who, according to him and my mother, was at the top of our chimney. So I was told to listen out for him. My father reached back to the cupboard door and knocked a couple of times, 'Are you there, Santy?', he asked. A voice from way up the chimney replied, 'I'm here'. 'Are you coming?', asked Dad. 'Yes, I'm coming', this other voice replied. Was there any other child in the land whose Dad made a personal call to Santa, years before we had a telephone in the house?

A few days before Christmas, the same procedure just to confirm that there would be presents at the foot of the bed on Christmas morning. And not just a stocking. A pillow case was put there. There wasn't enough money for presents at any other time of the year except for my birthday in October. So the Christmas gifts had to last a long time.

The illusion of my father's personal call to Santa Claus - always 'Santy' to him - lasted another two or three years. The spell was broken when I started school. Someone told me that it was really my parents who provided the presents. Spoilsports! So that year I paid more attention to where the voice in the chimney came from and found that my father was an amateur ventriloquist. I promptly got off his knee. The magic was over. I'm lucky enough to be a believer that Christmas wonder can still be seen in the eyes of a child. It just doesn't last as long for them as it did for me.

There was another magic happening that year, 1922. Christmas Eve brought a fall of snow so that, when I was told to open the kitchen door and look outside, I saw about six inches of the white stuff in our yard. There wasn't another Christmas Eve like that, right up to the end of the 20th century round here at any rate. Boy and man, child, parent and grandparent, I've seen them all. Even the one when I got out of hospital in Nottingham just in time for Christmas Eve. So that was another magic day - 70 years after the first one.

The preparations for Christmas 1922 were fascinating for me. We didn't have a proper Christmas tree. Instead, it was several boughs of holly, brightly berried, hanging from a hook in the kitchen ceiling. That year, for the first time, I stood on a chair, held by my mother, to fasten lovely coloured baubles to the holly boughs.

There was a special reason why my mother could not do it herself that year. My sister, Ida, was born in February 1923 so that was only eight weeks away. Not that I knew anything about it, I was much too preoccupied with Christmas and all it meant.

There was very little leisure time for my parents. That memory is one of the things that unites everyone of my generation, if they are still around. In our kitchen, on the opposite side to the wooden cupboard, was the kitchen sink. Cold water came from the pump outside in the yard. There was no piped water, no electricity, no gas, no central heating and no inside toilet. We didn't miss any of those things because we didn't know what they were. Bedroom furniture included the chamber pot, kept under the bed and used as required.

Our outside lavatory was at the end of the garden, about 30 yards from the house. It had two seats, one for adults and a lower one for children. Earth closets, these structures were called. On a cold winter's evening, I would try to make the journey with a lighted candle in my hands. Which was satisfactory until the wind blew the candle out. Next door to the house was the cowshed. The channel at the back of the cows was there for a purpose and it was a useful place for me to go when answering a call of nature. Provided the cow didn't get a call at the same time. If that happened, there was a bit of personal cleaning-up to do.

I remember one Christmas, when I was about seven years old, my mother wanted to buy me a toy wheelbarrow. But Dad had one eye on the future. 'No' he said, 'The lad'll soon be big enough to manage the big one'. And, sure enough, by the time next winter came, I was wheeling that barrow to the muck-heap.

We lived on what was known as a small-holding. Around 14 acres, which my parents rented from the family of Sir Matthew Ingle Joyce. I remember that they were able to buy it later. Judge Joyce, as he was then, came to enquire if we wanted to buy the holding. He said to my father, 'I think £800, what would you say?' Father said, 'I think 750'. 'If you give me 750, it's yours' said the great man. Father afterwards always wished he'd offered 700. I think they would probably have finished up at a mid-point anyway. That would be in the early 1930s. Concluded with a handshake, the legal requirements would follow. Around 30 years later, I bought a house myself, agreement reached with a handshake. But that's a story of a time now gone.

Even then, the money coming in from a holding of our size wouldn't keep a family. My father was a glutton for work - he'd never known anything else. Once he pointed to a man some little way off in the village and said to me, 'That chap's got gawber ruttles'. 'Whatever is gawber ruttles, Dad?', says I. 'Two stomachs for eating and never a one for work', says Dad. Except he pronounced it 'wok' like the Chinese cooking implement. You still hear that in Leicestershire.

Another example of my father's local dialect was when he mentioned 'Sarniper Bridge'. It took me many years to find out where Sarniper Bridge was.

Then one day, on the way to Coalville via Coleorton, I came to the next village, Sinope. A little settlement of cottages built for railway workers, with six or seven houses on each side of the road, and a bridge over the railway line from Leicester to Burton. There was his Sarniper Bridge.

Running a smallholding was a diversion from Dad's job at the Cloud Hill Limeworks, where he worked on the Sercombes kiln as a lime-burner. Eighty-four hours a week for a wage of 72 shillings. Two men covered every hour of the day and night. Five o'clock in the afternoon, Monday to Friday, was the change-over time. And there was no extra pay for night or week-end work. The basic wage covered everything.

'At twenty pun ten I'm bid. At twenty pun ten I'm bid. Twenty pun ten. Twenty pun ten. At twenty pun ten I'm bid.' The voice of the auctioneer at the Monday cattle market, Ashby-de-la-Zouch. 'Pun' of course was pound. The ten -mature readers, please forgive me - is 10 shillings, there being 20 to the pound then. He was talking up the bids for the cow which my father and I had walked with from Tonge to Ashby in 1926. And a minute or so later, the price had reached £22 10s. the hammer had fallen and the cow had a new owner

It was the first and the last time that I ever walked a cow to market. Cattle were already being transported by motor vehicles and the big farmers were moving them to Derby. My father soon came to accept this new way even though he had been walking cattle to market for most of his life.

Tonge & Breedon station, closed to passengers in 1930. From our home we could walk down the railway line to this little station, and our father would buy tickets. Traffic from the limeworks at Breedon was loaded into the wagons in the sidings in the 1920s. The line was taken over by the army in wartime and became the Melbourne Military Railway.
Author's Collection

The sidings at Worthington station, next up the line from Breedon in 1885. A Midland Railway locomotive is on the right. The wagons are destined for New Lount Colliery. The siding leads to Cloud Hill Limeworks. The Hoffman Kiln is seen in the distance beyond the locomotive, the great limestone hill that forms the backdrop is long gone, but limestone is still extracted from a deep hole in the ground here. *Author's Collection*

Sercombe's Kiln at Cloud Hill in 1905. Notice the Midland Railway wagons being shunted by a team of horses. It was around 20 years later that I first set foot on the kiln. By then the cabin on the top had gone, and the two men who each worked 84 hours a week had a proper cabin down below. Coal slack was barrowed up the incline by 'slack-wheelers'. The railway line from Derby is on the left. *Winters of Derby*

That had been the way of it countrywide, for a good many years. The old drovers routes are chronicled and still visible. On that day in 1926, we had walked about six miles but the old drovers covered immense distances. That was when the only other traffic on the highways was the stagecoach and the horse.

Think of taking animals along the A453 today – impossible! We did it then without any problems - except that I should have been in school that Monday morning. Obviously, the need for 'twenty-two pun ten' exceeded the need for me to be educated - just for that one morning. My father was over 60 so I may have been some real help. Trouble was that we had to pass the school on the way to market, but the windows were so high that there was no chance of us being seen as we walked by. Blasting the rock face of Breedon Hill was taking place around the village school and the windows, small as they were, were still covered with metal screens to prevent any damage from flying rocks.

There is nothing else I remember about the journey - just the voice of the auctioneer, a member of the firm of German, Stephenson & Stimpson. Just John German & Co. now. And cattle markets aren't what they were; changing customs - plus foot and mouth and BSE.

Way back then, there would be an embargo on the movement of animals from farm to farm, that would last two to three weeks at most. Nobody would have done anything so stupid as to feed cattle with processed waste of animal remains. Grass in the spring and summer, hay and cattle cake in the winter were the staple diet of young and old stock.

Cattle cake came in big slabs which had to be broken up in crushers kept for the purpose. Smallholders - like my parents - didn't have the resources of a big farmer, who could close a field - or several - to make hay for the winter fodder.

When my father set aside a field for haymaking, there was a period of about six to eight weeks in May and June when our cattle, around five or six of them, would be taken out to graze on the verges alongside the country lanes. This practice was called 'tenting'. I never understood the term until quite recently. Quite a literal explanation really. Before there was much traffic on the road, it was normal for a young man to take cattle out and to take a tent with him so that he could stay overnight. The cattle would simply lie down overnight just as they would in a field. A friendly farmer would provide meals for the lad in the tent.

It would only be young stock, 'yearlings' or the two-year-old stirks, that would be kept out for several nights. To do that with cows in milk you would have to take a bucket and a measuring jug. Cows have to be milked morning and evening seven days a week. The process of growing up included learning to milk by hand. Again, rural readers forgive me, but cows have an udder with four teats. We mankind, with two hands, grip the front two and squeeze them so that the milk runs into the bucket which is held between your knees. When you are finding it hard to get any more, you move on to the back two. This is all done while you are sitting on a three-legged stool with your head resting up against the flank of the cow. First time, you do this, the cow realises that you are a novice and the milk won't run quickly. And they always take the chance to teach you a lesson - just once. Waiting until the bucket is nearly full, the cow will - quite deliberately and accurately - kick out sideways so all the milk is spilt. Next time, you're ready for it.

Two studio portraits of Ida and myself with our mother. These could well have been taken on holiday. Our father would not accompany us on seaside holidays. Mother would have to plan our trips in secret, and announce just a day or two before we went away that we would be going, as to give him any further notice of her intentions would cause him to think of reasons why we should not go. He of course would not leave his job and the smallholding.
(Both) Author's Collection

During those weeks in May and June, Dad would take the cows out, Monday to Friday, and I would go with them on Saturday and Sunday mornings. By the time I was eight years old, I was reckoned to be well able to take care of stock. It wasn't too difficult, largely because there were few cars on the road. The first one in our village belonged to Alfred White of Tonge Hall Farm. There would only be a car coming along the A447 - Castle Donington to Hinckley - about once every 10 minutes and the verges were wide and well-provided with grass.

Moving the stock along occasionally, we would get to a place called Redwood where there was a side road which went off to Belton and Diseworth. I used to wonder why it was called that. If there had been a group of red cedars, that would have been the answer. There wasn't, though. Instead, at the base of a signpost pointing the way to those two villages, there was a small pile of red bricks, just a dozen or so. It didn't occur to me as a child that there might have been a house there once. Years later, though, looking at the census returns for our parish, I found the entry for a house called Redwood Toll Gate. That was part of the answer. Up to around 1870, the house was there to collect tolls from road users. People on horses, in jaunting carts or driving farm animals. Less than a mile further on is Brandgate Farm. The people who live there now - Mr and Mrs Dilks - have a field called Redwood. In it, they have found a good many musket balls, turned up by the plough. Away beyond that, going towards Belton, stands a wood. My own theory is that, in the English Civil War, there was a battle here and the fields around the wood were red with the blood of the soldiers – makes sense.

Further still along the road, where there is a junction, that would be the site of Brandgate Toll House. That was mentioned, I believe, in 1841 but not afterwards. Beyond that is the area known as Breedon Brand and the road there is still called Top Brand. Between that and middle or Lower Brand, there were once around 40 households. Now, it's down to two or three farms and a couple of cottages. I never got far beyond Redwood with our cows before it was time to make our way home. It was those days out which allowed Dad to close a field for haymaking.

As soon as my sister and I were old enough, we used to help out with the haymaking. Yet another country pursuit which was entirely dependent on the weather. Not having a mower of our own - or the horses to pull one - we had to wait until one of the local farmers had finished their own hay-making. That was before tractors replaced horses and farming was still labour intensive.

Dad was working 84 hours a week at Sercombes Kiln in Cloud Hill. The smallholding we had, first 14 then 18 acres, was a means of filling up his spare time. So it could never have functioned without wife and children lending several hands, all part of the ethic of the time.

It was always a gamble whether you could get a field of grass cut, dried, turned and dried again without some rain. Turning was done by hand, with a rake, until a machine was devised to make the job quicker. And it had to be done. Grass lying next to the earth won't dry unless it is turned to face the sun. If you were lucky with the weather, got the hay dry and built it up into cocks, big round bundles, it still had to be carried home to the stack-yard. Like every other part of the whole business, this had to fit around Dad's working day and our schooling. The men required to load the wagon were all at work during the daytime. So, as many as Dad could get were enlisted to help and it meant a long evening of hard work.

One year we had to carry the hay home when it wasn't properly dry and it wasn't going to be. The weather had been unkind. A few weeks later, the stack had heated up so much that it was smouldering. Father had to get his massive hay-knife, which was normally used once the hay had settled. But this was a crisis. Save the stack before it went up in flames. He had to cut a channel right through the middle to let enough air in to stop a disastrous end to that year's hay harvest. But that was the only bad year I remember.

Hay and corn in open yards were thatched with straw, bought in for the purpose in our case as we didn't have a corn harvest of our own. Thatching a stack of hay is much the same as thatching a house except that it doesn't have to last as long. But Dad could do it all. He had left school at 11 and gone into full-time farm service at 12. Running a smallholding on top of his 84-hour a week job kept him busy - and also passed on the idea of hard work to his children.

By the time I left school and was in full-time employment, he was 68 so his long working day had finished. But he continued to keep a small herd of cows and to take them 'tenting' in the early summer until the end of his life. By then, he was in his 84th year. It's true that hard work never killed anybody - provided that the work didn't start when you were really too young for it. And he lived most of his life when work was conducted at a steady pace with no distractions from the regular rhythm of country life.

When I was taking the cows out as a boy of eight, there were sights to see and sounds to hear that we don't witness in our part of the world any more. At Redwood, there was a field of spring wheat one year. Fifty feet in the air above it, a skylark was singing. The bird had a nest on the ground. The wheat was only a few inches high. When the bird suddenly came down, I watched exactly where it landed and then climbed over the hedge to find the nest. It wasn't there. The bird landed somewhere else and then ran along the ground to its nest. It was too clever for me and I never did find that nest. I also regularly heard the harsh call of the corncrake: a shy bird, often heard, rarely seen.

Going up and down the country by train, in later years, I can remember a time when sheep and cattle would run away from the noise of the engine. Now I see the occasional flock or herd in a field alongside a motorway. They simply ignore the noise, it's just part of their life.

There are many other aspects of life in the country that we shall never see again. I don't remember whether we had to pay anything at Lount Toll Gate on the way to Ashby with our cow. Up until 1930 when the passenger train service ran from Derby to Ashby, the railway crossed over the A453 at a level crossing. Can you imagine that as the road is now - or was before the A42 took the traffic away? If you know where to look, on the road running out of Ashby towards Smisby, you can still see part of the embankment where the trains continued on their journey to Ashby.

It is now over 80 years since I helped my father with a walk to Ashby along with a cow to sell at the market. I expect she went to her next home in a cattle truck. Never again did we repeat that journey. But I still remember that first sight and sound of the auctioneer, 'At twenty pun ten I'm bid'. A voice from a time long since gone.

Chapter Two

Home and Hearth

Before I was old enough to help my father outside, I helped my mother indoors. And so I learned enough about cookery to be able to make myself a meal throughout my working life. I mentioned the cold-water pump outside. Hot water was provided by a small boiler on one side of the fireplace, on the other was the oven. So a fire was always needed – winter or summer.

Washday Monday we spent in a small washroom at the end of the house, with a boiler which had to be filled from buckets of water drawn from the pump. The water was heated by a fire which we started in the fire-grate below the boiler and then when the water was hot, the clothes were put into a tub with soap flakes. Then we used an implement known as a 'ponch' which knocked any dirt out of the clothes. The rinsing was done in a big bucket and the clothes were dried on a line slung out between the plum trees. So it took most of the day to do the washing for a family of four.

And then there was the mangle. This was used to dry the clothes - to some extent - before they were hung on the line. This made it a job for two people - one to hold the garment and the other to swing the handle which made the rollers go round. A nice little job for me. They used to say that a woman's work was never done and I think Mum appreciated the extra pair of hands. In the winter-time, out would trot the old clothes-horse and the drying would be done in front of the fire.

One week, mother would be up at five in the morning to get my dad his cooked breakfast before he went to work at six. That would be the week he finished at five in the evening. The following week, he would go to work at that time and spend most of the day in bed.

I remember the days when my mother would say, 'I'm just going to have 10 minutes' and would lie down on the sofa in the kitchen. That 10 minutes would sometimes last an hour. Meanwhile, I would try to amuse myself with something that would not disturb her. I did a lot of reading as a child. And I could tell the time before I went to school. That may sound silly now but not many children could read the clock-face as accurately as I could at the age of five. I even drew pencil clocks on the kitchen wallpaper to amuse myself while my mother was asleep.

Before we could make a cup of tea in the morning, the fire had to be lit; that was the only way of cooking and boiling water. There were always some dry sticks handy so it didn't take too long.

My father would be 54 when I was born, my mother far younger - about 32, I would guess. He was a widower when they first met. His first wife, Agnes, died relatively young and he brought up the three children, Gertrude, Edith and George, on his own for 12 years.

Gertie was the little mother to the other two. She once told me a nice story about that time. With no electricity, the only lighting came from candles and the oil-lamp which stood in the centre of the table. They were all supposed to go to

Right: We think that this is our grandmother, Ann Throsby, as a young girl. At the age of 12 she worked an embroidered sampler which hung above my bed at White House. The text was much more detailed than you would normally find in a working class house of the sort that reads 'Bless This House' or 'Home Sweet Home'. The embroidery reads as follows:

Lord at thy foot ashamed I lie
Upward I dare not look
Pardon my sins before I die
And blot them from my book

And if our fellowship below
In Jesus be so sweet
What heights of rapture shall we know
When round thy throne we meet

Subdue, O Lord, this heart of mine
To thy most holy will
And place me on that safe, good way
That leads to Zion's hill.

Ann Throsby ag'd 12 yrs
1857

This photograph was probably taken in 1887. Our mother, born in February of that year, is the babe in arms. The proud parents are my grandfather, Thomas Eyre (a shoe finisher), and his wife Ann (née Throsby). The other children are Lydia on the left, and Edith (later known to me as Aunt Edie Allen) on the right. In the centre is my uncle, Albert Throsby Eyre. I only ever knew my aunts as Uncle Albert died about 1915 and is buried in Isley Walton churchyard some two miles from Breedon. His death led, in a round-about way, to my parents meeting. Clara Harriett, our mother, was only one year old when her mother Ann died, so she was brought up by her father with Edith's help. *(Both) Author's Collection*

bed at nine o'clock which, of course, was just what happened when Dad was home in the evenings. When he was on the night shift, and came home in the morning, he would look at the level of oil in the lamp and work out what time they had gone to bed. 'We soon got wise to that', said Gertie. 'We used to top up the lamp with oil before we turned in'.

It had been a hard life, in many respects, for Josiah Weston's first wife. And even harder for him, leaving school at 11, to stand in a field, acting as a human scarecrow for sixpence a week. In the census returns of the last half of the 19th century, such children were described as 'bird tenders'. And one boy, eight years old, was listed as a 'ploughboy'. Which meant he led the horses. Just as I led a pony in 1934 but I was 14 by then and it wasn't on arable land either.

Victorian values will stand a bit more examination. My father, Josiah, was hired out in farm service at Ashby Statute Fair to Mr Goodacre of Worthington Fields Farm for £5 a year and his keep. Read that bit again, it isn't a misprint. £5 a year! He lived with the family and took his washing home to mother on Sundays. It isn't my story but knowing it has given me the impetus to see that it is recorded. He also said that he could milk 12 cows in one hour - by hand of course. Even in the 1920s, he could still milk a cow faster than I could - it's like riding a bicycle, you never forget. You will notice that I could milk the cow as well as wheel the barrow. It's a lot easier writing about it.

My mother was a town girl from Leicester. Her mother had died while she was just a toddler. Her father is noted down in the 1881 census as Thomas Eyre, a shoe finisher. On some occasions, my mother must have got a bit tired of life in the country and I remember going with her to visit her eldest sister, Edith. Aunt Edith lived in Friars Causeway in Leicester near Central station. She had been a widow for ages and kept a boarding-house. As children do, I remember her voice - it was a great booming thing and she called me, 'Little Johnny Weston from Tonge'. I couldn't argue with that.

They obviously wanted a sisterly heart-to heart so they sent me up to the railway station to watch the trains. Before I went, I heard them talking about one of Aunt Edith's boarders who was known as the 'Racer'. He wasn't an athlete or a cyclist; he was a professional gambler. The business of studying horses to make a living is quite respectable now but I don't think it would have been considered proper conduct then. But gambling certainly went on and the pawnbrokers kept money flowing into the houses. People used to leave their most valued possessions with the man known as 'uncle'. I thought he was called that because he was kind enough to give people money and keep their treasures safe for them until they could afford to redeem them. But it may have been that his clients didn't want to talk about it directly. It was a form of money-lending, of course, but it seemed less cruel than the loan sharks of today. 'Uncle' might charge a few pence. What people were never able to redeem, he was able to sell. In its way, it was an honest living.

Never did I get the impression that my parents had fallen out with each other. It was just that sometimes my mother needed a break from the constant grind of country life. I know that she was never kept short of money because dad brought his wage-packet home unopened on Fridays. He had no need of money for gambling, smoking or drinking. His only leisure-time came once a fortnight in the winter-time and that was after being at work from five o'clock on Friday evening until noon on Saturday.

So how was that little bit of leisure-time utilized? On something that both my sister and I could share in from the time that we were five years old. Here are some extracts from an article my sister once wrote. It was called, 'When Dad took us to watch the "Rams"*'.

He came home, about a mile walk, bolted his dinner, had a wash, changed his collar to a cotton collar and front, put on his suit and he was ready.

It was always a rush. The train came from Derby and went to Ashby, where it turned round. When it came back, we got on it at Tonge and Breedon station which was about half a mile away from where we lived.

We all listened and when we heard the train go up, we knew it was time to leave. 'The train's gone up.' We gathered ourselves together, locked the door, crossed the road and, going round the back of Mrs Bird's house, went down the path which slanted down the steep bank. Then we were on the track and walking to the station. I was about five years old and my mother had got me, my brother and herself ready and, in spite of the rush, we always seemed to manage it.

We walked up onto the platform and we were never there long before the train arrived. John and I watched for the stations and when Peartree and Normanton went by, we knew there was not much longer to go. We got off the train and went to the match.

The time went quickly enough because of the excitement. That was when the half-back line read Nicholas, Barker, Keen and the left-winger Mee, who was not above swearing at the supporters when they made remarks to him, before breaking off to tackle a suddenly advancing opponent.

After the match we got on to a tram and went into the town. There we bought two pounds of butter at the Maypole, where a man in a white apron would cut a piece from a big lump a bit like a barrel before shaping it into a nice oblong with his butter pats and wrapping it up for us.

When the assistant took the money, he put it in a little wooden pot, pulled a handle and it flew up on a wire to a cashier in a kind of glass-fronted pulpit. In a minute, down came another little pot with your receipt and cash. How I longed to be an assistant and to be allowed to pull that handle.

We went to one or two other shops and then to the market. Dad would go into a pub or hotel with some steps and we would have to wait outside while he had a pint of Offilers ale.

It was winter and dark by now as we went round the market. The gas jets flared and the market people called their wares and my dad would bid for some teaspoons or half a dozen willow-pattern plates.

Sometimes we would have a cup of tea in the Market Hall and would sit at a table where there was a curtain down the middle and you could peep underneath it at our mother sitting on the other side.

Soon we were on our way home again, really tired. The train drew up into Tonge station and we got off. I held tightly to my mother's hand as we walked past the engine with its huge wheels and connecting rods. Then my father put me on his back, Mother took John's hand and we walked down the platform under the bridge and into the darkness, knowing that in a minute we would have to step back as the train passed us. It came with the noise, the fire, the sparks in the darkness and then it was gone on its way to Ashby and we could resume our peaceful walk home.

When we got there, Mother made a fire of sticks and boiled the kettle. Then she cleaned and floured the herrings we'd bought and put them in the pan on the fire. Meanwhile, dad had picked up a bucket and gone to milk his one or two cows and

* The Rams is the nickname of Derby County Football Club.

suckle his calves. When we had had our tea, I lay on the sofa and mother would pick me up to take me to bed. I would always let her think that I was more tired than I really was, so that she would carry me and I wouldn't have to walk upstairs.

When I was five years old, it was time to go to school. There were no nursery schools in those days, and what early education we had was learned from our parents. It's well over 80 years since I went to school in Breedon and over 70 since I left Castle Donington school to start my working life. My recollection of the 10 years from 1925 to 1934 only covers the high points and the low points so I'll deal with them as honestly as I can.

Education at Breedon began in a small building on the side of a hill, which is now a private house. It is unlikely that there is anyone left alive in the parish of Breedon-on-the-Hill who was taught there. It was known as 'The Boy's School'. In my time, both boys and girls went to the school on the main road through the village. Children from Tonge, where I was born, and Wilson, the other village in the parish, had to walk nearly a mile four times a day. We always went home at mid-day for our dinner and went back for the afternoon lessons. Our mothers were always at home and with none of the machines and modern cooking methods, their days were long and hard. Family life was closely knit in the years between two World Wars.

Whatever the weather, we made those four journeys a day, Monday to Friday, except when a childhood illness kept us at home. There was a school attendance officer who would soon be visiting the home of any child who wasn't attending every day, to make sure that it really was illness and not idleness that was the cause of the absence.

We didn't have electricity, gas or piped water when I was young. We didn't have television, computers or school meals but we had a sort of play area on the Berry Field. With a morning and afternoon playtime, that meant crossing the road eight times a day. There were not many motor cars around then and horses and carts didn't knock anybody down. Why did I run across the road one day and almost become the first child at Breedon school to be killed by a motor vehicle? For no reason at all that I can remember. The car ran up the school bank to avoid me. I don't remember telling my parents because I wasn't upset about it. They found out just the same and my father was very soon letting the head teacher, F.W. Roberts, know what he thought about unsupervised children crossing a main road. So after that little episode, someone had to see us across at playtime.

My first teacher in the infants section was Miss Barsby. Our lessons were truly the 'three Rs' - reading, writing and arithmetic. I'm told that my mother asked about my progress in class and Miss Barsby said, 'Oh, Mrs Weston, he is a plodder'. Possibly because I didn't hold my pen properly. To this day, I write with my thumb across the top of the pen instead of the first finger. Does it matter? Of course not, but they did expect everyone to conform. So I was instructed in writing the proper way - but it didn't stick. Some left-handed people didn't escape being instructed to do it the 'right' way.

Reading came easily to me. Before *The Beano* and similar comics, I remember *Tiger Tim's Weekly*. I also read bits of the *Farmer's Weekly* which had pictures of men with heavy Victorian beards and whiskers; just like King George V.

This photograph, taken in the late 1920s, is of my sister Ida and I in fancy dress for a garden fête at Breedon. I am dressed as a chimney sweep, my face blackened with soot and Ida is Red Riding Hood. *Author's Collection*

One name stuck with me for many years, because it was uncommon. Mr E. W. Lobjoit. I know now that there was a variety of lettuce which bore his name, Lobjoit's Green Cos. Another uncommon name I remember, belonged to an engine driver, a cockney who moved to Derby. His name was Harry Clarricoats.

Reading by candlelight in the bedroom equipped me with the knowledge to master spelling, too. So, when we were tested at school, I was a benchmark. Never lost a mark at reading in 10 years. Not bad for a plodder.

Writing, they could mark me down for because of that thumb wrapped round the pen. My grammar is not always right, either - but when we had a spelling competition, it was no contest. They were run on a knockout basis just like *Spellbound* on the television. Each child had to spell five words read out for them by their opponents - and then he or she returned the favour. If I chose from my 'A' list - words like pneumonia or phlegm, the teacher would rule them out even though I could spell them. That didn't matter, though, because I had the 'B' list ready. If only examinations had been limited to spelling, reading and mental arithmetic, I would have been on easy street.

One day, Frank Taylor, who was the school governor, came in and set us a little test to win a penny. His question, 'How much would I have to pay for 20 penny buns and 23 half-penny ones?' Someone added up 1*s*. 8*d*. plus 11½*d*., quite quickly. 'Two shillings, seven and a half pence'. 'No', that was wrong. Two more attempts, both of them wrong. Then I put my hand up, having added 2*s*. 6*d*. to 1*s*. 8*d*. to make 4*s*. 2*d*. and won the penny. It all depends on what you mean by '23 half-penny ones' and remember that 'three ha'pence' was a common measure back then. I won the penny, which had a bit of value in those days. I think those tiny triumphs at school stay with us longer and more vividly than other greater events later on. The moments of sadness do too.

So, what wasn't I much good at? Pretty well everything else. That didn't cover many subjects. Our written arithmetic wasn't very complicated. If you could add, subtract, multiply and divide, that was about it. Still, I wouldn't get 50 marks out of 50, which was what I got for reading and mental arithmetic. Mathematics and algebra, we never heard anything about them. Or foreign languages. We would not be expecting to travel abroad anyway, not when a journey to Derby was a big day out.

I don't remember anything at all about geography. A large part of the world seemed to belong to the British Empire. Somewhere, the sun would always be shining, but we would always have to put up with the cold and the rain. And history, that was all about kings and queens, the really important people. The British had fought various battles on land and sea, most of which they seemed to have won.

There were about six or seven of us walking from Tonge every day. I remember there was a rather big holly tree about halfway to Breedon. The older boys tried to frighten us by telling us of a bogeyman who was lurking in the tree.

However, did I come to be involved in a fight one day? I had no quarrel with Arthur Coxon but somehow it was arranged that we would fight each other one playtime. So everybody gathered round. We sparred a little and then Arthur struck me one blow on the chest. I fell down, soon got up again but then a teacher appeared on the scene and everybody dispersed quickly, leaving Arthur and me to take the rap. But there was no visible damage so we didn't get into trouble.

A pair of photographs that may have been taken on the same day. Above, Mother and Father stand with one of the family's cows. Working a smallholding was something that our father did in addition to a working week of 84 hours at the the limeworks. In the view below, Ida and I pose with our parents. I am standing on a tree stump behind the rest of the family.

(Both) Author's Collection

One summer's day at Tonge, five or six of us boys went into the field just beyond the railway bridge where there was a public footpath to Cloud Hill. I was set up as a fall-guy for a trick that can only be played once. It was suggested that I should be blindfolded and then given a stick which had been put in a cowpat. Then I was to whirl it around and see who got spattered. I fell for it and was handed the stick. Of course, I was handed the mucky end so my hand got filthy and I had to wipe it on the grass. If ever you hear that someone has got the dirty end of the stick, that's the way it's done.

Those are the bits I remember. Why did I not pass the 11-plus examination and go to Ashby grammar school? There are several reasons but it all comes down to one thing. I didn't do well enough on the day. Now, if there had been a second chance, or if a year's work had been taken into consideration, who knows? Anyway, I just missed out so it was Castle Donington for my secondary education.

My parents wanted me to go to Ashby, and they would have paid for that. Foolishly, I said they had done enough for me already and I ought to take my chance. I wasn't to know that they would have received some financial assistance. It isn't surprising that they didn't know that either. Neither my father nor my mother had the time to research it all so that was the end of it.

One thing which they did do was to arrange for me to have a cooked meal at mid-day. This festival was celebrated with a lady who lived near the main road, a Mrs Morris, so that I missed any of the rough and tumble that was all part of school playtime. We had a bus in the morning and the evening to take us to and from Castle Donington. That was the first bus ever to come through Tonge village. It's quite possible that we were the first from Tonge to go to Donington. I don't remember older boys and girls going there.

At nine o'clock, we all had to march around the school hall, while Mrs Handford played a tune on the piano. That was the beginning - and the end - of our introduction to music.

Woodwork class was a disaster for me. Quite simple for most boys - for me extremely complicated. Given a plane and a block of wood, I could never take the right amount off which made Billy Batten (really!) the teacher quite angry. But it didn't make me any more competent.

Whilst learning to ride my mother's bicycle, I turned round on Tonge Lane and fell into a ditch. We had a nurse in the village. She examined my wrist, which had taken the brunt of the fall and pronounced it 'just bruised'. A few weeks later, it still looked a bit bowed and I went to Melbourne to see the doctor. He was rather annoyed - why had I not been to see him before. When I told him that I'd seen the nurse, that calmed him down a bit and he sent me off to the Derbyshire Royal Infirmary. There it was diagnosed as a greenstick fracture and it had to be broken again and reset. I was given gas for this operation and I don't recall it with any pleasure.

For some time afterwards, my mother had to take me into Derby once a week on the bus - no hardship to me since I missed the woodwork class on that day. By the time all this was finished, I was regarded as being too far behind everyone else in the class so I was excused woodwork from then on, and I was quite happy about that.

I think on my first examination at Donington, I got 188 out of 200. Because it was just the basics, written and mental arithmetic, reading and writing. This was a level I never reached again.

So that's what my education was like in the 1920s and 1930s. Goodness knows how I was persuaded by my parents to stay on for an extra term. It was a time of very high unemployment and the chances of getting a job were not good - so it wasn't just a matter of 'leave school and start earning'. If it had been, I think I would have been off at the first opportunity.

We knew very little about the education that was available to the children of rich people. Although my schooling was better than my father's had been - 50 years before - the end product was much the same. We were expected to work hard, to speak when we were spoken to and to be grateful for the alleged kindness of our employers.

When the time came for me to leave school, those were the attitudes I took with me into the world. And there would be very little change until after World War II. We had been educated to accept that kind of life.

It is only recently, now that I am over 80, that I have found out the lessons of history that we were never taught. Television can be a menace; but it can also be a huge force for education and enlightenment - as it has been for me.

Our parents, Dad has his shirt sleeves rolled up, ready for work as always.
Author's Collection

Chapter Three

All in a Day's Work

A lifetime of hard work starts one Monday morning in April 1934. This will be my first experience of paid employment. I am starting work as a gardener's boy. Not quite in a mansion but in a large country house. Langley Priory is roughly midway between my home village of Tonge and another village - Diseworth - about three miles away.

Work was not regarded as a right in those days. It was something you almost had to beg for. So I had been to see my prospective employer about a week before to make sure that I was suitably qualified. The main qualifications, in fact, were respect and obedience. The pay would be 10 shillings for the working week of 48 hours. So it took a fortnight to earn one English pound.

We all have to start somewhere and this was not as demanding or as demeaning as the jobs which many other boys of my age took on. To start with, it was neither dangerous nor dirty - except for a bit of superficial mud. My parents were realistic in seeking something out for me which wouldn't make me old before my time. For which I have cause to be grateful.

By now my father was 68 and only semi-retired. He was no longer working 84 hours a week but still employed by Breedon & Cloud Hill Limeworks on a job called 'unbearing', which involved digging away the soil from the top of limestone rock. The rock would then be drilled with explosives. When detonated, these would blast the rock face down to ground level. Hard physical labour was involved, pick and shovel. The limestone rock, used for road-building and carriage drives, was then loaded into tubs and transported by horses to a big machine called a 'cracker'. For this, the men were paid *6d.* a tub. Those men who had a good 'stall' - not too many hard lumps - could fill 20 tubs a day. But they had to work harder than the horses to do that. My father knew what was involved and he wasn't going to see me worn out while I was still young.

So he must have asked some questions about the chances of employment for me at Langley Priory. One of the farm workers there, George Barber, also lived at Tonge, so he would know what was going on. The young man, Jack Barker - who had already been there several years - was now about 18 so it was time for him to move on. Boys of 14 didn't get much money. Some of them might be apprentices learning a trade. Then they had to hope for an adult vacancy to turn up.

But even the pay for adult workers wasn't much in the 1920s and 1930s. Two pounds a week was a standard wage for farm labourers, the same for railway track workers, known as platelayers. No-one expected an 18-year-old boy to manage on 10 to 15 shillings a week, so that was why the gardener's boy at Langley Priory was ready to leave, if he was lucky, to another job.

That is how I came to work for a country squire, which is how these gentlemen in the country were known. Their workers, male or female, were known as being in 'gentleman's service' working for the squire and his family.

Charles Bowles Shakespear was the head of the household at Langley Priory. It was ownership of land which gave these people their very exclusive lifestyle.

A number of tenant farmers paid rent for their land on 25th March and 25th September each year.

I was destined to move on myself, as well, when I was nearly 18. We didn't know then, of course, that we were going to be involved in a second World War within 21 years of the previous one. When that war ended, the pattern of country life changed very quickly.

During my 3½ years on the outdoor staff, young, and sometimes not so young, women came to work indoors. And, wherever they came from, far or near, they lived as inferior members of the household. Housemaids, a cook, parlour maids, kitchen maids, all under the control of the housekeeper. My sister went to work there, sometime after I left. Even though her home was less than two miles away, she still had to 'live in'. There were no exceptions to that rule.

The turnover of indoor staff was in complete contrast to the adult outdoor workers. I sometimes think that Mrs Shakespear was a rather demanding employer - or perhaps the young women who came to work for her didn't care much for having just one day a week off. Whichever it was, none of the young girls stayed with the family for more than a year or two.

Employment opportunities, especially for women, increased a great deal during the war years. Afterwards, the supply of girls prepared to leave home for domestic service soon dried up. Men, too, had job chances that never existed before 1939. This meant a big change to the life of a country gentleman - no longer could he pick and choose and pay the lowest possible wages.

Langley Priory where I worked, from Easter 1934 to September 1937, as a gardener's boy. This picture was taken before my time there, and by then the climbing plants on the front wall had gone. The entrance on the right had also been blocked off, and this became the gun room. I cleaned the family's shoes in the building on the left, which is hidden by trees. The kitchen was on the left in the foreground. *Author's Collection*

Many people remembered the way it had been. Almost 50 years later, I remember listening to a radio phone-in. When I called with some of my memories, I was asked, 'Did you tip your cap to the squire?' 'Yes', I replied, 'to show respect'. And that was true, too. Respect was regarded as a vital attribute for a member of staff - especially the younger ones. And respect was to be shown not only to the master and mistress of the house, but to the son and daughter, Mister John and Miss Roseia. Neither of them married. Miss Roseia was a lovely-looking girl who died relatively young of some obscure disease. So, when Mr and Mrs Shakespear died, there was only Mister John left. But let's not get too far ahead.

Here I am, on that April morning, setting off on my mother's bicycle, to collect the papers from a newsagent in Castle Donington. There were also assorted magazines, all wrapped up in a cylinder, tied up in a loop of string. The paper-shop was right at the bottom of a long hill and it was hard work pedalling back up on a single-geared ladies' bike. At the Nags' Head, the public house at the top of the hill, I turned left. You can't get to Langley that way now. That road would take you right across the runway of the East Midlands airport.

Skirting the edge of the village of Diseworth, I turned right towards Belton. Another right turn and I was then on the carriage drive leading to the big house. After riding about a mile I came to the big white gate at the end of a shrubbery where there were many fine trees. Past these, the house itself came into view. Eight o'clock in the morning and my day's work was about to begin, having left home just after seven o'clock.

I was greeted at the far end of the house by an old chap who introduced himself as Harry Moore. He would be my foreman for the next 3½ years. The bundle of newspapers was handed in at the kitchen. The main house, I remember, was in an enclosed courtyard, a three-storey building with a wing at each end. The kitchen had a door but the other wing could only be reached from the inside. Later on, I found out that it was the gunroom.

Harry Moore explained to me how my time would be occupied until five in the afternoon. There would be a one-hour break for lunch - which we always called dinner in those days. First of all, there were the family shoes to be cleaned, after which I was to take them to the kitchen, the staff employed there being a cook and a kitchen-maid.

There I would be given what they called a 'mid-morning lunch', after which I was to report to Harry for seasonal work in the garden. That comprised a big area of grass lawn, a tennis court, several beds of roses and a shrubbery at each end of the house.

Shoe-cleaning was done in a sort of open shed: around nine or ten pairs of shoes every day, worn by the four members of the family. The ladies' footwear was relatively easy to clean, and Mr Shakespear always seemed to wipe his shoes on a mat before entering the house. I thought well of him for that - as a servant, you tend to judge people by these things. As for Mr John's shoes, though, they were always caked deep in thick mud, even in high summer. He always managed to find some way of getting them into this state - and the worst, of course, was during shooting parties in the wintertime. Getting caked mud off a pair of boots takes quite a while. But I managed to do it and then applied a liberal coating of dubbin. Next morning, all the Dubbin would be off and all the mud would be back on. Once - and once only - Mrs Shakespear descended from on high and let me know that her son's shoes were not clean enough. So, after that warning, shoe cleaning took even longer.

The mid-morning lunch was always the family leftovers from the previous day. Which was either moderate or bad. Brawn I particularly hated but I still had to eat it. The cook would always engage me in a bit of conversation. Meanwhile the kitchen-maid would be washing the kitchen floor in a skirt which rode up quite short at the back so a fair amount of leg was visible above her stocking-tops. That didn't make me like the brawn any better but it took my mind off it.

All the indoor staff lived in the servants' quarters. I remember the housekeeper who was there when I started work, a very warm-hearted and down-to-earth North country lady. Her name was Alice Sample. When Mrs Shakespear wanted her in attendance, she would walk down the corridor shouting, 'Saaample! Saaample!' in a voice like a foghorn. I could hear it easily in the outside shed. Alice Sample became Mrs Monkman when she married Benny Monkman the gamekeeper.

I met most of the outside staff at dinnertime on the first day. We all ate our sandwiches in one of the farm outbuildings. Even Tommy Brooks, who had a house in the yard but who liked to eat with the other staff. There was George Barber, a very quiet man who kept the off-licence in Tonge village. He didn't need to say much because there was a constant dialogue between Tommy Brooks and the cowman, Jimmy Marvin. Well, not so much of a dialogue as two competing monologues. They always struck sparks off each other and the language was a revelation to me. It was all effing this and effing that or bloody well something else. The cowman was the first person I ever met - I've met one or two since - who couldn't frame a sentence without a swear-word in it. I always wondered how he managed to talk at all at home. Perhaps he wasn't allowed to.

Also in houses attached to the estate lived Benny Monkman the gamekeeper and Rushton the chauffeur. We didn't see much of Rushton as he had several cars to care for. There was the big one which rolled up to the front of the house every Wednesday to take Squire Shakespear to Loughborough where he was chairman of the magistrates. Miss Roseia drove her own car and so did Mister John. If he treated his car like he did his shoes, Rushton would have plenty to keep him occupied.

The other man on the outdoor staff was George Mason, a Breedon man who looked after the walled garden. If I could have worked with him, I might have learned a lot more than I did with Harry, who was very reluctant to share his knowledge.

Many crops can be grown to a high standard in a walled garden. I remember going up there once or twice with a message. Seeing peaches and nectarines on trained trees in early summer was a revelation to me. At home, we had good plum, pear and apple trees but this was very different. I remember being taken with a terrible temptation to pick a ripe peach the first time I saw one. But fear is a marvellous policeman.

There was a big area of grass to mow in the spring and summer. We had a 30-inch mower and it was pulled by a pony, led by me. While I was cleaning shoes, Harry was getting the machine and the pony ready for work. Both proceeded at a very steady pace and it took two days to do the lot. The pony, which we called 'Tommy Dodd', was led up and down, up and down until the grass box was full. He wore special leather shoes which protected the grass from hoof-marks. At the bottom end of the biggest lawn, there was a pond on which sailed a couple of swans. Their droppings were obstacles I had to avoid as neither I nor Tommy Dodd wanted to pick them up. They just went into the box along with the grass.

Winters were less intense but still busy. During October and November, I was fully occupied in sweeping up fallen leaves. The equipment was basic, a besom broom, a wheelbarrow and two boards. Besoms are still around, a bundle of birch twigs, two or three ft long, secured to a wooden pole. Up and down I went, sweeping with a side-to-side movement. The boards were used to pick up bundles of leaves which I then placed in the wheelbarrow. When that was full, I wheeled it off to the shrubbery among the rhododendrons.

It's hard to believe now but I was rather proud of my work when I finished sweeping. So much so that, if half a dozen leaves came down behind me, I would pick them up by hand. But there would be many thousands of the little so-and-sos waiting for me next morning.

Harry Moore cut the grass in the courtyard and the tennis court with a hand mower. There were several rosebeds and, at the back of the house, two areas of bedding dahlias. Red was the colour, the variety the new Coltness gem. Knowing where they were was the limit of my knowledge. Harry had no intention of teaching his apprentice rose pruning, planting beds or anything that might be useful. That was often the way in rural areas, just the fear of an older man that a younger one might replace him.

When I had been there just over a year, I asked the squire for a rise. Very grudgingly, he made my 10 shillings up to 12. Fifteen months later, I asked again. Even more grudgingly, he made it up to 14. By that time, he was getting a strong and experienced 17-year-old man for 14 bob a week. Still, his shoes didn't take much cleaning.

Miss Roseia had tennis parties in the summer. She was a real looker but never started courting. Some of us reckoned that the 'Hooray Henries' of the day were scared of Mrs Shakespear. Plenty of them turned up for these parties but we were always given jobs to do which kept us well away from the tennis court.

The two men of the house had shooting parties in the winter. The pheasants were reared in the surrounding woods by Benny Monkman. Sometimes, I would go out 'beating' with the other workers. This involved slowly walking through the woods beating the trees with a stick. And, at the end of the day, the beaters were allowed to take a pheasant home - but only in lieu of a day's wages. My pay for the day would be 2*s*. 4*d*., the pheasant would have cost the older men 7*s*. They didn't believe in giving anything away, these landed gentry.

Normally, rabbits on the estate belonged to the tenant farmers. Just once, I went out on a rabbit shooting expedition and witnessed a little cameo that stayed with me. The ferrets put up a rabbit which raced away, white tail bobbing. Mister John let fly with both barrels of his 12-bore but didn't hit the rabbit. Probably too much mud on his shoes. Benny Monkman, though, took aim at the disappearing target and brought it down with a single shot. There was rather a frosty silence as the echoes of the shot faded away. I had to make sure that nobody saw me smiling.

Gamekeepers, of course, had to be good shots. Their job depended on two things - the supply of birds for the shooting parties and the control of predators. My stepsister, Edith, married a gamekeeper in the nearby village of Wilson, Harry Cooper. I remember my father saying that Harry had once made 97 kills in 100 shots. That would take a bit of beating.

Approaching 18 years of age, I knew that there was no future for me at Langley. And I was not learning enough to qualify me as an apprentice gardener anywhere else. I had told Harry Moore that I hoped to get a job on the railways as I knew he had two sons working as railwaymen in the Derby area. Several of my uncles were also railway workers. One uncle, Harry had been a driver on the Canadian Pacific Railway. My step-brother, George, was an engine driver firstly at Coalville, later at Burton.

I tried to get a job at Derby once. If I had been living there, they would have taken me on as a caller-up at No. 4 shed. But they didn't recruit engine cleaners until they were nearly 18. Which - by the summer of 1937 - I was. And, once again, my father was able to help me. From one of the trainmen who came up to Worthington, where he had once worked, he learned that engine cleaners were once again being recruited in Derby. So I asked for a day off work so that I could check out my chances of employment there. I remember having to ask the permission of the watchman of the overbridge to the locomotive works before I was allowed to cross.

Once I got there, I was told to see the chief clerk. He looked me up and down and decided that I was tall enough, had good eyesight without glasses and looked fit enough for him to ask some more questions. Could I obtain two references to prove that I was of good character? 'Yes', I said. Would I be prepared to live away from home or to travel to wherever the railway wanted me to work? Once again, the answer had to be 'Yes'. Anything else would have ruled me out. There would be many other questions to answer later.

So I was given a date to start work as an engine cleaner. In September 1937, I cleaned the family shoes for the last time and left before the autumn winds had the chance to blow the leaves from the trees.

Chapter Four

The Tramp of Many Feet

On 13th September, 1937, I entered the service of the London, Midland & Scottish Railway Company (LMS). A young man, born and bred in the country, was starting work in the town. And not just any town, but Derby - one of the great railway centres of England.

My home was only about 11 miles away. Journeys to Derby, first by train and later by bus, had become a regular part of my childhood. From the age of five, my father and I would watch Derby County on a Saturday afternoon and then join the queue for a tram to the town centre. A cup of tea on the balcony of the old market hall then a short walk to the fish market. Having bought some herrings or maybe mussels, it would be time for the trip home.

I had also been a patient at the Derbyshire Royal Infirmary, then a very austere and forbidding place for a small child. Fortunately, minor ailments would not prevent me from passing the medical and eyesight tests that were part of the entrance examination for railway workers. These were a routine part of the job, particularly for the man who aspired to the footplate grades.

Medical tests were one thing - the rules and regulations were something else. Take my word for it, I know the following extract from the LMS rule book by heart. Rule 1, Clause A was as follows:

> Employees MUST reside at such places as may be appointed, attend at such hours as shall be required, pay strict obedience to all persons placed in authority over them, conform to all rules and regulations of the Company and, apart from the Company's business, must not engage in trade.

Note the word 'MUST'. And that is just the start. In the 1930s, discipline was the top and bottom line. I noticed this early on during our 30-minute lunch break. We ate - not in a staff room, canteen or bothy - but in a mess. The military origins were clear and so was the discipline.

In the early years of the last century, the Midland Railway recruited many men who were returning home from the Boer War. One such was Lieutenant-Colonel Harold Rudgard. He would have been quite a young man then and, in 1937, was still pursuing his railway career. He was then the superintendent of motive power for the Midlands region of the LMS. So it was easy to see where the army-type discipline had its origins.

None of this was known to the young man who made his second journey across the Hulland Street bridge on that autumn morning in 1937. The first journey had been to look for employment. The second was to start work. I was just one of thousands who flocked over the bridge between 7.15 and 7.55 in the morning.

Some of the people came on foot, from the streets surrounding the area of St Andrew's and Holy Trinity churches. Many more came in buses run by Derby Corporation and the Trent Omnibus Company.

A line-up of locomotives around the turntable outside No. 4 shed on 9th October, 1938. *Left to right:* Stanier class '5' 4-6-0 No. 5180 and Compound 4-4-0s Nos. 933, 1053 and 1025.
A.N.H. Glover/Kidderminster Railway Museum

Johnson class '3F' 0-6-0 No. 3400 stands next to the water tank at Derby on 9th October, 1938, by which time I had been made redundant. *L.W. Perkins/Kidderminster Railway Museum*

At the street end of the bridge were three small flights of steps. On the level, this solid metal structure with a tarmac floor stood over the railway lines at the south end of Derby Midland station. Solid though it was, at around 7.45 in the morning, it shivered and shook with the tramp of many feet .

At the far end of the bridge was a gradual slope down to ground level. Most of the workmen turned left to the many workshops covering a vast area. A few went straight ahead. The young lad from the country turned right across the railway lines to Running Department, No. 4 shed, just another young man entering the line of promotion. From cleaner to fireman to driver. That particular journey would take 18 years. But this was the beginning

By Wednesday of my first week cleaning railway engines, I was beginning to settle in. The routine became familiar. We stood waiting for a few minutes while the man in charge completed his paper-work. So much depended on how many of the senior cleaners were needed for firing duties. Then the rest of us were detailed off, four at a time, to a particular engine. That is how we worked, in gangs of four. You just had to listen for your name to be called and it was usually about 20 names later that he got to 'Weston'.

We worked two shifts. Day turn was 7.55 am, 30 minutes meal break and finish at 4.25 pm. Night turn, start at 7.55 pm, finishing at 4.25 next morning. It was hard, repetitive work but we didn't let ourselves think of it as onerous or boring because it was a living and we were grateful. We preferred the day shift, of course. Cold and tired at the end of the shift, you did sometimes wonder whether there was anything more to life.

Day or night, though, the routine was much the same. Report to the stores, give the storekeeper the number of the engine you are working on. He hands you over a bundle of cotton waste, some rather brown cloths and a box of black wax. It takes two of you to carry this because there are also two cans of paraffin mixture, always known as 'jazz', or sometimes 'lightning'. I didn't work as quick as lightning!

Your two mates have gone to find a couple of trestles - just a plank with a sturdy leg at each end and braced with metal arms. These were substantial constructions and they needed to be because they were all you had to stand on to apply the wax to the tender. There was nothing to stop you falling off if you took one step too far - so you didn't take one step too far. There were various Factory Acts to do with safety but they didn't apply to the railway industry. But at least there were four of us working together so we could keep an eye out for each other.

Two men worked on each side of the engine. Start at the top and work down so it's one on the boiler and one on the tender, with a lump of black wax. We toss a coin. The winner will always take the boiler graft. Not only is it a bit safer because there is a bigger and firmer foothold. But it's quicker and easier, too. The boiler would sometimes still be a bit warm so the wax would run more freely. The tender would be full of cold water and that black wax would stay hard and unresponsive in your hands. Winning that toss would be a good start to the shift. Win or lose, though, there would be a lot of elbow grease involved. No slacking on the job. We had to get one engine cleaned by the meal break. Now, I don't want these memories of mine to suggest that, things were better then. In very many ways, they certainly were not. But we were a cheerful and easy-going bunch. In all those years, I don't remember anyone grumbling that they were always losing the toss. We tended to grin and get on with it.

Once the top part of the tender has been waxed, the remainder can be cleaned from floor level. Better working on the ground. Next we start on the engine wheels, connecting rod and side rods. The wheels have a thick layer of 'swarf' which we remove with the metal scraper. 'Swarf' is simply a mixture of oil and dust which builds up on the wheels. When the scraper has removed most of it, vigorous rubbing with 'jazz' on a cloth will remove the rest. As the engine stands over a pit, one man goes underneath to clean the inside motions, and one cleans the cab area.

Around about ten o'clock, we get a short break. One of the gang takes his tea and sugar in a can to the messroom. The mashing can is a most essential item in our personal belongings. The break is unofficial so the journey is made furtively, dodging round the backs of engines. No doubt the chargehand cleaner knew full well what was going on but it wouldn't do for higher management to see.

This unofficial tea break was repeated at about 3 pm. By that time, we would be working on our second engine. The first one would have been finished at about 12.25. Then it was the job of removing the morning's accumulated dirt from our hands. If you had been working with 'jazz', pour some of that on to your hands and rub vigorously with a cloth. Black wax was too ingrained for that. The only thing that would shift it was sand from the sandhole. Just imagine rubbing sand vigorously between your hands followed by a good going-over with carbolic soap. The afternoon engine didn't get quite the same attention as the morning one: not so much time and fewer visits from the chargeman.

Washing your hands took place in the locker room and bath-house. When that was built, two baths had been included and I think they were the two least-used baths that anyone ever saw. In all the years from 1937 to 1974 I never saw or heard of anyone using them. There were two good reasons for this. The first is that the bath-house with its ever-open door got more than its share of dust and dirt. The second was that the idea of bringing a change of clothing to work and having a bath before going home was not the way that railwaymen's minds worked.

For drivers and firemen, the places they were going to after work didn't expect fresh clothing. Not having a car meant you weren't going to travel very far. For the teetotallers, straight home. For those who liked a drink, there were plenty of pubs in the area. They were not open all day in those days, just four hours in the morning and four in the evening.

The washbasins were fully utilized, though. Five minutes was the allowed time for cleaning up and walking to the time clock. Sometimes, the chargeman stood outside and wouldn't allow any cleaners in until the appointed time. If he wasn't there, some of us would be in earlier. Just as well, there were only 12 washbasins and between 20 and 30 cleaners on the day shift.

At 4.23 pm, a queue would form up at the time clock. Always first there was one of the shed labourers and he would try to urge the clock forward to 4.25 by banging on the handle several times before putting his card in. It made no difference but he thought it did! For me, there was a walk back across the bridge and then catch a trolleybus back to Madison Avenue, Chaddesden, where I was lodging. I had finished my first day's work for the LMS.

On that first day, though, there was only one question which needed answering. Would young John turn up for work on the Tuesday? Of course I did. This was 1937, you didn't just walk out of a job. The other advantages were that the future would follow a set pattern - and that I was getting more than double the pay that I had been making at Langley Priory.

But there was another big question which we had to answer during that first week. Would we pass the medical and eyesight tests? If we didn't, that was end of your career on the footplate. On that Thursday morning of the first week, the chargeman told me to report to the medical officer at 9.30 am and to come straight back from there and carry on with my cleaning duties. Of course, the other lads who have been for medical and eyesight tests tell you what to expect. But, when the test comes, you are not one of the gang. You're on your own.

After a short wait, I was called into a sort of corridor where the eyesight test is conducted. First there is what they call the form vision test. That's where you have to read the bottom line on a chart - first with the left eye only, then with the right eye and finally with both together. So that's out of the way. Then onto the colour vision test. If you fail this, your chance of a career as an engineman has gone – just like that! All you have to do is to read correctly about eight pinpoints of different coloured lights. You know that there are only four colours you have to identify - white, green, yellow and red. So why eight pinpoints? Because there are different shades and sometimes they threw in a maverick. You have been warned about this so when it comes up - orange - you simply say, 'Red'. A vital call - and you have got it right.

After this, you go to another room to see the medical officer. Just answer a few questions about childhood illnesses, he already knows you are fit and active because of the job you are doing. After that, it's the old clarion call of 'Drop your trousers'. That's just to confirm that you are, in fact, male, and also that you are not suffering from a hernia which we used to call a rupture. My father had a rupture and had to wear a cumbersome belt from the age of 19. I didn't wear underpants at the time, very few working men did, so dropping my trousers told the doctor all he needed to know.

Back to the shed then to start working again. And to talk about the next test - being passed for firing duties, which the older lads had already taken. So we talked about it when we got together in the cab to finish off our first engine. If the chargeman found you there as a group at any other time, you were ordered down and no nonsense.

On 14th October, 1937, I reached 18 years of age. That meant that I would be working nights for the first time in my life and I didn't enjoy it. I didn't like my eating and sleeping patterns being disrupted. But I had to get used to it - it would be part of my life for the next 37 years.

Life in a big steam shed mirrored life outside at that time. The ranks and hierarchies were rigid and well-defended. I was a cleaner who would move on to be a fireman and maybe a driver. But there were many other ranks and

Compound 4-4-0 No. 1105 in steam on No. 4 shed on 9th October, 1938.
L.W. Perkins/Kidderminster Railway Museum

Ex-Midland Railway passenger engine (note the full cab roof) class '1P' 0-4-4T No. 1228 at Derby on 13th March, 1938 - at this time I was cleaning engines on shed.
A.N.H. Glover/Kidderminster Railway Museum

grades as well. The job titles make it clear what they actually did: boiler washers, tube cleaners, shed labourers, coaling plant attendants, foreman cleaners, telephone attendants, caller-ups. Then there was the running foreman in charge, the inside foreman whose duties were largely clerical and supervisory. He was the main link to top management and reported to them on a daily basis. His assistants were responsible for rostering drivers and firemen on all their goods trains and local trips. His opposite number was the outside foreman who dealt with the stabling and marshalling of goods and passenger engines. The shed was open 24 hours a day, seven days a week.

At the depot, there were also a number of fitting staff in at least two categories. First, there were those who were called leading hands and leading hand fitters who worked on the most important jobs. There would be other less skilled, and a few tender fitters who only worked on that part of the engine. In the walkway between the locomotives, we always had to dodge round items that all of these men were working on, notably leaf springs. In some museums, I have seen motor cars with exactly the same kind of spring - built up in a series of metal plates, starting at the bottom with small ones and increasing in size, plate by plate. All enclosed in a buckle.

The fitters had their own supervisors called RE (repairing engines) foremen. The running foreman was properly referred to as WE (working engine) foreman. Three shifts made up the 24 hours of one day and night.

Two more grades, ending with the - to us - most important of the lot. There were all the clerical staff who kept records of what everyone was doing in the course of their day's work. And then there was the pay clerk. He it was who drew cash from the bank on Fridays to pay us between twelve noon and 5 pm. The money was always handed out in a small building at the street end of the works overbridge.

No. 1 shed at Derby was the world's first railway locomotive running shed, although Barrow Hill also lays claim to this title. It should have been made a World Heritage site and I believe that in another country it would have been. We have a great and glorious history in this country - but, despite that, we tend to overlook great assets of which many other countries would be very proud.

No. 1 shed , like Nos. 2 and 3, has long since been closed. Commonly known as the 'Roundhouse', No. 1 shed was restored in 2009, and taken over by Derby College. No. 4 shed, where I spent so many years, is also now no more.

So - with a few diversions - that is the story of my first few weeks as a railwayman. Engine cleaner J.A. Weston, check No. 1137. One month in 44 years. But perhaps it was the most important month of all.

Ex-MR '3F' class 0-6-0 No. 3510 north of Ambergate with a coal train, destined for Rowsley sidings. The 'white feather' of steam comes from the safety valves.
Kidderminster Railway Museum

Chapter Five

A Job for Life?

In 1937 as a young engine cleaner, I had a dream that one day I would become the driver of the steam engines I was cleaning. It would take a long time, but the time would come. That was the promise that tempted us all in the line of promotion. Everyone was subject to the same disciplines, a long straight road ahead but with hard work you will get there. The incentive to stay all those years ago was the prospect of a job for life.

The day I began my employment on the railway, 13th September, 1937, was my seniority date, the key to a completely rigid system. It did not matter what age you were when you started on the railway, and some were as young as 14. You were not allowed to start as an engine cleaner until you were 17, and then on day work only, but there were plenty of other jobs for younger boys at a big depot like Derby.

This is the way it worked for me, a late starter in the 1934 to 1937 intake of engine cleaners. After just one month of regular day turns, I was put onto shift work, having turned eighteen. The upside of turning 18 was that I was now old enough to be passed out for firing duties. Our rate of pay was 30*s.* per week at age 17, rising to 36*s.* at 18.

The process of being passed for firing duty was quite straightforward. We were expected to gain a working knowledge of the working parts of the steam engine as part of our cleaning operations. We were also supplied with a copy of the Rule Book, which outlined at a basic level the duties of a fireman. Management knew that the most important part of our learning would come from being paired with different drivers almost every day.

In early November 1937, I and a few others were sent to see Mr H.H. Basford, the assistant superintendent. Having asked a few basic questions, he told us we were qualified to act as fireman. With a warning to pay strict obedience to all persons placed in authority over us – a reminder of what it said in the Rule Book.

So what did this mean for us financially? Starting wage as a fireman was 57*s.* a week. All wage increases after that were decided by the 'turn' system. If an engine cleaner worked as a fireman one day in a six day week, that counted as one 'turn'. A total of 313 turns represented a year (that's six turns a week for 52 weeks, plus one). Every wage increase, from 57*s.* to the top rate for drivers of 90*s.* was graduated. After 626 turns as a fireman, you would be on 63*s.*, after another 313, it would be 66*s.* It would take 10 years of firing turns to reach the top rate of 72*s.*, and another 10 to progress to 90*s.* a week as driver. It was only after 1945 that these long intervals started to come down. About 1947, when I had eight years and nine months turns, that 10 years was reduced to five. In practice, many footplatemen from 1900 to 1947 did not attain the top rate of pay until they were between 45 and 50 years of age. At some depots, such as in London, it could be shorter, but in others, even longer than that.

The men who started at Derby in 1934 became drivers in around 11 to 13 years. By my time that had risen to over 18 years, of which for around 14½ years I was firing in main line 'links'. Pre-war, a link at Derby consisted of eight weeks work. In the nine goods links, three of those eight weeks involved lodging turns of duty, four weeks of main line goods work out and home on the same day, and a week of local or shunting work. So every week in any two months was different. In addition to the nine main line goods links at Derby there were four passenger links, and two more which worked *both* passenger and goods turns over the old North Staffordshire Railway, going to Stoke and Crewe.

After 12 months paired with the same driver, a firemen would move to another link with another driver. This system gave every one of us a wide range of experience, and knowledge of train management, a system that worked very well for a very long time.

The general procedure for drivers was that they worked firstly through shed and local links up to the 'Spare' link. There they provided day to day, or week to week cover for drivers who were off sick, on annual leave or route learning. From there, in strict seniority order, they progressed into one of the main line goods links, and eventually onto passenger work.

That is the system which operated at Derby No. 4 shed for many years. In 1919, the eight-hour day had been introduced, and that 48-hour week remained unchanged for the next 30 years. Prior to that, 10- and 12-hours shifts were the norm. World War II would bring more changes.

You might think that drivers would always be older than the fireman they were paired with. Often that would be the case, but there were exceptions. In 1939, at No. 4 shed driver Billy Kirkman was working with fireman Charlie Farnsworth, a man 18 months older than he was. Billy later told me how this came about. He had volunteered for war service, though under the age limit, as some young men did. On active service in France he was shot in the stomach area, which resulted in him wearing a belt round his middle for the rest of his life. Invalided out of the army he was sent back to England, and by 1916 he was working at No. 4 shed, first as cleaner, then later fireman. So his seniority date was some time in 1916. Something else he told me was that, due to an administrative error, he was listed as killed in action. Outside the Midland Hotel, on Midland Road in Derby, is a war memorial, and there amongst the other names is 'KIRKMAN, W.H.' It's still there!

Tommy Farnsworth was called up to fight in the same war, and like Billy he was one of the lucky ones who came home. He, however, had served until 1919, and started on the railway on his return. That means his seniority date was sometime in 1919. Hence although he was older than Billy, in railway terms he was the junior man. By 1939 he was the senior fireman at the depot. Every man in front of him had been passed for driving. Eight or 10 firemen might be passed at a time, then it could be six months or as much as three years before more drivers were required. That is what happened to me, between sometime in 1952, and October 1955, no men were passed for driving at Derby. (It might have been longer, but I was able to do something about that, but that will come later.) In later years, some men found a way round the problem by moving to other depots. Some Derby men went to Burton, where junior men were being passed, and eventually some of them returned to Derby.

So there you have it. A fireman working with a driver over a year younger than he is. Bill and Tommy had a saying at the time, 'What would you do mate, as one driver to another?' You just have to laugh about it and get on with the job.

To illustrate how cruel the system could be, I'll tell you about another man, who joined the LMS at Shrewsbury in 1924. Trevor Adamson was moved from pillar to post in his first 10 years of railway service. Railway management tried very hard to get Trevor to pack the job in. They moved him seven times in the 10 years between 1924 and 1934. I don't remember now where they sent him, but certainly some of those moves were what was called 'out of grade', and three of the moves involved him moving home. One regular tactic was to send footplatemen to act as porters at small country stations. That happened to several young men at Derby.

All this means that it takes a long time to get the number of turns required for a pay rise. I wonder if anyone had less firing experience than Trevor in any 10 year period on any railway? When he came to Derby, he had worked 39 firing turns in 10 years. Or to put it another way, one every three months.

So why didn't he, like many other young railwaymen treated like pawns on a chessboard, pack it in? The answer is that there wasn't anything any better to be had. Work in the 1920s and 1930s was hard to come by. The General Strike in 1926 and the Jarrow March in 1936 were both before my working life, but I was later to find out how difficult it was to find regular employment in the winter of 1938/1939.

Trevor Adamson's second 10 years in railway service were much better, for a while. At Derby, he soon got a regular firing turn. When war came along, promotion quickened up. Earlier I wrote of the main line goods links having eight weeks work. In the early part of 1941, this increased to 10, by adding a week of control relief and a week of shed duties to each of the goods links. At an open meeting called by the staff representatives, some of the older men spoke against it, but they were outvoted by men who had waited a long time to see an improvement in their promotion prospects. It was in June 1941 that I became a registered fireman, and in December of that year, moved up to the London goods link. By then, with bombing raids taking place, it was taking too long to get to London with goods trains, so we didn't go beyond Wellingborough.

In due course, Trevor was passed out for driving. But then he had the bad luck to suffer an accident in blackout conditions. On the north side of No. 4 shed, for many years the goods engines were stabled on lines N1, N2 and N3, where they were prepared for their next trip. Trevor Adamson was there one night in the winter of 1944, with no lighting except the small flare torches we had to use. He was moving from one line to another when he fell and hit his head on the opposite rail. That accident resulted in him losing the sight of one eye – a disaster for his career on the footplate.

Finding suitable work for Trevor was taken up by the union at national, as well as local level. Negotiations took some time, but eventually it was agreed that he could continue as a driver, but not of course on the main line, and only on a day turn. So he was given a preparation duty, based at the shed, and that lasted until the time came for him to retire or take redundancy. This sort of agreement had never happened before, to the best of my knowledge. It was visible progress in railway industrial relations.

Another man at Derby called George Rhodes had lost the sight of an eye some years previously, in a firework accident. At that time, there was no chance of him continuing on the footplate. He was found a position as lodging house keeper, at the trainmen's lodging house in Derby. I know that he was still there in 1939. The lodging house closed around 1950, and was later let to a firm of mowing machine manufacturers.

Pre-World War II, the management used every trick in the book to prevent people getting the higher rate of pay by virtue of the turn system. The passed firemen of the time, men often around 45 years of age, kept a strict record of every higher grade duty. About the only thing management could not do anything about to keep wages down was when heavy falls of snow caused trains to be stuck in drifts. Snowploughs had to be called out, and a great deal of overtime was worked.

These movements of men were governed by the Promotion, Transfer and Redundancy Agreement (PT&R). A very important undertaking in that agreement was the clause that gave men the right to return to their home station. If management moved a man away from home, then any cleaners recruited in their absence would not be allowed to take up our position in the line of promotion. In due course, I had reason to be grateful for this.

In addition to the PT&R agreement, operated on a national basis, there was some scope for men to take grievances, or requests to local management. From 1923 onwards, Local Departmental Committees (LDCs) were set up. Very few working men at the time had this kind of representation. Later you will find that I served for some time on the LDC at No. 4 shed. Unpaid and voluntary of course. The story of my life!

So, as a 'passed cleaner'- someone who had proved his worth in the hard, dirty and repetitive business of cleaning railway engines - my first rung up the promotion ladder was to think about firing duties. More than a step - a huge leap forward. Cleaning engines - 6*s*. a day, firing rate minimum 9*s*. 6*d*. When 2*s*. could buy you a good night out, that extra 3*s*. 6*d*. sounded like paradise.

The drivers, of course, didn't see it as part of their duty to be too encouraging to young firemen. They were simply telling it exactly as it was. One of my early firing turns was on a Friday night, 'Seven o'clock Carriage Works Shunt'. In a quiet moment, the driver turned to me and said, 'Now then, my lad, do you think you are going to like this job?' I couldn't give a quick answer to that, simply because I'm still finding my feet. He continued,

> Well, young man, it's like this. Tonight you have to come to work at seven o'clock. Your mates on the day shift are just getting ready for their Friday night out. Home at three in the morning - bed. You may think you are going to make up for it next week but suppose you are put down for a job at two in the morning. You'll be going to bed at six o'clock the night before. So it can seem like all work and sleep. Still, if you behave yourself and don't pinch anything, it's a job for life.

And that mattered in those days. I'm not saying it was right but you were honestly grateful for 'a job for life'. Many people - most people - didn't have that and 25 to 30 years' service without earning top rate until you were nearly 50 years old seemed a small price to pay.

The young passed cleaner is called on for firing duties as and when required. In 1937, that meant, for me, around 10 or a dozen turns in six weeks. In 1938, just one turn in six months. And that one was followed by transfer and redundancy.

I still remember my very first turn of duty as a fireman. It was November 1937 and a very foggy day. My driver was Albert Ault, then in one of the main line links. His regular fireman, Alf Jacquest, was off duty for a funeral. Turning up at 7.55 for cleaning, I was told not to clock on, but to report to the running foreman. At his window, I am given a timecard and instructed to sign on at 8 o'clock for yard trial. We were entering a short period where winter weather means a little more work for the passed cleaners. It lasted all of six weeks and I was given perhaps a dozen or so firing turns in that time. The time card for drivers and firemen doesn't have to go into a machine. It shows two rates of pay, 36*s*. a week when you are cleaning, 57*s*. when you are on a firing turn. So I shall get 9*s*. 6*d*. for this day.

We were given an engine to take out on this little run. And it's the shortest possible run, just beyond the shed signals, perhaps a quarter of a mile. Up to the departure signal at Engine Sidings No. 2, when that clears up to Engine Sidings No. 1 home signal. At that point the fireman gets off the engine to ring out on the bell push below the signal post. The code tells the signalman where we want to go - one for the passenger station, two for St Mary's or north of there, three for Chaddesden and four for a return to No. 4 shed. These yard trials are for passenger engines going from the loco works to their allocated depots - which could be anywhere in the LMS system

Before the days of power controlled signal boxes, lineside boxes were a familiar feature. Many small passenger stations had a siding where goods traffic could be unloaded. Almost every road crossing was controlled from a signal box. Sometimes the gates were opened and closed by a crossing keeper who lived in a house close to the gates. When the trains were running, the crossing keeper had to get permission from the signal box before he could open the gates to let road vehicles through.

All the busy signal boxes were linked to each other by the block telegraph system. Messages respecting trains were passed from box to box by the bell code. Every type of train and every kind of occurrence was provided for. Just as a driver had to know the routes he signed for, so the signalman had to be thoroughly acquainted with his box. Ring that bell, pull that lever. One of the finer arts of communications, basic though it may seem.

Gongs were used in certain places, usually where the curvature of the line or an overbridge restricted visibility. New Lount colliery sidings is a very good example. We used to take a train of empty wagons up the branch line from Chaddesden to New Lount. When we arrived at the empty side of New Lount colliery, with around 40 wagons, we used to run under the bridge which still carries the road from Melbourne to Coalville, the B587. Through this bridge,

EX-MR class '3F' No. 3229 at Derby. In the background we can see the roof of Derby's No. 3 shed. *P.M. Alexander/Kidderminster Railway Museum*

Derby Engine Sidings No. 1 signal box photographed in the 1960s. The locomotive works are in the background. *D. Wittamore/Kidderminster Railway Museum*

and on a bend, we could see only the first five or six wagons. So we were stopped and restarted by a gong. This was controlled by a wire running alongside the track, operated by the shunter from his little cabin. With noise from passing traffic on the road and also on the engine, you rarely heard the gong unless you were stopped right close to it. So the procedure was to watch the wire. Pulled once, that meant stop. Pause, while the brake van was uncoupled and turned on to loaded wagons and the points set for an empty siding. Then the wire would be pulled several times. Seeing this movement was made easier in fog or darkness by tying small pieces of cloth to the wire, that system worked very well.

Before we leave New Lount sidings, I must tell you of an incident between there and Worthington. Just to show how, sometime, somewhere, human fallibility catches us all out. After detaching empties and picking up the shunter, we proceeded back down the branch line to the point where the loaded wagons were waiting. Here, three or four sidings all converge into one exit line. This is fitted with what are called trap points. A safety device in case loaded wagons run away, in which case they will run off the rails and pile up causing great damage to wagons and contents. A job for the steam crane.

The gradient from New Lount to Worthington falls quite sharply. There is no signal box at New Lount, it's the end of the branch. So the shunter is in charge of the ground frame from which the trap points are controlled. He and the guard are responsible, also, for the handbrakes being applied on those loaded wagons until the engine is turned into them. After which, we used to hold them by the engine's braking system until it was time to go.

This particular mishap didn't happen to me and the enginemen were not in any way to blame. One day, the engine was turned onto a siding to pick up some wagons, On the adjoining siding stood the major portion of the train with three or four handbrakes on wagons applied. The guard picked most of these up. Nothing happened until the engine moved on to the next line. A slight tremor was all that was needed. Slowly the wagons started to move, towards the open points. When the guard and shunter realized what had happened, they tried to apply wagon brakes. Too late, the wagons were in control – disaster loomed.

Another turn quickly coming my way was a shunting duty on the workshops. It could be any one of four or five turns in the loco works and roughly the same in the carriage and wagon works. The drivers on these jobs did not have regular firemen, just whoever was first in line for firing work.

Apart from one carriage works turn, which runs on the three shifts, it was all morning and afternoon turns. The shunting staff were nearly all on regular day work. All the engines had to be serviced, preparation in the mornings, disposal in the evenings so there were two sets of men to look after the engines. Morning shift on at 6.40 for loco works and finish at 2.40. Afternoon men on at 2.10 relieve the day men. So they shunt until 5 o'clock or thereabouts, after which there was a 20 minutes meal break. Two of the afternoon sets take out of the works all the engines that are available from the paint shop: some new, some having had major overhauls, all require a running-in period. And that is where the young firemen get their muscles working.

All these engines had to be coaled and watered. Fortunately there was a mechanical coaling plant. The engines were known as 'dead engines', meaning they were not in steam. We were the first link in the chain that carries them into service. They all move stiffly, like arthritic old men.

After a struggle, two shunting engines together, we get them to the water crane. Two firemen, up and down steps, on to the tender, pull the leather bag round, put it in the big hole below in the tank. Driver turns the water on, says 'tell me when it's three-quarters full'. In service, of course, you fill them to the top. Much the same with coal and all to do with economy. If you send every engine away with a tender full of coal and water, Derby will show 'excessive consumption'.

There was still some heavy work to do. The sandboxes have to be part filled. The engines are groaning again on their way to the shed. We stop outside the top door of the shed and the two firemen fill the sand buckets. These are something like a two gallon bucket with a wide spout. Our drivers stand on the framing and we pass the buckets up to them, one at a time. This was a form of weight-training, swinging the heavy buckets up to footplate level. Then we stable the engines on the south side of the shed.

The following day, these 'dead' engines were drawn out of the sidings and propelled on to the weighbridge. Here they were carefully set so that the bogie wheels and the driving wheels are weighed. Assuming everything is OK - and it always seems to be - the engines can be fired up. The engine is taken round Derby yard a few times; the next day it will be sent a little bit further.

For the young fireman, this is where the job gets a bit more interesting. All my early firing turns were local. Shunting turns in the loco works and the carriage works. Later, shunting turns at Chaddesden and St Mary's. All the time, of course, you are learning your trade.

In the fullness of time, I was called upon for the 8 o'clock Trent trial. This was the next stage in the running-in process for the newly-painted passenger engine, which we brought off the loco works a day or two before. Not quite a main line trip, but a chance to see a little more of the countryside around Derby.

Here we have the usual duties under the heading of 'preparation of engine'. Once it was established that the new boy was going to stay the course - and subject to his medical - he is issued with the Rule Book (we'll give it the capital letters it deserves). Naturally, the first thing you read, learn and inwardly digest is the part that relates to what you already know.

While cleaning engines, the general layout has become familiar. The first lesson is to keep a sharp look-out at all times. For your own safety first and foremost but then you'll also be looking out for your mates in the gang. There are some differences now, of course. No longer are you working with three mates of about your own age. You are now with a driver who may be anything from 20 to 40 years older than yourself.

When you go to the stores and give the engine number to the storekeeper, you are given a bucket of tools and - most importantly - a firing shovel. Your badge of office. Now then, what else is there in the bucket? It's all laid down in the rule book. Four spanners, of varying sizes, a brush, and a tin containing 12 detonators. And two red flags. Why 12 detonators and two red flags? It's all to do with safe working. If you are unfortunate enough to be involved in real trouble, then both your train and others need to be protected. Your driver - hopefully - will be well versed in Protection of Trains and the use of Wrong Line Orders: rules 178 to 188 in the British Railways Rule Book.

Hopefully, we won't need any of this today; but the possibility has always to be at the forefront of our thinking. If it is just the driver and the fireman who are available to protect their train - and that could happen - there is a procedure to follow. Briefly, each man will set off with six detonators and one flag, the minimum to protect a disabled train. You may well be thinking - what happens if there is an accident at night? What use will a red flag be then? You might as well wrap your sandwiches in it. But that has been thought through. With every engine going out on a running line, there will be two headlamps. And each of these will have a red shade. So, in a night-time emergency, both men will set off with a headlamp set to a red aspect. The fireman goes forward to protect the opposite running line. The guard goes back to protect the line on which his train is standing; only if the guard is not available will the driver need to protect his train in the rear. Right at the end of Rule No. 188, there is a clause covering the whole purpose of the Protection Rules. From memory, it goes something like, 'In all circumstances, the safety of the travelling public must be the ultimate concern of the train crew'. That's it.

But, as I say, we hope the safety procedures won't be needed today. So my first duty, as the fireman, is to check the steam and water position. Do we have a reasonably good fire? What is the boiler water level? Do we have enough coal for the journey? And is the water tank almost full? All these are visual checks. The first three before we collect the tools from the stores. After that we attend to the headlamps.

Now two other checks are necessary. Do we have the right fire irons? Three are needed. A straight dart, a bent dart and a clinker shovel. The darts are a long iron with a chisel-shaped end, in the case of the bent dart, right-angled at 90 degrees. Both are used to break up clinker, an accumulation of spent coal. If the unlikely happens and both injectors fail - they are the bits of kit that put water into the boilers - then we shall have to lift the fire out of the firebox with the clinker shovel to prevent damage to the firebox crown. We also need a coalpick to break up the very large lumps of coal. For many years, I had a rather unsightly mark on one of my fingers, this was caused by throwing a large lump of coal into the firebox. On the way in, my finger was trapped between the coal and the baffle plate.

The baffle plate, like everything else, it has a purpose. We don't live for very long without air. And the fire in a steam locomotive won't function without air. This is taken into the firebox through one - sometimes two - dampers. There are two devices in the firebox to ensure that cold air doesn't blow straight on to the firebox tube plate and cause stresses and strains. One is the baffle plate, up to 18 inches long and semicircular in shape. The other is the brick arch - just like any other brick arch - but nowhere near a semi-circle, just slightly raised in the middle. Together, they ensure that the cold air warms up before it hits the tube plate. From time to time, the brick arch may need renewing. And very occasionally, it can completely collapse. The fireman and the driver are not required to deal with this, but as a passed cleaner, I could, on occasions, be required to report for labouring duties. On one such occasion, I had to throw out a collapsed brick arch from the firebox. And - also just once - to throw out badly bent firebars. Once was enough - or once too many in fact. I'm quite claustrophobic. It didn't scare me too much at the time - although I was very glad to scramble out again. Now I get upset just writing about it. Climbing in and out of a firebox through a fire hole door? Never again. Not ever.

There are two other checks to make from the foot framing in front of the cab. Sandboxes - six of them. Are they reasonably full? And last comes one of the most important checks of all. Amongst our four spanners, we have one which is seven-eighths of an inch. We check the smokebox door which is secured by six metal lugs. Always check the amount of ash in the smokebox. It should be only a small amount. That's what the seven-eighths spanner is for, to operate the securing lugs on small engines.

So what remains to be done? Go to the messroom and make a cup of tea, that's what. By this time, we are almost due off the shed – 45 minutes preparation time for all the small engines. For the big ones, class '5' and '5XP', one hour. While all this is happening, the driver is oiling the engine and making all his visual checks as well.

If you think that all this is rather a long-winded explanation, you would be right. But I have my reasons. Today, people make long journeys just to photograph the occasional steam engine running over the iron road. And we have some very successful heritage railways up and down the British Isles. The magic of steam they call it and so it is. But there's no sleight of hand involved. Just a lot of hard, back-breaking toil. And a very long apprenticeship. Eighteen years as cleaner and fireman before I became a passed fireman. Then a route card that involved me in working every class of train that there's ever been on the Midland Division of the LMS – bar one. I was never called on to work a Royal Train. Thousands of drivers never were.

We have followed the engine as it was pulled and pushed around by the shunting engine, everything stiff and unyielding like a frightened virgin. Once in steam, and having made that journey round the Derby yard, it is ready for something else. We proceed from the shed signal to Engine Sidings No. 2 signal box and then to No. 1 and the ringing out point. This time I ring three to indicate that we are running towards Chaddesden. And the journey begins.

The engine loosens up a little as we pass the curve round from Derby Junction. This, for me, is a new experience. We pass the sidings at Chaddesden where trains from north, south and west enter to be split up and remarshalled. No surprise this, Chaddesden is correctly called a marshalling yard. Next is Turntable Sidings - cleverly called that because there's a turntable there. Not for Derby engines to use, though, this would mainly be for Nottingham or Leicester men who work a train in and then take another out from the south end. It's an old-fashioned turntable, balancing the engine is a work of art. A few inches too far and it's very difficult to move the table at all. Set back a little, the table queedles. Now there's a word - 'queedle'. It doesn't mention it in my old dictionary, it means what happens to a turntable with a well-balanced engine on it. Anyone who's tried it will know what I mean.

Next we arrive at Spondon Junction. Here we wait until a passenger train comes along from Derby South, via Etches Park. Some passenger trains run into Derby via Chaddesden, but not very many. All the expresses run on the other line and they take precedence. Once the fast train clears Spondon station, the signal clears for us.

The engine gathers her skirts up, in a manner of speaking, and we're off. Now I have to get used to firing on the move. Like everything else, it takes some working out. All part of the learning process. We pass Spondon, Borrowash, Draycott and Old Sawley; once, passenger trains stopped at Old Sawley, about a mile from anywhere. To this day, there is a road crossing there. Next we arrive at Sawley station (now Long Eaton station), where there used to be a diversion from the main line. It isn't there any more and a housing estate has taken its place. The diversion was called the North Curve and curve it certainly did at the Trent end. The old Trent station was one of the draughtiest places in the Midlands. Just two platforms, simply a place for changing trains, really.

The North Curve is the line we take with the engines we are running in. Here, the driver will check the engine axleboxes. A fast run for seven or eight miles is the ideal test. If the lubrication system isn't working properly, the axleboxes will be overheating. We would then return to No. 4 shed, if the axleboxes were overheating, that would be at a reduced speed.

Now we have followed a steam engine on its journey from the Derby works. The Trent trial run carried on for many years, until the North Curve was cut out. It was only the passenger engines which were sent out for the Trent trial. All the goods engines were sent out coupled to goods trains, to their own depots. I remember in the mid-1950s, after I became a driver, passenger engines were still going out 'light', that means under their own steam but without a train, which was all part of the running-in process. It would also have dislocated diagrammed programmes to have added them onto another train.

I can tell you of two good examples of how this operated in practice when I was a driver. Several times when I was not required for anything more important, I was called for duty at two o'clock in the morning to work a coupled goods engine to Rotherham Masborough. The engine would be bound for Canklow shed, and it would be coupled onto this train to save an additional journey. At two o'clock in the morning this is the 'rough' side of the job.

The second example illustrates the 'smooth'. After I signed for route knowledge to Chester, there were occasions when I was brought on duty at seven or eight o'clock in the morning to take a passenger engine light to Chester shed, I being the only Derby driver who could go beyond Crewe, the story of that will come later.

Stanier 'Jubilee' class 4-6-0 No. 5559 (later to carry the name *British Columbia*) climbs Camden bank with an express passsenger train *circa* 1934. *Kidderminster Railway Museum*

LMS 'Patriot' class 4-6-0 No. 5533 *Lord Rathmore* on Camden shed on 2nd April, 1938. We called these locomotives 'Baby Scots'. I spent two weeks at Camden in June 1938, prior to being made redundant. *H.C. Doyle/Gresley Society*

Chapter Six

Up the Smoke

In a lifetime of footplate work, there are many defining moments. Assuming that you spent the major part of it on train working, which is what I did, I have had my share of good and bad days, weeks and years. Very near the top of the list of bad days was the morning I came out of the time office, with a message and a ticket to ride. The message was very simple,

> You are being transferred away from Derby. As from the 13th June, 1938, you will be a passed cleaner at Camden Town, London. Report to the running foreman there, on that day, for further instructions.

Having said this, the chief clerk handed me a railway ticket.

In something of a daze, I looked at this ticket outside the time office. The message it conveyed was clear and stark. 'PASS. JA Weston from DERBY to CAMDEN TOWN.' And after this it would normally say 'and back'. But that had been carefully crossed out. As though it were yesterday, I remember the first thought that came into my head – bloody hell, have I got to spend the rest of my life there?

A body blow to me, but not really a big surprise. After almost a straight six months cleaning engines with just one firing turn in that time, we knew that something like that would happen, as it had already happened to so many passed cleaners and firemen from 1922 to 1934. The drivers who asked us to make the Associated Society of Locomotive Engineers & Firemen (ASLEF) our union had seen this coming, and they had told us what we should do when filling out a preference form. That form was given out to footplatemen who were to be transferred away from their depot, as part of the Promotion, Transfer and Redundancy Agreement.

This agreement had been negotiated by the railway trade unions, to provide some protection for staff who were moved around like pawns on a chessboard by railway management, who had almost absolute power over the lives of their employees. Footplate work is specialized. The only opportunity to fire or drive a locomotive other than for the main line railway companies was on colliery or industrial shunting engines. This was reflected in the wages paid to a highly skilled work-force, whose training in those days took place over a long period of time. There were absolutely no short cuts to becoming a driver unless you were prepared to move to another depot in another town, where promotion was swifter. Even then, you would be talking about an apprenticeship of years rather than months.

Birmingham or London were places that in later life I might have moved to for a quicker climb up the ladder. But this was 1938, how could a young man with just nine months' experience of railway work be expected to cope with this sudden upset in career prospects? And what about seeing my family? I was in comfortable lodgings in Moore Street, Derby, from where I could get home every other Saturday night, and come back to Derby on Sunday, because there was a very reliable bus service. There would be no going home for the weekend from London.

So I was aggrieved, but there wasn't any way I could feel sorry for myself. After all, my father had left home at 12 years of age, and I was 18. That's the same age my Uncle Harry was when he emigrated to Canada, and he didn't have a job to go to, which I still had. Life isn't all we want, but it's what we've got. So have it.

I was not alone. In August and September 1937, around 30 young men had started work as engine cleaners at No. 4 shed. The two or three lads junior to me were made redundant without the option of transferring away. About six of us were sent to London, those who had started in August were going north, to Fleetwood and Barrow-in-Furness. There wasn't anything we could do about it, if any one of us had refused to go, we would have been of no further use to the LMS. We did not know then, that we were only 15 months away from another World War. Or, that by 1948, the railway system of the country would be taken over by a Labour Government.

So that was it. I told my landlady on Monday evening that it would be my last week in Derby. And then I wrote a letter to my parents, giving them some warning of what was going to happen. I had what might be my last Sunday at home on 12th June, 1938, for perhaps a very long time.

I remember being about 200 yards from the bus-stop at Breedon when I saw the bus in the distance on that Monday morning. With a heavy suitcase, I couldn't run, so I missed the bus. We had not been told to catch any particular train, so I caught a later bus, and a later train. Therefore I was very much on my own when I got to London, but of course I found my way to Camden Town station, and from there to the motive power depot. It was a busy day for them, finding lodgings for the new arrivals, as it would be at some other LMS running sheds, certainly at Fleetwood and Barrow-in-Furness.

We were soon to find out that young men from these depots had been sent to Camden. All part of the game of chess. The railways didn't send young men to depots 20 or 30 miles away, in case they found their way home for the weekend. When you are over 100 miles from home, there's no chance of that! So there I was, almost alone in the big city. The foreman's office in Camden sent me to No. 122, Gloucester Road, for my place to stay. The next day, I realized how many of us were affected. At Derby, I was next in seniority to Wilf Ward, who started work one week before I did. At Camden, there were two or three lads between us.

I know now why the LMS did all this in 1938. Before then, competition from bus companies had forced them to close many branch lines up and down the system. Now they were competing with airlines, but they had one other problem. As public companies, they had investors: shareholders, who expected a return on their invested wealth. That is why we had to go, economies of scale, they called it. Well, I had invested something myself – my life, which I feel was rather more important.

After one week, I was called into the office at Camden, and given seven days notice, to the effect that my services were no longer required. Just like that. Well I wasn't sorry in any way about that. The only memory I have of the place is that

I didn't like it one bit. Of course, I would not have packed it in. Our family history shows that we are workers not shirkers, and so we accept such things.

After nine months at Derby, and two weeks at Camden Town, my railway career had come to a halt. Wilf Ward told me afterwards that he remained at Camden for two or three months, and that he even had a few firing turns. For every one of us who had been transferred to Camden, over a few weeks, or a few months, the end result was the same, 'Your services are no longer required', and we were given a ticket back to our home depot.

It had of course been a paper exercise. The decision to sack us had already been taken, but the LMS had to show their authority. As our Rule Book said: 'You MUST reside at such places as may be appointed ...'

There was, however, a redeeming feature in all of this. Before the LMS could employ another man in the line of promotion, they had to give every one of us a chance to take up our position again. Where they asked you to restart was at their discretion. I would never have gone back to Camden Town, of that I'm certain.

From this nine months and two weeks in railway service, I had learned much more than you might think. There had been some very important lessons, which would stand me in good stead in the future. It had been a pleasure to work in a gang of four, all of us about the same age, within a few months. Cleaning dirty steam engines, enjoying the unofficial tea breaks and beginning to learn our trade. Afterwards, a few of us would meet up in the evening for a drink and a game of darts. Around a dozen firing turns had given me an insight into the work of the crew on a steam engine. Most of the drivers, themselves approaching retirement, treated their young mate very fairly. We were simply starting out, as they themselves had done 30 or 40 years previously. These were men who had no fear. They had almost without exception been in the footplate grade for well over 20 years before reaching the top rate of pay, and they saw us as their natural successors, after a similar period had elapsed. Working at all hours of the day and night, with one week's holiday a year, was simply a way of life to them. We listened to what they told us, and learned accordingly.

Being treated as I was in the month of June 1938 made me the more determined to fight my corner, against any perceived injustice, all through my working life. And to enjoy the comradeship of men, who trod the same path together. All the ups and downs of this life ensured that we were well aware of our own worth, and that everyone else would recognise that. But now I was leaving railway service, at least for the time being. What, I wondered, would the future hold?

We have been following my story for the years 1937-1938. Just a small part of a much bigger story of what was happening to railways in general. For the people who worked for the four great railway companies of the era, 1934 to 1937 had been a very busy time. From 1924 onwards, there had been virtually no recruitment to the footplate grades, due to the Depression. From 1934 onwards, recruitment began once more. Later, you will find out what a huge influence this had on my railway career.

Two of the four Grouping companies, the LMS and London & North Eastern Railway (LNER) had been building up for the 1937 'Race to the North'. The LMS worked express trains from London (Euston) to Glasgow (Central) – the West Coast main line; the LNER from London (King's Cross) to Edinburgh (Waverley) – the East Coast main line. The LMS introduced the streamlined 'Coronation Scot' express in June 1937 to compete with the LNER's fastest passenger trains. It wasn't the first such race. There had been one 50 years before but the names were different then. There were so many more companies. Now it was down to the two big names: the LMS with their great railway workshops at Crewe and Derby; the LNER building mighty railway locomotives at Darlington, Doncaster and York. The legendary designers, Stanier (LMS) and Gresley (LNER) – successors to George Stephenson and Daniel Gooch except that Gooch worked for what was then the Great Western Railway (GWR). I have seen the wall of white bricks at the former Swindon locomotive works. Each one bearing the name of a former employee. And there are four or five bearing the name 'Weston'.

The GWR was once the brand leader. For two reasons. Their great locomotives, the 'Kings' and 'Castles' could match anything produced anywhere else. And they had the first automatic warning system in Britain, forerunner of today's train protection and warning system, which came to the LMS about 20 years later. The GWR ran trains from London to Bristol and the West of England. From London to Brighton and the south, the Southern Railway (SR) ran famous trains to the continent of Europe: the 'Night Ferry' and the 'Golden Arrow'. These crack, named trains, the glamour girls of their time, were not the main revenue earners.

When coal was king, the coalfields of England, Scotland and Wales used the railways to carry mineral traffic all over the country. Many of the collieries had their own designated fleets of railway wagons – these were known as private owner wagons. The railway companies' wagons were known as 'common users'. Any man, or any company, could transport their goods and chattels over the length and breadth of the land, and the railway companies could not refuse to take a load if they had a suitable vehicle. Truly, the great age of the railway.

Thanks to the efforts of two former colleagues, Barry Gordon and Ben Taylor, I have some of the service records of footplatemen from the 1900s onwards. They give a very detailed insight into the working lives of these people. How they were nearly all around 20 years of age when they entered the line of promotion. That was the bed-rock of our foundations. Your seniority date, the day you became an engine-cleaner, governed everything else that would happen in your working life. It certainly did for me.

The line of promotion is rigid and unyielding. From cleaner to fireman to driver. With a very few exceptions, that would take 20 to 25 years for these men. That's if they remained in good health, didn't get involved in major railway accidents, loss of limbs or loss of life. All of which happened to men I have known. That's a long apprenticeship by any standards. I worked for many years afterwards with men who had done exactly that sort of thing. It could be worse. There were men at some depots still firing regularly at 45 years of age.

When you finally passed out for driving, in those days, there was still some way to go before you reached the drivers' top rate of pay: the magic figure of 90s. per working week of 48 hours. Five years main line driving turns, that was the qualifying period. That could take up to 10 years. It wasn't all that much better in my time. When I was passed out for driving in November 1955, I then had 18 years' service as cleaner and fireman. Because the qualifying period had been reduced, I achieved top driving rate after 21 years. When we weren't very busy, I could still be utilized for firing work at a lower rate of pay.

Unlike so many men in the 1930s, these old drivers were in no danger of losing their job. There had been mass unemployment in a decade from 1924 onwards, a General Strike in 1926 because of adverse working conditions and, later still, the march of unemployed men from Jarrow to London. And I lost my job in 1938, but I never suffered as so many did.

But there I was, in June 1938, going home. It had been a funny old year. Twelve months earlier I was leading the pony up and down the lawn at Langley Priory for 14*s*. a week. Twelve days previously, I was cleaning engines at Camden Town for 36*s*. a week. Now I was unemployed. Whatever happened to the job for life?

It was a new experience, unemployment. But I had learnt so much in the preceding nine months that I could cope. The footplatemen, more than most employed people, knew so much about imposed discipline. That means that the management can tell you where you will work, and when. To reinforce that, the footplateman knows even more about self-discipline. When the caller-up bangs on your wall at two o'clock in the morning, to tell you that you are required to be at work at three o'clock, you sure need it. Maybe you were on duty at six o'clock the day before and expected the same today. Don't turn over and go back to sleep. Do that a few times and you've made a passport to the dole queue for yourself.

And that is where I was in 1938. Not because of any failings on my part but simply that I was surplus to requirements. The message was very clear - your services are no longer required. Maybe someone else will require my services; but that will only happen if I go out and look for work. Once again, mother's old bike was called into action. First stop was the Ministry of Labour sub-office in Melbourne, three miles away. It turns out to be a rather small cubby-hole in a building called, grandly enough, 'The Athenaeum', in Potter Street (better known now as 'Wesley Hall'). The man there has no work for me and no money either, not until I've been out of work long enough to qualify for unemployment benefit.

No matter. I was lucky enough to have a home where money was not a constant problem. The virtues of thrift and only buying what you can afford have been drummed into me from very early days. Determination, not desperation, is the key to my future. The fire in the locomotive firebox is one thing; the fire in your belly is another. Stick a feather in your hat and be happy (the old engine-drivers had another version of that which involved the feather being in a completely different location).

Chapter Seven

A Return to my Roots

Towards the end of September, I still had no job prospects. Nothing moved in the labour market. Neville Chamberlain returned from a trip to Germany, assuring us that he had negotiated 'Peace in our time'. Seventy years on and I still don't trust the promises of politicians.

In the rural areas, the farming year had reached a decisive moment. Corn, cut by the binder and harvested by men, working with horse and cart, had reached the farmyard. In Canada and the US, they already had the combine harvester. One man dealt with the golden grain. Here in England, in 1938, I became part of the chain reaching from the plough to the baker's shop.

It was my father, of course, who had nudged me towards a career as a railwayman. Now he suggested that I seek casual labour with the threshing machine. 'Casual', of course, had nothing to with a dress code. We all had corduroy trousers and hob-nailed boots. No, it simply meant short-term. One day at a time or two if you were lucky.

The threshing outfit, which is the collective term for a traction engine, a drum a chopper and a tyer, rumbled round the country lanes, farm to farm, village to village. The owner of the whole shebang was Oswald Sharpe of Melbourne Parks Farm. One of his full-time employees was Edwin Johnson, who lived in Breedon and was known to everyone as Neddy. So it was Neddy that I went to see one evening. He was non-committal as older men in the country were with their younger brethren. Still, I could turn up and take my chance, see if the farmer they were going to the following day would employ me.

As with my first day at Langley Priory, as with my first day at the Running Department of the LMS Railway, so it would be again. There was very little formal training, just basic instruction that you have to learn quickly. That is no problem for a young man, willing to work, willing to learn and used to discipline. Always you start at the bottom and work your way up and in that one winter I did pretty well every job connected with threshing corn, starting with 'chaffing and pulsing'.

Our language changes with the years. 'Pulse' nowadays means the seeds of leguminous plants as well as the rhythmic beating of the arteries. When threshing corn, it meant the small sheath which protects grain from the elements. Along with chaff, the remains of broken straw, it was deposited underneath the drum. My very first day's work with the outfit consisted of raking this apparent waste onto a hessian sheet and then carrying it off for storage. By the time you got back, the heap waiting would fill the sheet again so there were no idle moments, you just kept going as long as the wheels were turning. We started at eight o'clock with a break at 10 o'clock for a cup of tea provided by the farmer. After 10 minutes, off we went again until 12 noon and a break for lunch - your own sandwiches with more tea. At one o'clock, start again with another small break mid-afternoon until the bay in the dutch barn was emptied - usually before 5 pm. Often, the farmer preferred his own men to carry the heavy sacks of grain to the building where they were stored. Somewhere, though, I remember that I had a day or two at this heavy work.

My first day had been hard, because I had to carry the chaff quite a way. It was, of course, intended to be. That was the test, could the young man stand the pace? It very soon got easier. I don't think they ever had someone else willing to travel everywhere the machine went, which is just what I did. South to Long Whatton, north to Barrow-on-Trent and Allenton. Most of the work however, was in Diseworth and Breedon. Wherever we went, some local would turn up, just to work the odd day or two in their own village.

Moving from one farm to another, often every one or two days, usually involved taking the whole outfit, and setting up ready for the next day's work. The drum had to be exactly level. It wasn't long before Neddy asked me if I would help out. He and the driver, Arthur Howe, set off from Breedon, rattling along the country lanes to Diseworth with the whole outfit. Bringing up the rear, a young man on a bicycle. The extra pair of hands was useful. The farmer would use his own men when threshing started, but Arthur and Neddy got no help setting up, except from me. They were full time, and paid every week. For the casual labourer, the money for a full day was 10 shillings. Very good money that was, 10 bob a day, in 1938. But we, the casuals, never made a full week. Two days in one village, sometimes just one, then back on the road again.

John Fowler & Co. of Leeds built this traction engine. It is seen towing a threshing machine at an unknown location. The engine we worked in 1938/39 did not have a cab roof, and it had a flywheel to drive the drum. *H.W. Burman/Kidderminster Railway Museum*

When we were working on the thresher there would always be two men on the stack, throwing the sheaves onto the drum. That was easy enough in the morning when you were above it. Harder as the day wore on when all the sheaves had to be lifted up. As winter came, I was usually employed on the stack or the drum. The whole operation would take two men on the stack, one carrying corn, one behind the tyer, dealing with straw, and one more chaffing and pulsing. Neddy Johnson looked after the tyer or the chopper, Arthur looked after the engine.

Two men on the drum: one - the bunt-cutter - and the other feeding the drum. You carried your own knife for cutting bunts, which is just another name for the string which bound the sheaves. As a sheaf landed on the drum, the bunt-cutter picked it up, cut the string as near to the knot as possible and dropped it into the arms of the feeder. He stood in a well and fed the sheaf through his hands into a small aperture where it was caught up by the knife blades whirling round. This job demanded total concentration, those knives did not distinguish between sheaves and fingers.

At the end of the process, the straw was reconstituted as a sheaf complete with string, by the tyer, but without the golden grain. In the case of wheat that was destined for the flour mill. Oats were, in the main, used as animal feed and barley went to the brewers where it was produced as malt.

Many factors could affect the working day, though. For a start, you were entirely dependent on the weather. If it was raining before you left home, you didn't start. The heavy belt running between the large fly-wheel on the traction engine and the smaller one on the drum didn't like rain at all and would come off if it got wet. Arthur Howe, the driver and Neddy Johnson would manhandle it back on again once but if it came off a second time, that was it. A day's work gone. If we got through to mid-day we would get half a day's pay - but there was nothing to show for it at all if we had to give up mid-morning.

One other crop I noted in my diary of that time was beans. Broad beans. Beans fly everywhere so there was a special way of dealing with them. A frame was erected on the drum, rather like a tent. The well was no place to stand because of all the flying ammunition. I stood on the drum itself, picked the small sheaf up, cut the string and threw it as loosely as possible into the clutches of the knives. Quite an experience.

That was at Alf Marshall's farm at Diseworth: two days threshing corn, the third day beans. And that was Wednesday, 1st February, 1939. The whole threshing season finished in April and then it would be on the bike again to sign on or to look for work - which almost always was not forthcoming.

If the thresher wasn't working, I would ride to Melbourne, and sign on for unemployment benefit. One day, the man at the Ministry of Labout didn't like the fact that I couldn't make either a full week at work or on the dole. I told him I was looking for work. If he could find me some, I would go to it. If not, I would do the best I could for myself. That shut him up. The matter was never raised again.

I learnt a lot that winter; and I was happy to learn - and to earn. But I was a spirited lad and I remember two episodes when farmers didn't get their own way - and that was an unusual experience for a farmer in those days. The first was at a farmyard in Allenton on the outskirts of Derby – owned by Mr Smith, butcher and farmer. The job was chopping hay for animal feed. That only took half a day.

For the casual labourer wishing to keep his benefits card, there was a special procedure. Whoever employed you on your first working day of the week was responsible for the employer's contribution to the national insurance stamp. As I remember, it was a shilling a week for the employer, *6d.* for the employee. Some of the farmers grumbled about this - not many of them were keen on parting with their money - but the vast majority paid up. Not so Mr Smith – from him there was a point blank refusal.

This was a test of resolve for a 19-year-old. I went home and wrote a letter asking for my stamp money – I got no reply. I gave it a week and then wrote to the Ministry of Labour in Derby. They did reply confirming that I was within my rights. So I wrote again to Mr Smith, notifying him of what would happen if he didn't pay up. He never did send me any money - but, by return, came a National Insurance stamp. The young man had put down a marker. No credit to me. Credit to the people who had trained me. Don't mess me about.

During that winter, I had the same trouble with Sammy Jarrom of Diseworth. This time, the two permanent workers on the thresher intervened on my behalf and told Sammy what had happened at Allenton. Sammy got more than a bit annoyed. He gave me the money but told me not to set foot on his land again.

There was a sequel. Sometime later, the machine was due at S. Jarrom's again. I wanted to stay at home but my father told me that Sammy would have forgotten all about it by now. Up on the drum I went and, after about an hour, out comes Sammy. Either I will work this day for a shilling less than anyone else or I could make my own way home. Honour was more important to me than a shilling so I walked to the old bike, got on it and rode to Melbourne to sign on. You could say that I lost that one but, when the machine moved on, I was back at work.

Apart from those two, most of the farmers were pretty good and a couple were excellent. Those were the ones who provided beer at lunchtime instead of tea, William Jarrom at Diseworth and Arthur Wheatley at Worthington Fields Farm, which is only a mile and a half from where I sit now.

Arthur Wheatley's grandson, also Arthur, is farming there now. His grandfather was a jolly, thick-set man, who liked a drink himself. So the jug of ale came round three times a day. And my diary for the 20th and 21st February faithfully records that I had seven glasses of beer on each of those days.

Those are my outstanding memories of my winter season as a casual labourer; another slice of useful experience and all on my mother's old push-bike.

Johnson '0F' class 0-6-0ST No. 1509 inside No. 4 shed on 26th October, 1947. Visible in the background are '3F' class 0-6-0 No. 3598 and class '4' 2-6-4T No. 2340.

L.W. Perkins/Kidderminster Railway Museum

Johnson class '3P' 4-4-0 No. 743 on shed at Derby on 11th May, 1946, 'Jubilee' class 4-6-0 No. 5640 *Frobisher* is obscured behind it. A group of enginemen are chatting at the north end of No. 4 shed. The class '3P' worked express trains from Derby to Bristol, Leeds, London and Manchester, before the Compounds were built. *H.C. Casserley*

Chapter Eight

Back to No. 4 Shed

By the Spring, the railway was recruiting again and I was back where I wanted to be by May 1939. There were many highpoints as well as some low ones in that last summer before the war. Getting back to No. 4 shed was the big bonus. I would never have gone back to Camden Town, that much was certain. Making Derby my home station, as I was advised to do, took care of that.

Always, for the young passed cleaner, there was uncertainty. Would I get a firing turn - or maybe several - in a particular week? The difference in pay - 3*s.* 6*d.* - it doesn't sound much; but you could do a lot with three and a tanner in 1939. That sort of money would take you to the cinema several times. And it would more than cover a good night out in a public house, such as the 'Green Dragon' on the Spot, in Derby.

In 1939, at first, I was the junior passed cleaner on one shift. So, when I got a firing turn, it meant that everyone else had to have one as well. That meant there was no meeting up in the pub any more. Sometimes I would go the pub with the driver. But that depended both on the time of day and the driver's attitude to drink. Now, in May 1939, it was a new beginning for me. For a few weeks, that meant a mixture of cleaning, labouring and some firing duties. Local management considered their options and slowly, laboriously, the country prepared for war.

Most of the young men who had been told in 1938 that, 'Your services are no longer required' had come back to No. 4 shed. Simply because, like me, they had not found a better job. In 1938 there had been three or four men junior to me in the line of promotion. Now there was only one although several more youngsters of 14 or 15 had been recruited while we were still redundant.

Their position was accepted and understood. They could not become firemen until they were 18, and until all the men who had been made redundant had been given the opportunity of coming back to No. 4 shed. Those were the foundation stones of the PT&R agreement.

For a few months, the two shift system meant that I was the youngest passed cleaner on one shift, not in age but in seniority. The gang of four system for cleaning engines didn't operate anymore. There was a long list of passed cleaners and most of them were needed for firing duties on a daily basis.

There were so many turns on the shed and shunting yards that the drivers didn't have a regular firemen. On main line work, there were many firemen of 40-45 not yet passed out for driving. They, as the senior men, all had regular firing positions. As and when they became passed firemen, they would move on to become drivers. That meant there was always a pool of spare men, who would cover for men who were off sick or on annual leave. The railway companies never - never - cancelled trains due to staff shortages and very rarely for any other reason.

We learnt our railway lines quickly, doing something different every day. Most of those days, we were with a driver who was getting near retirement. For many of his years, he would have experienced the much harsher discipline of the old Midland Railway. That company had a famous system of fines and punishment which became gradually more lenient - some would say more sensible - after the integration into the LMS in 1923. Derby had been the headquarters of the old Midland Railway. It still was in 1937 and for some years after that, not in name, but in practice.

Now, I know I'm on sensitive ground here but the young trainee firemen were always called 'nig-nogs', I don't know why. It simply meant a young man learning his trade, but 'nig-nogs' they always were and I simply record that fact. Different drivers treated their 'nig-nogs' in different ways. At worst you were treated with suspicion. You would not be given proper instructions but you would always be blamed if anything went wrong.

Preparation of engines, before they go out to work, was one thing. Disposal, when they came back to the shed, was quite another. Those were the jobs that footplatemen do. There is a lot more to maintenance of the steam locomotive and many more people involved.

Another example of the worst kind of driver for the young fireman to be paired with was the one who refused to give you a proper understanding of what the job you're doing involved. So you don't manage the fire in the firebox as well as you should. The class '2' and class '3' engines were relatively easy. Anywhere you put the coal in will make a good head of steam. With the class '4' engines, it was quite different. On these, you have to build up a body of fire at the back of the firebox. And feed the front of it with coal very thinly, a bit at a time. Once you understood this, management of the class '4' goods engines was easy. Just keep the back topped up, the coal will roll down to the front. So it has to be a sloping fire, not an evenly spread one.

If you were lucky, your first experience of this engine would be with a driver who told you how to do it. The other kind would leave you to it and then grumble when things went wrong. That would only happen once but there would be other ways of making you feel inferior: such as the classic, 'You're not paid to think'.

The best were the young passed firemen who said, 'I'm not going to treat my firemen the way I was treated'. They recognised that, if you are eager and willing to learn, as I was, a little bit of tuition will make everybody's life that much easier. And some of the older drivers were also very good with their young trainees.

'Now my lad' they would say. It was always 'my lad'. 'There are only two of us on this engine. If we can't get on together, the job will be much harder. But if we do get on, then the job will be like going out to tea'. The very fact that they talked to you like this meant that you were going to be treated as an equal even though you were still learning.

Sometimes you heard about a particular driver from one of the other passed cleaners. One such was an old driver, Francis, working on the carriage and wagon works shunting engines. He had been given the nickname 'Damper' simply because, if the engine blew off steam, he would curtly say 'Damper'. That was the big flap that controlled the admission of air through the ashpan underneath the firebox. The fire doesn't burn without air through the fire hole door when that is open or by the damper which is controlled by a lever on the fireman's side of the engine.

Well, I had one day with this old man. And I didn't have any trouble at all. 'Forewarned is forearmed' was the bit of wisdom that covered those instances. And, of course, I had early experience of shunting in the carriage works where they had thousands of tons of timber stacked around between the lines. That had been one of the times when smoking in the works was strictly forbidden, even on the footplate where you had a fire going anyway. You could understand it! If any of that timber caught fire, there would have been no stopping it.

When you took the afternoon carriage works' shunting engines on the shed, it was usually three engines coupled together. That was after about four hours of duty so engines had to be 'disposed of' as they used to say. Briefly, that meant cleaning the fire, the smokebox and the ashpan. When a shunting engine is out from 12 to 24 hours, clinker builds up on the fire bars. That clinker was broken up by a metal rod, four or five feet long with a chisel end. Once moved, it was lifted out with a clinker shovel, slightly longer. Heavy work if you didn't get any help from the driver taking a turn. The smokebox, where fine dust accumulates, is secured by six metal lugs, each secured in turn by a ⅞ in. nut. We used one of our four spanners to loosen these nuts and the lugs, then, with the firing shovel, threw out the fine dust from the smokebox.

All this work was carried out in the ashpits; a long pit, where, in due course, the ashpan has to be raked out. Not at all dangerous but very dirty. After which, we checked the sandboxes and topped them up if need be. Sand, to prevent the wheels slipping, can be absolutely vital in some situations and in certain weather conditions. Pre-World War II the supply of sand was assured. It was one of the first commodities to run short after the war started, however. Understandably, the supply of sand to railway depots was a low priority.

The other shunting yard near to the shed was the locomotive works. As with the carriage and wagon works, the afternoon sets of men came back to the shed after about four hours' work. But there was a major difference. Two of the afternoon shunting engines were scheduled to pick up new and refurbished engines turned out by the locomotive workshops, Monday to Friday.

There could be the occasional goods engine. Mostly, they were class '3' or '4' passenger tank engines bound for depots all over the LMS system. In one respect, they were all treated the same. They had to be supplied with coal, water and sand before they could be sent to their home station. So, it was a procession of 'dead' engines, engines that are not yet in steam. If you filled the water tank, the coal bunker and the sandboxes, it would be a big chunk out of the depot resources.

So there was an agreement to restrict the amount of coal, water and sand that they were supplied with. The fireman was grateful that he didn't have to lift 12 or more buckets of sand up to the foot framing. Most of the drivers would stand up there, empty the bucket into the sandbox and pass it back to his mate for refilling. But I remember at least one driver who left the whole lot to me. So it was quite a chore, filling, lifting up, climbing the steps, emptying the bucket, climbing down, refilling and repeating the whole business five or six times.

As always, tomorrow was another day. There was a good chance that you would be on some other job because there were shunting engines at Chaddesden and St Mary's sidings. This was such an important part of railway work at Derby, that I will devote the next chapter to describing it.

The signal gantry at Derby North Junction in 1932. Cattle trucks stand in the siding to the left. The tracks off to the left lead towards Ambergate and those to the right to Chaddesden sidings and Spondon Junction. *D.J. Powell Collection/Kidderminster Railway Museum*

Railway companies were bound to accept any traffic, provided they had suitable wagons or vans to carry the goods and that they were within the loading gauge - a good example is shown here. Farmer Mr Dibb-Smith of Breedon decided to relocate to Cornwall. His cattle are seen being guided into cattle wagons which were 'common user'. Some extra staff have been sent to deal with the loading. The coach is there for the family and their belongings. *Author's Collection*

Chapter Nine

Shunting and Marshalling Yards

There's no glamour, no prestige, to be found in some aspects of railway operations. Just a lot of hard work, performed by a lot of hard men. Before the Beeching era, the travelling public could get on a passenger train and go to almost anywhere in the British Isles. In the course of even a short journey in my time, they would see, from the carriage windows, goods trains and mineral wagons, but they would never see what went on in the goods and marshalling yards.

As a young passed cleaner at No. 4 shed, Derby, going out on a firing turn, I was soon working on shunting engines. No two days would be the same. This is because there were four local yards where drivers and firemen would be working.

The principal purpose of shunting yards falls into two headings. One is the breaking up and re-forming of trains coming in from outlying areas. The other is the internal movements made to move wagons and coaches to the required locations within the yard. At Derby, there were four main shunting yards, Chaddesden, St Mary's, the locomotive works, and the carriage and wagon works. Chaddesden and St Mary's dealt with goods carried for the railway's customers, principally coal, steel and minerals. Goods trains in those days carried anything and everything from a box of goods to heavy industrial plant and machinery. The shunting yards at the Loco and C&W works were there to ensure that goods were delivered straight to the area where they were required for the building of the railway's own rolling stock.

At Derby, there were three or four permanent firemen, men who could not go forward to become drivers, principally for health reasons. One of these men worked at Chaddesden, one at St Mary's, one or sometimes two in the carriage and wagon works. A few turns in the locomotive works, and the other yards, would be covered by men from the main line goods links, they would spend one week in an eight week rota there. That way everyone was kept in touch with the harsh realities of shunting duties.

Even then, there would be around 10 spare firing jobs to be covered on the day shift, and 20 on afternoons and nights. Those shifts would call for the passed cleaners to act as firemen. From November 1937 until June 1941, except for those 10 months when I was made redundant, I would often be working as fireman on one or the other of the shunting and shed turns. Hard and dirty jobs were always allocated to the young men at the bottom of the railway ladder.

I remember one train every weekday which went from Chaddesden to the loco works. This train carried the raw materials to make steam engines, the tools of my trade. Starting sometime in the 1850s, many hundreds were turned out at Derby. Some new, some refurbished or re-boilered. As fireman and driver, I worked over many thousands of miles with them, and they never let you down. In the loco works, there was no shunting after around six o'clock in the evening, so just two sets of enginemen were required on three engines – all class '1' goods engines.

Class '1' engines also did all the shunting in the carriage and wagon works, where there was just one night turn. Again, three engines went off from No. 4 shed to work with the shunters, leaving the shed at around 7.30 am, to ensure they were at the works by the time the shunters started work at eight o'clock. Two of them came back to the shed at around 5.30 pm, the remaining engine stayed to work the night shift. In between those hours, they went backwards and forwards, in and out of miles of railway sidings. Goods and mineral wagons were turned out in their thousands from the carriage and wagon works. Again, the raw materials came in by rail from Chaddesden. Timber and steel were the main raw materials used to build carriages and wagons. As with the loco works, many tradesmen spent their working lives building these vehicles.

At St Mary's they dealt with a wide variety of goods. Two engines worked 24 hours a day, a third engine worked for 16 hours. The morning and afternoon shifts of one of these engines dealt with the shunting of 'bonded' goods, chiefly spirits and tobacco. These goods were subject to Customs & Excise duties, and were taken into the bond stores. In the spring and early summer, fruit and vegetables came into St Mary's direct from the Peterborough area; even banana trains! All this traffic went into the Town goods shed. There it was unloaded into road drays, first pulled by horses, later by motor vehicles. Some went to the wholesale market, some to greengrocers shops. Fish, and sometimes cattle, were sent in vans coupled up to local passenger trains. Cattle were also forwarded on goods trains. Then they would have to endure a long and uncomfortable journey. All cattle wagons had to be taken to the cattle dock, about half a mile out of Derby station, going north. We had a shunting engine there every Friday, when there was a weekly cattle market at Derby.

At St Mary's and Chaddesden we did the shunting with class '2' and '3' goods engines. The class '1' engines used in the carriage and wagon and loco works could get round curves in those yards because they had a short wheelbase. That wasn't necessary at St Mary's and Chaddesden. The work there was also heavier, so the bigger engines were required for that reason too.

There were two occasions every day when men had to walk to St Mary's to relieve the shunting engines and the men they relieved had to walk back to No. 4 shed. One afternoon, I had to walk out with an old driver called Joe Allen. I was surprised at how fast he could walk. I had to go hard to keep up with him. He had long legs, and took long steps. I can still take those long steps, walking like Joe Allen. (Up until I was 80 years of age, I could cover a mile quite quickly, and 10 miles, more slowly. But those days are gone.) There were only a few trains which went out of St Mary's, mostly empty vans and wagons to Chaddesden. Daily trips were made each way between the two yards.

The sidings at Chaddesden were designed for hump shunting. The principles are quite straightforward. Push a wagon over a hill, it will run down the incline. For a relatively short distance there is no engine power to control it. So you use manpower to do so, until mechanical retarders were installed (which happened in some places but never happened there). When Chaddesden was at its most productive they dealt with 1,600 wagons in a shift of eight hours. I only heard that figure once, but it came from someone who spent seven hard years on one job in the sidings. He was a man who had the most dangerous of the various duties connected with the management of railway wagons. Yes, it was 'Wagons roll' alright in those days. As a fireman from time to time on one of the two shunting engines in the middle part of the operation, I can tell you how it was done.

All this work was being performed in a stretch of sidings covering around 1½ miles. You may wonder where all this is happening in relation to Derby as it is today. Today, the sidings are long gone, replaced by the Wyvern Centre. The only remaining evidence of the operations is the old wagon repair shop building, which is now a showroom for the Fireplace Company. In those days, near to the sidings in Highfield Lane, Chaddesden, were a number of railway workers' houses. Staff and their families would hear the banging and clanging as wagons buffered up to other wagons from 6 am on Monday morning to 6 am on Sunday morning. They were almost living on the job.

Receiving trains, breaking them up and then reassembling the wagons into another set of trains was a major operation, which started at the North End of Chaddesden sidings. All movements were controlled from the signal box at Chaddesden North End. No matter from which part of the country they were arriving, the trains all entered the sidings at the North End. Here, in a small cabin was the train receiver. Goods trains coming in from the North and West had the engine leading. The last vehicle in the train would be the guard's brake van. As the guard passed the cabin, he would hand a slip of paper to the waiting train receiver. This contained the details of where the train was from, the number of wagons and the engine number. This basic information was entered into the log book by the train receiver. Normally the incoming trains run down No. 7 line, known as the running road. Nos. 1 to 6 and 8, 9 and 10 could all be used to stable trains which cannot be dealt with immediately (which could happen if there was a derailment at the Centre).

Trains from the South and East were dealt with in a different way. The initial movement towards the sidings for these trains was controlled by the signalman. He had signals controlling the movement of all trains destined for the sidings. When the train receiver was ready to accept a train from the South, these trains were drawn up past the sidings towards Derby North Junction. When the train has cleared the signal for setting back into the sidings, that signal was lowered, and the propelling movement began.

There were special regulations controlling the propelling of trains, which must be carried out by experienced men. The incoming trains from the South were almost always worked into the sidings by Derby men, sent out to relieve the train crews from Nottingham or Leicester. The relieving train crew waited in the train receiver's cabin. Derby men working trains from Wellingborough or Peterborough were often relieved too, because they had already been on duty for over eight hours by the time they reached the sidings.

Returning to our train from the South, which was being propelled so that the brake van was leading. As before, the guard handed his train details to the train receiver, who told him on which line the train was being dealt with. It was up to the driver to make this movement quite slowly, because he was following in another train, from the North or West.

Now we come to operations at Chaddesden Centre. Here, was No. 4 Centre Shunt engine, an engine which was used to go around and couple up to the brakevan of all trains from the North and West. The leading engine was detached and left the sidings, so it was always a propelling movement on No. 7 line (wagons leading and the engine at the rear). The young fireman would see all of this. He was, as always, learning his trade.

Movements at this point were controlled by the inspector in charge, operating a signal which was lowered for go, and raised to horizontal for stop. At the Centre, wagons were detached. As each train arrives, two men, one on each side, walk up the line. One, the head shunter, would read the wagon label, step back a pace or two, and chalk up the number of the road which the wagon was destined for on his side of the wagon. The under-shunter, just like me, was learning his trade. He also chalks the road number on his side of the wagon. On one side it would be read by the inspector, on the other by the 'Steadiers' and the signalman in the sidings signal box. The signalman must set the points for the line on which any particular wagon, or group or wagons, had to be stabled. Nos. 16 to 30 were the lines to which wagons were diverted. No. 31 was for 'cripples' – damaged wagons. Nos. 1 to 13 were relatively short sidings, traffic in these was dealt with at the south end of the yard.

Now to the business of detaching wagons. The two men chalking up line numbers on wagons now moved on to the next part of their job. The under-shunter, seeing that the first wagon was for line 19, the second for line 26, for example, would uncouple them. So we have a wagon for line 19 running free downhill. If it isn't 'steadied', there will be one big bang, when it hits the other wagons on the line.

This was the primitive way of dealing with the run-away wagon. Running alongside the wagon was the steadier. He would drop the handbrake on the wagon, applying pressure with the brakestick to slow it down, still running alongside the wagon. When it was sufficiently retarded, he lifts the handbrake, and it rolls more gently into line No. 19. The wagon for No. 26 follows, controlled by another steadier. Can you imagine the hardships endured by these men? A wagon load of coal running downhill – even in fine weather and daylight, you had to be young, fit and nimble to do this for over seven hours every shift. My old friend Jack Wakefield did this job for seven years. When promotion to shunter was at a standstill, unemployment was the only alternative in the Depression years. No wonder Jack Wakefield walked with a limp, after seven years chasing wagons.

Sometimes, the brakestick could get caught in a wheel, resulting in flying shards of wood. Keep out of the way, or you may be hit by a piece. What happens if the steadier slips? Years later, I was the fireman on Centre '4' engine. We were standing on one side, with a train coming in from the South, and the wagons are rolling. We didn't see what happened, but we heard the screams of the young man whose leg had gone under the wheel. Just one of the many unfortunate accidents that can happen to railway workers.

What made all this work necessary? The key words are 'common carrier' and 'single wagon load'. The railways of Britain before, and during my time, could not refuse to transport any commodity, provided they had a suitable wagon to convey that load. So if a farmer at Breedon wants to send a load of sugar beet to Liverpool, the railway cannot say, 'No thanks, your load won't be profitable'. They are common carriers, as defined by law. So, the empty wagon is sent from

Chaddesden and put into the sidings at Tonge and Breedon station. The farmer sends several cartloads down to the station, his sugar beet is loaded up from the ramp, so it hasn't got to be thrown up from ground level. The loaded wagon will be picked up by the 'trip' engine, which serves all the sidings on the line. The wagon goes back to Chaddesden North End, then to the Centre, and is detached, and steadied into the line which deals with traffic for Liverpool. And when the time comes, is forwarded with the other traffic for that area.

We have dealt with trains arriving at Chaddesden North End, and now we move to the South End, at the other end of the sidings. Here again, there was an inspector in charge of four or more engines, each of them working with a head shunter and an under-shunter. The shunting engines at the south end were Nos. 1, 2, 3 and 6. No. 4 engine, as you know, is at the Centre. Also at the Centre, No. 5, which worked in a short group of sidings, off to one side of the main sidings. No. 5 was only a two-shift engine, no night turn. They got one very special goods train ready, the night train to Gloucester, and a couple of local trips.

No. 1 shunt engine dealt with sidings traffic on line Nos. 1 to 13. These were relatively short sidings, dealing with special loads. No. 2 moved wagons from the south end to the new sidings, on the other side of the main running lines. And once there shunts about seven or eight sidings.

No. 3 shunt engine dealt with traffic from sidings 16 to 21 or thereabouts, making trains up for North and West, Ambergate, Ripley, New Lount, Burton, Birmingham and points beyond. There were four departure lines for these trains with always a lot of shunting involved. Trains had to be properly marshalled. Take New Lount trains. Traffic for Chellaston Quarry was put at the front of the train. Then there would be several wagons for Melbourne, one or two for Tonge and Breedon, a few more for Worthington. The rest, at the back end, would be empty wagons for New Lount Colliery. All the wagons had to be in the proper sequence, otherwise a lot of time would be taken up by trains occupying the running line on the branch, making unnecessary shunting movements.

Then there was No. 6 engine, familiarly known to everybody as 'Strikem', which dealt with wagons from roads 21 to 30, traffic for places south of Derby. This engine pulled out wagons on to No. 7 line, perhaps 15 or more wagons at a time. Because of the adverse gradient, the wagons needing 'hitting up', that's why it was known as 'Strikem'. Movements made more slowly were described as 'all together'. This engine drew out trains for Wellingborough, Nottingham and Leicester. They were taken down No. 7 line and the engine would return up No. 6.

All of these shunting engines at Chaddesden ('Chadd') worked three shifts except No. 5. Unlike St Mary's, we didn't have to walk to the sidings. Every day, except Sunday, one engine with a guard's brakevan left the shed at 5.45 am, 1.45 pm and 9.45 pm. All the relief sets, of 10 and sometimes 12 men, rode out in the brakevan, which made a swift journey across 'the Branch' from Etches Park to Spondon Junction, then up to Chadd. At Chadd, all the men got out, and relieved their colleagues on the various shunt engines. The one time this did not apply was on Monday morning. Since all the engines came in to No. 4 shed on Sunday morning, they all went off the shed on Monday morning.

The young fireman, on his first Chadd shunt turn, knew the basic essentials of his job: keeping the proper steam and water levels. There was one occasion, on the No. 3 engine, where the fireman was instructed to watch for a signal. That happened when we had drawn a train out, and the engine returned up No. 5 line. There was one small red signal, like a dinner plate, at ground level. We knew them as 'dummies' (sometimes 'dollies'), one dummy for each line 1 to 5, leading up to a signal with a frame on one side. This exhibited one of these cut-outs, or stencils. We would get an indication 'US' (meaning up sidings). Driver Billy Gunn would refer to this signal with the phrase, 'He winked his eye, and said "Upstairs"'. Another indication which could be used was 'DS' for down sidings. These, properly known as the storage sidings, were on the other side of the main line. They were used to hold trains of empty wagons for the various collieries. The only other signal indication was 'ML' (main line).

There were two extra engines which came into use around September 1939. One was called the Stowing Engine and was used at Chaddesden North End as an addition to Centre 4 engine, and also to deal with trains on lines 8, 9 and 10.

The other was Chadd No. 7, used as an addition to No. 3, and for the same purpose. Once blackout conditions came into operation, everything moved more slowly, so extra engines were required.

I have a little story from each of the three locations at Chaddesden sidings. One of the train receivers at the north end was Teddy Angus. Known to the old drivers as 'Teddy Anxious'. A descriptive nickname, which fitted. When he retired, his position was taken by Bill Ingram, for some reason known as 'Jocky' Ingram. (His son Gerald became a fireman at No. 4 shed, sometime during the war. He, too, was known as 'Jocky'.)

When the train receiver called the trains from the South back into the sidings, they would mount a few steps to a small platform, and call the train back in daylight by the prescribed hand signal. After dark, or in foggy weather, the hand lamp provided for guards and shunters was used to call the train back. For some reason, Jocky Ingram would always swing the hand-lamp quite vigorously, as if to encourage the driver to move the train more quickly. despite the speed restriction for propelling movements, which I think was 10 mph. No driver was going to exceed that, propelling about 40 wagons down the running line, No. 7, often occupied by another train. This wasn't fast enough for Jocky. Sometimes he would swing the lamp so hard that it would break up and fly over the hedge into the adjoining field. Curse, and more curses!

For many years until around 1942/1943, the shunters at Chadd south end and St Mary's worked to one rigorous schedule. Unless their engine was waiting for a signal, it must *never* stand still. If that involved making work where it didn't really exist, that is what they would do. The drivers knew when this was happening. The practice went on from the Depression years: fear of the sack, if they went into the cabin, except at meal times.

The laid down procedure for locomen involved in shed work and shunting duties was this. There must be a meal break of 20 minutes between the third and fifth hour on duty. Men working trains had to get a meal as and when the opportunity arose. You must never, ever, stop a main line train to take a meal break. (Although on some branch lines up and down the country it has been known for a driver to stop for the purpose of picking mushrooms - but not at Derby.) So, sometime when convenient, the head shunter would say, 'Get your twenty, driver'.

And you could bet that after 22 minutes or so, they would be back with the engine, looking for work. Anything to avoid the inspector saying, 'Have you no work?'

Nos. 1 and 2 engines had their own little cabin. No. 3, and sometimes No. 7 would use the big cabin provided for 'Strikem'. On these engines, the drivers and firemen would also go to the shunters cabin. I was in that cabin, as a fireman, when a major change began. For countless years, head shunters dared not break the tradition: 20 minutes meal break.

During wartime a young man, 'Bill' we will call him, was appointed head shunter on No. 6 engine 'Strikem'. He had been the under-shunter, and knew all the rules. But this man had no fear. On the morning turn, after several hours hard work, 'Meal-time, driver' he would say. After washing his hands, he would get out his egg and bacon, and put it on the lowest possible setting on the gas burner, so that it would take about 20 minutes to cook. Meantime, he would make the tea, and read a newspaper. Only when he was ready, would he eat his breakfast. So his 20 minutes became 40.

I was there when the inspector came into the cabin, trying to enforce discipline. 'Have you done so-and-so?', he said to Bill. 'Yes, we've done that', said Bill. 'Have you done so-and-so', the inspector tried again. 'Yes, we've done that', said Bill. The Inspector retired, defeated. Bill knew all the moves, better than he did. So of course, when the other head shunters saw this, a sea change took place. They too had 40 minutes meal break. And the work got done, just the same.

Bill was the last head shunter left at Chaddesden South End, before it closed down altogether. My very last week's work as a driver, December 1974, was with him on No. 6 shunt engine. All the other shunters, and inspectors, had long gone. But Bill still had the same extended meal break.

There were marshalling yards at all the big towns on the LMS. All working to the same general principles that I have described. It is possible that, in some of the places, discipline was as strict as it was at Derby, in relation to the 20 minutes meal break. Possibly yes, but not really very likely.

In some yards, footplatemen going into the shunters cabin were not welcome, because they went in for hot water to make tea, and forgot to top the big kettle up again. The shunters would have to wait a while before they could mash.

Like all other railway procedures at the time, shunting yards were labour intensive. A lot of people were employed in these yards, and a lot of work was done. For the young fireman, at the beginning of his railway career, it was all useful experience. The day would not be far distant when the driver would say after the meal break, 'Come over this side, mate'. By that he meant that it's your turn to do the driving now. There is a big difference between a town with just a railway station and a town with both goods and passenger facilities - a Railway Town. And, in Derby's case, a great railway town.

A general view of locomotives in the interior of Kentish Town engine shed's roundhouse *circa* 1949. Some of our lodging turns were to Kentish Town, London.

W. Potter/Kidderminster Railway Museum

We also lodged at Wellingborough. '2F' class 0-6-0 No. 58193 stands alongside '3F' class 0-6-0 No. 43529, which has been detached from its tender, in the roundhouse at Wellingborough on 24th September, 1955. Note the smoke troughs, suspended from the shed roof.

Kidderminster Railway Museum

Chapter Ten

Homes from Home

I have mentioned the way in which the railway used to expect us to move about at their behest. That led to a major factor in our lives - lodging turns of duty known as double home work. All of us who started work in the footplate grades at Derby in 1937 had our full share of it right up to 1948. After that only a few lodging turns remained, chiefly on passenger trains.

Pre-war there were 11 main line goods links at Derby. Being roughly in the centre of the country, we went out north, south and west with goods trains. We only went out east as far as Peterborough. Each of these links had eight weeks work and three of those were lodging turns. In my time, I have lodged in railway barracks at Crewe, Birmingham, Holbeck (Leeds), Wellingborough, Peterborough, as well as Kentish Town and Cricklewood in London. There were various railway depots where no railway barracks existed. In these places, several householders were prepared to take train crews as lodgers. Different drivers had their own favourites which they would return to. I remember Gloucester, Bristol, Canklow and one or two more obscure places. So I'm well qualified to write about my lodging experiences both in railway barracks and in private houses.

One of the places I lodged at only once was Aintree. Derby men used to work a goods train to Liverpool, in fact they called it the Liverpool link. Only a month or two before Derby lost the working, I was booked on the Sunday night turn with driver Cyril Dence. That was my first ever trip up the Manchester bank. Later on, I often worked to Manchester Central as both fireman and driver. Sadly it's no longer there.

I remember that trip for two reasons. One, we had a 'Black 5', a lovely engine for a young man learning his trade. And for something that Cyril Dence told me about on the way. He said that when we arrived and went to our lodging, we would be asked our foot size. He was right, we were and we were then issued with a pair of carpet slippers. Hob-nailed boots, standard wear for firemen and drivers, were strictly not allowed in that building. It seems that it was first and foremost a hotel for the Aintree races but someone had the bright idea of using it all year round. So the likes of us were allowed to stay there. But we weren't allowed to wear our boots. It was carpet slippers for us until we were ready for the return journey.

There were long trips, there were short trips. There were also some when you were off duty for a long time at the away station. Alsager was the one that most Derby men disliked. We didn't actually lodge there but that's where the outward train finished. As I remember, the signing-on time in Derby was 10.32 am. The train ran from Chaddesden sidings to Alsager, where there was an engine shed and a comparatively small goods yard. Arriving at about six in the evening, you left the engine there and caught a passenger train down to Crewe to lodge at the Gresty Road railway barracks.

The snag was that you didn't book on again until the following afternoon. Nineteen hours off duty and in Crewe of all places. One of the very worst places for anything more entertaining than railway workshops and sidings. Miles of them, there were and two engine sheds, Crewe North and South. I only worked that particular turn on one or two occasions in the summer of 1939. All the regular men in the link hated it because you were away from home for so long. It was said that one or two of the men did a moonlight flit, in a manner of speaking. Instead of catching the passenger train to Crewe, they went the other way - back to Derby - and spent the night at home. Obviously it was possible but there would have been hell to pay if the management had found out. In any event, they would get back to Crewe in time to start work the next afternoon. So possible yes, but very, very risky.

Gresty Road barracks, though, was like nowhere else I ever went as far as cooking facilities were concerned. And I've cooked bacon and eggs on a firing shovel - which makes them taste better than any other way. Later, during the war, there were railway canteens at some barracks, Wellingborough certainly. Pre-war all the drivers could take their steak, chops or whatever and cook their own meals. At Gresty Road, though, summer and winter, there was just a huge open fire like in some baronial hall, but there weren't any rounds of beef or suckling pigs. What we had here was a brick hearth in a semi-circle raised one brick high. On this raised brick semicircle stood a variety of rectangular pans. Not a round tin anywhere. All of them cooked slowly and equally. It was almost a continuous process - as one man picks up his tin another is ready to take his place. That's because it's about seven o'clock in the evening, just the right time for a cooked meal. And I can still savour the moment when my own meal was ready. This was before the days of rationing - and before gas cookers came to Gresty Road barracks.

Before the winter of 1939/1940 had run its course, I was called on for one more lodging turn in Crewe. This was at a different time altogether, around 1.00 am. Thank goodness there was no repeat of the 19 hours off on the Alsager turn. This one was around 12 hours off as I remember. The one other thing I recall is that my driver was an old chap named Shaylor Smith – not Sailor but Shaylor. I expect it was a nickname. There were around 10 or a dozen drivers named Smith. Long Smithy, there was, and 'Happy Frank' Smith, who never let the shadow of a smile cross his face, and Ambergate Smith, these were just three of them. And an old passed fireman, Cockerel Smith, I never did find out how he got that nickname which might be just as well. You may be wondering if I had one. Yes, sometimes 'Honest John' but more often 'Farmer John'. One middle-aged passed fireman, Willy Thompson, regularly used to ask me if I had milked the cows. Just smile and say 'yes' is the answer. Don't let them get to you. But that's by the way. After those two isolated instances, it was several years before I lodged again at Crewe. By which time, they had discovered gas cookers. Which saved having to keep that big fire going, winter and summer.

But back to tales of lodgings. The nearest to Derby was at Saltley just 38 miles away and only a mile or so from Birmingham (New Street). It was only for the period during the war that we lodged at Saltley, and I was lodging there on the night that Tommy Sherrin was killed by enemy action.

Tommy's was quite a story. Thomas Edward Sherrin, born on 6th May, 1902. In April 1933, he was still a passed cleaner at Derby. But the entry on his service record for that month reads 'left the service having refused a position as porter'.

We don't know what he did or where he went for the next 16 months. The next entry - on 8th August, 1934, says, 're-engaged at Crewe', and two months later, 're-engaged at Derby'. His rate of pay at Crewe was 63*s*. for firing and 57*s*. for cleaning. At Derby, 66*s*. for firing, still 57*s*. for cleaning. And this gives us a clue to the more humane side of LMS management; because the first year fireman's rate of pay was 57*s*. So someone, somewhere had been sensible and flexible enough to say, 'Welcome back, Mr Sherrin. Take a couple of months work at Crewe and then come back to Derby on a higher rate of pay'. They didn't have to do that. But they did.

The last entry on his service record is sad reading. It is dated 24th October, 1940 and reads, 'Killed by enemy action at New Street, Birmingham. Severe injuries to back of head, neck and back. Died on way to hospital'. Tommy was on an engine standing in the station. The German plane dropped incendiary bombs on the roof of the station. Tommy's driver, Frank Newton, stayed on the engine and survived. Tommy himself, together with a porter, found his way on to the roof of the station. They tried to put the incendiary bombs out but the high explosive bombs followed and both of them were killed. Heroism? Of course. But there were many heroes at that time. We were told about Tommy in Saltley just as we were signing on at about three in the morning. We were only a mile or so away from New Street at the time. Sadness and fear; quite a common combination at that time.

Years later, I was able to play a part in getting Tommy's name on a memorial in the old Market Place area of Derby. A man with strong connections to the town, Roy Northridge, put a proposal to the local council to recognize all the people of the town who, as civilians, had been killed by enemy action during World War II. Having found just one person in the Derby telephone area with the name Sherrin, I asked my daughter to ring the number. And we found out that this lady, well into her 90s, was indeed the widow of Tommy Sherrin. And,

A general view of the shed yard at Saltley, Birmingham, in 1949. A variety of locomotives are in attendance including 'Crab' class 2-6-0s and '3F' and '4F' 0-6-0s. The coaling tower can be seen on the left. *W. Potter/Kidderminster Railway Museum*

despite having been married twice more and lost those husbands as well, she had continued to bear his name. When I met her and her daughter, they told me that they had been trying to get Tommy's death recognised as being due to enemy action. Being able to supply them, and Roy Northridge, with a photocopy of his service record was a clincher.

So, on a cold November day in 1999, we sat in Derby Market Place when the Mayor of Derby, Councillor Sarah Bolton, dedicated a section of the city's War Memorial to all the civilians killed in the course of their duties. Tommy's name was there and we met Mrs Sherrin and her daughter again at the reception afterwards. Incidentally, someone else was anxious that Tommy's name should be included. This was my friend, Val Hughes, who left the railway service in about 1960 to keep a public house in Leicestershire. He had been engaged as a caller-up and had got to know Tommy Sherrin during that time when all the men who had to be on duty between midnight and 6 am had to be called. And his wife's father, Fred Shaw, was a foreman's assistant, and would have been about the same age as Tommy. So Saltley has sad memories for me.

The war memorial on Midland Road in Derby in 2012. The plaques on the wall behind the memorial carry the names of the fallen, amongst them (in error), the name of W.H. (Billy) Kirkman. *Helen Devaney*

In the same manner that Saltley was a just a wartime lodging, so was the one at Holbeck where we stayed after working a goods train to Leeds on a Saturday evening. Here they built the lodging house as close to the running shed as they possibly could, right in the middle of the yard. Talk about living on the job. Sleep in the daytime was almost impossible with the noise of the wagonloads of coal being hoisted up to the top of the coaling plant; followed by an almighty thump when the black diamonds cascaded into a huge hopper. There were two reasons not to grumble, though. One was that without coal we would have had no livelihood. The second was that a lot of people were being deprived of sleep for altogether more sinister reasons in those war years.

Being on nights anyway, there was no chance of a Saturday night out. Same again on Sunday with the Holbeck turn because our return was on the 5.20 pm express passenger from Leeds to Derby. Before the war, not many goods trains ran on Saturday nights because of the Sunday rate of pay - time and a half, later time and three-quarters. This rate ran from midnight Saturday to midnight Sunday and management had their own way of making sure they didn't pay out too much.

On a three-shift system, with the depot working all the time, there were bound to be a certain number of men working on Sunday rates of pay - steam raisers particularly. Pre-war a lot of engines were stood down on a Saturday afternoon and evening. Steam pressure soon falls when the fire is shovelled out of the firebox. Just enough remains to line the engines up behind one another on three roads north of the No. 4 shed. They all stand there in their serried ranks, quietly awaiting Sunday evening.

It took around eight hours to get a cold engine into steam. The procedure is quite simple and drivers and fireman were often called on to carry it out. First off, you collect a shovelful of firelighters, plus some cotton waste and 'lightning' - the same stuff we used as engine cleaners. Putting this to one side, you then start shovelling coal into the firebox. When you have a hundredweight or two in the middle of the box, it's time to light up the firelighters, soak the cotton waste with lightning and chuck it on top of the coal. Give it a few minutes to take hold and then carefully put three or four shovelfuls of coal on top. And that's it.

Slowly, the fire will spread. Very slowly, in fact, because everything around it is cold. So you go on to the next job and let nature take its course. Four or five hours later, go back and see how things are getting on. Usually, the fire will be taking a good hold by now but the steam pressure gauge won't have moved. Some way still to go. Pile some more coal in. Come back a little later. Things are warming up nicely. Tap the steam pressure gauge. It gives a little jerk and then settles back to zero. Then, a few minutes later, it'll begin to move. Many an engine has gone slowly away from the shed with a hot fire and full boiler but with only 80 lb. of steam, all the way to Chaddesden sidings. By the time you get there, everything is OK. The only difference for the steam raisers is that they get more firelighters. We get three or four, they get seven or eight. It's understandable, as they have a lot more engines to get steamed up.

Weekend working was a regular feature during the war, but management didn't want to pay too many men at Sunday rates of pay. To avoid this, a shift would be called into work at 12.05 am Monday morning. All the shunting engines at Chaddesden and St Mary's had to be prepared by a shift of men starting at this time. Also a number of main line goods turns ran in the early hours of the morning.

A feature of passed cleaners' work for one summer only in 1939 gives us an insight into how management saved money. We would be instructed to travel away on a Friday, work on the Saturday and travel back on the Sunday. This sounds alright. Three days pay for one day's work. But there were two advantages for management. On the travelling days, they only paid us at the cleaners' rate - 6*s.* for the day as opposed to the fireman's scale of 9*s.* 6*d*. The other advantage for management was that they liked the power it gave them. You, young man, will go to work where we tell you and when we tell you. Just think yourself lucky getting three days pay for a day's work. And we did.

On one of these Fridays, three or four of us were sent to Blackpool. We all travelled together on the same train. Derby to Manchester Central, walk across to Manchester Victoria and catch the Blackpool train. Arriving there, we ask where the locomotive depot is. Another walk with the small amount of luggage we needed. So here we are in a strange town, but we are young, we're willing workers and we like a bit of adventure and, to most people then, this would have been a real adventure. The vast majority of the working population hardly travelled at all. Very few had private cars, air travel was scarcely born and you were granted one week's holiday after working for a year, and that would be allocated to you any time between April and October.

When we found the running foreman's office at the depot, it's allocation time. First question - where do we stay for two nights? The railway barracks are full because some young men have been transferred to Blackpool for the summer. Two of us are given an address and told how to get there. We are also told what time we have to report for duty on the Saturday. I am given the doubtful privilege of a 4 pm start. Still, it's main line work, much better than the shed. Before splitting up, we arrange to meet that evening. Friday night in Blackpool, money in your pocket, young and fancy free. It's not all bad. Off the two of us go, me and Arthur Wharam. We are staying with a Mrs Kearsley. Her husband, Oswald, is also a passed cleaner. But we are 19, he is 48. When he comes home from his turn of duty, we are told all about the Blackpool system.

They don't have much work there in winter. So he is cleaning engines or on labouring duties at the adult rate of pay, whatever that is. For 10 years now, he has been 'red-inked' on a regular firing turn in the summer. In the winter, back to menial tasks. 'Red-inking' simply meant he was allocated work a week at a time. It was a living and, if he had been a registered fireman, he would have received the full fireman's pay. The railway, ever anxious to save a few bob, deferred registering him as long as possible. I think Oswald Kearsley was the most extreme example I ever met of someone who, nearing 50, still hadn't got his foot on the second rung of the ladder. Some climbed slowly, some more quickly. But Oswald never climbed at all.

So why did he put up with it? A glance at his date of birth gives a clue – 1891. Twenty-three years of age when World War I broke out. Put simply, he would spend the rest of his life being both surprised and thankful that he was not killed as many of his mates would have been. Also, in Blackpool, most of the population would have been used to seasonal work, one way or the other. So he and Mrs Kearsley took in visitors in the summer and a regular supply of people coming to look at the illuminations. Oswald Kearsley was just on the lowest rung of the ladder. But he was glad to be alive.

Friday night would have included a pint or two. Then on to the next day, when we were all on different turns. When I reported at the depot that Saturday afternoon, it was all new to me. The driver is a stranger and he thinks the same about me. We are working on a passenger train - again a different experience for me. And the engine - a 'Claughton' - a big monster with a different arrangement on the footplate. Since I know how to shovel coal and to get water into a boiler, I shall cope all right. I remember that we went from Blackpool to Accrington and I asked the driver how far it was – 32 miles. One way, outward I think, we stopped everywhere. On the way back, it was non-stop to Blackpool. The driver was satisfied with me so I must have done something right.

I remember another trip to Lancashire - going to Southport in that same summer of 1939. This time I had a morning turn on the Saturday. Since I like brass bands and cinema organs, there was something for me to do in the evening. Not a brass band concert, unfortunately, but Reginald Foort, the organist. I had heard him on the radio which meant he was a magical and mysterious figure – and there he was performing at Southport's main theatre.

Rose Grove was another depot we were sent to. On our very last weekend away that summer, all of us were allocated morning turns on the Saturday. I remember we all went to Belle Vue for the evening to a speedway meeting. It would have been the last Saturday in August, which was not a bank holiday at the time.

I know exactly where I was on the following weekend. Friday night was my first trip on the Canklow turn, returning to Derby on the Saturday. On the Sunday morning, I finished work at 6 am and stayed up to listen to a radio broadcast by the Prime Minister Neville Chamberlain. He announced that we were at war with Germany. And the lives of every one of us changed for ever.

Ex-LNWR 'Claughton' class 4-6-0 No. 6001 at Derby No. 4 shed.

Kidderminster Railway Museum

Chapter Eleven

Some Personalities

It was 3rd September, 1939 – time now to draw breath. Many people all over Europe were wondering if each breath might be their last. But the forecasts of immediate, devastating and irresistible bombing did not happen straight away. But when it did come, it was devastating.

But we'll take a break from thinking about the horrors of war, to concentrate on the railway, and in particular some of the characters I came across. Of course there were so many - and so many genuine 'characters' that I can only give a flavour here. But it is that word 'genuine' that tells the tale. In an age where 'personalities' are so often created by marketing experts and style gurus we can sometimes lose sight of the fact that characters cannot be created, they simply grow naturally. And so it was on the railways. The background, of course, is the sense of sturdy independence and equality felt by railway workers.

There was a hierarchy, a very rigid one in many cases, but railwaymen did not easily bend the knee. They were, for the most part, honest, fearless and forthright men; old-fashioned men in a way. And certainly they had some old-fashioned names. Ezra Owen, I worked with him on the north Stafford link in 1945. Another driver called Abner Cowley; and the secretary of a working men's club in Alvaston, by the name of Enos Fisher.

It was Ezra – 'Ezzy' – who was with me during my closest brush with death. Coaling stages were often built so that there was as little space as possible between the engines and the walls. This was done so that coal was not wasted, considerations of human life came a poor second to that. Well, of course, from time to time, some poor fellow would get trapped in this confined space and lose his life, and one particular fellow had a very narrow escape from certain death – me!

Ezzy had said to me on one occasion, 'If we ever go on the coaling plant at Crewe South, keep your head in, the supporting pillars are very close on the cab side'. On this particular morning, we signed on as usual. Our train was cancelled but we couldn't escape the lodging part of our duty. We were given a light engine for one of the depots west of Crewe and instructed to take that as far as Crewe, which saved getting another set of men to work on it. We could not make an issue out of this so, unwillingly, we did as we were told.

The means of getting on to Crewe South shed from Basford Hall sidings involved going round a long curve, which had the effect of turning this engine round to face in the opposite direction and we were not allowed to go on to the shed from the passenger station, not with a light engine, so that was how it had to be. On arriving at the depot, we were told to clean the fire, coal and water the engine and turn it on the turntable ready for its onward journey.

Having filled the water tank and turned the engine round, we set back towards the coaling plant. I, on the fireman's side, thought I heard someone shouting. Doing what comes naturally, I put my head out of the open window of the cab. Doing what comes naturally, not seeing anyone, I drew my head back in again. And, as I did so, the concrete pillar supporting the coaling plant caught my left eyebrow. Ezzy, looking out on his side where there was no danger, stopped the engine. And turned his head to see me, in the middle of the cab, shaking mine. I had just a slight graze above my left eyebrow and a few drops of blood. A split second later and my head would have been compressed to about three or four inches. We have to take these things in our stride. So we coaled the engine, stabled it and signed off.

We walked to Gresty Road, talking about other things. Ezzy had only said 'Well, I did tell you to beware if we ever went under the coaling plant'. No doubt he would have said the same to an enquiry. Or to an inquest. It was only when I had had a wash and a sit down that this very narrow escape got to me. For about 10 minutes, I sat still, just shaking. It passed off just the same way it had come and I was all right afterwards. We never talked about it again which is the best way.

I might as well tell you now about the second occasion when I almost lost my life. As a driver, also at Crewe, 13 years later, I was once again inches away from instant death. It was one of those odd weeks on the day shift when I was on duty at a very reasonable time. I was to travel out to Crewe along with my fireman Walter Usher, as passengers to work a goods train from there to Chaddesden. This train started from Runcorn and the engine was never fully coaled up there. On this day, the train came to Crewe on the up fast line, and stood there as we took over.

It was Walter's turn to be the driver, because he was the regular fireman in the link. That was how we worked with experienced men. No problem there. What I didn't like was the fact that we had a class '4' goods engine with a 'horse-shoe tender'. So called because there were no means of getting the coal down except by going over the top. Crewe station, like most of the main lines in that area, had by this time been electrified.

So there was I, only 400 yards away from the scene of my earlier brush with death – once again, going about my everyday business. I looked at my watch and realized that, if we were here for another five minutes, we would be held for the passenger train to Derby – the 11.20 am departure. Five minutes passed. Time for action. Without a word to Walter, I picked up the coal pick and clambered over the back of the tender. Standing on the low level coal, I was in the act of raising my pick when something - sixth sense, divine providence, call it what you will – told me to look up. And there, only a few inches above my head, 25,000 volts were humming merrily away.

I thought to myself get down, you silly devil and made very sure that I didn't touch any of the wires as I clambered down to safety. As Walter said, 'My heart came into my mouth, when I saw where you were'. A set of men in the relief cabin came out to see what was going on but, for some reason, I wasn't at all upset. Just Crewe having another go at me. Those wires had to have a victim. Just a few months later, a fireman on a main line diesel engine, standing in Crewe station, clambered on to the front of the engine to clean the windows. And touched the wires. Bang! There had also been a case of a fireman who went on the tender to fill the water tank.

Railwaymen were hard men in those days, they had to be. Two items of clothing were certainly never worn. The first was underpants. Very few working men wore underpants at the time and I would certainly have scorned to do so. The only advantage in this omission, apart from a certain freedom in the walk, was that the doctor at the medical had an easy job establishing that you were in fact the male person you claimed to be.

Even more 'cissy' were gloves. With hindsight, this seems ridiculous. Firing was a dirty, dangerous and hot job. Gloves were obviously sensible. But the first man I remember wearing them was Ron Hemmings and he was subjected to a few taunts regarding his masculinity. 'Glamour boy' was the most repeatable of the insults. Of course, he was a trailblazer. It wasn't long before gloves came into widespread use and proper industrial gauntlets were soon to follow.

To be in charge of such independent men you needed to have a bit of backbone yourself. And our supervisor in the days when I was a cleaner certainly did. His name was H.L. Matthews universally known as 'Harry Butcher'. Butcher Matthews was a stocky man who imposed discipline with a simple warning, 'I'll see you round the corner'. Not in fact the physical challenge that this might imply but a warning that 'round the corner' lay the motive power superintendent H.B. Buckle. Although Harry Butcher used to come round and see his cleaner gangs from time to time, he never said much to us except, 'I'll see you round the corner'. It was his way of letting you know who was in charge.

The other chargeman cleaner was Charlie Turner, known to one and all as 'Popeye'. Not because of the strength of his forearms but because he only had one eye. If anyone lost the sight of an eye in those days, it was replaced with a glass one - colour-matched of course. He was very much Mr Turner to us - and only Popeye behind his back. He didn't miss much with that one eye. He was the foreman who checked up whether I was cleaning wheels properly and his method of doing so was to take a pure white duster from his pocket and give my wheels a rub. Thankfully, although I wasn't the fastest man in the depot, I was probably the most thorough. And the duster went back into his pocket without comment.

Although there was a line of promotion governing everyone's progress on the footplate, there was also a rank of 'permanent fireman'. The reasons for this particular grade were all medical. One such fireman was G.W. Pountain, otherwise known as 'Polly'. He was the only man among us who could say with certainty that he was not mad. Some time ago, apparently, he had been treated for some kind of mental condition and had been discharged with a certificate saying he was of sound mind. The rest of us assumed we were sane but only Polly Pountain had a certificate to prove it.

Another regular at the carriage works was Harold Jackson. Years before he had been struck on the head by a lump of coal, which fell off an engine. I don't think it had any lasting effect on him but the medical officer decided that he was not to go forward to be a driver. Later, he became only the second person in the country to have a particular type of operation - I think it was something to do with the removal and replacement of an artery. What I do remember, however, is the gruesome pleasure he took in describing the operation to us. This was in the days before keyhole surgery, remember, and Harold always said, 'They cut me open from throat to crotch'.

Also in the carriage works, there was George Trollope. A real star turn this one. He had been on light duty work for about seven years because he was not well. When the men around him were getting near to being passed out for driving, however, George began to feel better; so he asked to see the medical officer. The result was that he was allowed to go out on the main line again. And, when I was firing for Len Beard in the London to Manchester link, George was sent out learning the road to Manchester. That was in the winter of 1947/1948. Whatever his condition had been, he always managed to keep it a secret. For several years, I was in lodgings with his wife's mother and even his wife didn't know what was the trouble with him. My own view is that it was a very obscure complaint called 'Idle-itis'. There are subtle variations but there was a common result at least as far as footplatemen are concerned. It means that you avoid the heaviest kind of work and, while everyone else takes their turn, you don't.

Another star turn was a man who seemed to have served his time as a fireman but who became afflicted by a condition which blighted his career as a driver. Everyone knew him as 'Tired Ron'. Any kind of physical exertion caused a reaction, so he was always feeling tired. One of the few things he could manage was to stand up for a couple of hours to watch Derby County play football. Not that he ever talked about it, the very idea was tiring. One Saturday afternoon, I was making my way off the ground at the Osmaston end. There had been a big crowd there and, suddenly, I spotted Ron about 12 paces in front of me. It was very interesting to see his shoulders moving up and down with the rest of the crowd, almost as though he didn't suffer from this terrible affliction at all. A very strange event – 'Tired Ron' galvanized into life.

People! I won't say they are larger than life because I have always found life very large indeed. But, for all the work, for all the worries, for all the wondering what will happen next, it's humanity that shines through.

Ex-MR class '1F' class 0-4-4-T No. 1404 at Derby station on 25th March, 1944. In the background is Austerity 'WD' class 2-8-0 No. 7506. No. 1404 was the North End passenger shunting engine, seen here on platform 6. That line, and the siding line adjoining, were controlled by Derby Station North signal box, not visible. The other lines were controlled by the signal box at Engine Sidings No. 1, as seen behind No. 7506.

V.R. Webster/Kidderminster Railway Museum

Chapter Twelve

Whatever the Weather

In the 1930s and 1940s, we had more settled weather patterns through the seasons of the year. Not like that now, with global warming and extreme summer temperatures. Back then, winter, particularly November, usually brought fog and snow. We carried on, whether cleaning or firing, with the same routine, except that fog and falling snow slowed operations down. I remember one night outside the shed when I was standing on a trestle, rubbing black wax onto a big tender. Working away with my sleeves rolled up, the snow began to fall. With flakes falling all around, I carried on until the chargeman cleaner came out, and called us back into the shed.

Way back then, we had fog much thicker than we get nowadays, because the terraced houses in Derby, as in other towns, all had coal fires as the principal means of heating. Lots of chimney smoke damping down greatly reduced visibility. It wasn't too bad in the daytime, but nightfall closed in, and so did thick, clammy fog. Drivers and firemen peered through the gloom, trying to see semaphore signals. There were only a few coloured light signals then. There were two grades of railway worker at the time who are now just a distant memory: lampmen and fog-signalmen. Oil lamps were used to light semaphore signals. Some of them were quite high up, particularly where there were bridges in the area.

With loose-coupled goods trains, the only braking power is the engine, although when working down inclines, the guard would apply the handbrake in his van. We took about three-quarters of a mile to stop a heavy goods train with the engine brake, so that was the standard distance between distant signals and home signals. The distant signal, if it is in the caution position (horizontal), means that you will have to stop at the next home signal. If it is in the clear position, raised to 45 degrees, you expect to find the home signal at clear, and to be 'right away' through the section controlled by one signalman. But that must never be taken for granted.

At all the signal boxes, there would be a suitable cabin for the lampman to fill and trim the heavy signal lamps. They could be recognized by the strong smell of paraffin. Out on the line, there could be four or more stop signals, and two, or sometimes more, distant signals controlled by each signal box. That meant that there could be a journey of nearly two miles for the lampman. If he could ride a bike, in some locations, that would help. But there could be two heavy signal lamps to carry. Hot they were too, and in the daytime the heat wasn't always welcome, because you don't make the journey in the afternoon or evening to light the lamp, it is illuminated 24 hours a day.

When the lampman arrives at the distant signal, he has to climb a narrow metal ladder, carrying the heavy lamp up to the platform provided for him to stand on. He will, of course, have to carry the previous day's lamp back down the ladder. We never saw a fat lampman. For that matter, there weren't any fat firemen either. Not on main line work anyway.

Now suppose it is really foggy, and the fog-signalman has not yet arrived at his post. The signal can be quite high in the air, and the driver can't tell what aspect it is showing. How can the driver be certain that it is safe to proceed? There's only one way. That's for the fireman to climb that narrow metal ladder until he can see the signal aspect. And I remember just once having to do that. That was some fog, that was.

Lamping had to be done 365 days a year on main lines. Obviously you can't keep men in reserve for fog-signalling in two or three winter months, so that job was always done by the platelayers, better known as lengthmen. They were supervised by the ganger, and summoned when the signalman, or in some areas, the station master, called them out. A supply of handlamps and detonators were kept in each signal box.

The ganger would be 'fogging' the nearest home signal to the signal box, so that he could maintain contact with the signalman. Distant signals were, of course, some distance away. Each man going to a distant signal had to follow a recognized procedure. His first duty was to check the aspect of the signal. If it was green, he would turn his hand-lamp to show a green light. If it was at caution, he would show a yellow light. Then, he would put a detonator on the line, about 20 yards before the signal. The detonator is only needed when the signal is at caution, or stop. When that is done, he can attend to his personal requirements. He must keep warm on a cold and foggy night, so he would get a fire going, in the brazier. He would have brought some kindling wood, and paper. By some strange chance, lumps of coal often fell from the engine at these locations. Well they would, of course! When he had a fire going, he would lift up the fogman's hut, which had been lying face down at the side of the track. The fogman's hut was a small wooden hut, just big enough to accommodate one man, with a small plank to sit on - no luxuries whatsoever. I daresay they brought a flask, or more probable in those days, a bottle, of tea. And some sandwiches, they could be there all through the night. We enginemen were always glad to see their lamp on a foggy night. When you were out in a real pea-souper, it was sometimes impossible to see beyond the engine chimney.

I remember one such night, when I was working a goods train from Derby to Washwood Heath, Birmingham. We ran over one detonator, which had been put down by the guard of the previous train. There weren't any fogmen out that particular night, which was in 1954. What I remember well is setting the regulator in such a way that we were just crawling along. Being on the nearside, all I could look for between signals was the red sidelamp on the guard's van of the train in front. His white sidelamp would be on the offside, nearest the main line. This journey to Washwood Heath was when I was firing for Albert Harris. Working with him, I acted as driver every other day, 'Day about' we called it. The following year, with Billy Cass, I did no driving at all. He was too tired to take a turn with the firing shovel.

There were three lamps on a guard's van, one on each side, and one, the tail lamp, at the rear. When running on a main line at night, all three showed a red aspect. On a goods line, the side nearest the main line would show a white light. Each lamp had a red shade, so that it could be changed from white to red. Hand lamps, apart from the fogman's, could show white, green or red. At one time, even the water gauge lamp on the engine had a red shade on one side. That could be used as a hand lamp, in an emergency.

One night, when Birmingham was being heavily bombed, the driver said to me, 'Let's go under the tender for safety, in case they hit us'. So we sat there for a while, but nothing came near us: another once-only experience. There was nothing unusual about being behind six or seven other trains, all waiting until the 'all-clear' sounded. Then there would be a quick movement.

In 1939/1940, the platelayers were happy to be called out for fogging duties, because of the extra money, particularly in the weeks before Christmas. They would only earn around £2 a week for their normal duties. Later, another version of how to behave in bad weather appeared in relief cabins. This is how it went. 'During fog and falling snow, in the cabin we will go. In the cabin we will stay, until the fog has gone away'. Ah well, the times they were a-changing.

Snow lies on the ground as LMS class '5MT' 2-6-0 No. 13055 powers away from St Mary's Junction, Derby with the 11.00 am Derby to Liverpool service in February 1933. These engines were known as 'Crabs' because they were top-heavy, and had more sideways movement than any other engines. A fogman's hut can be seen on the right.

F. Carrier/Kidderminster Railway Museum

Chapter Thirteen

Travel by Rail

'Travel By Rail' – that's what the posters used to say. When advertising trips to Skegness, they used the picture of the 'Jolly Fisherman', bouncing along with a very big smile on his face. In recent years, a lot of people have not been smiling after a Saturday train journey to Skegness. It isn't the only destination that people have complained about, but more than any other railway journey from Derby, that's the one that gets the most complaints in our local newspaper. People have stated that they and their families have had to stand up all the way there, and sometimes, most of the way back. That the train was late arriving, or that the toilets were not working, and so on. Often, their letter finishes with the statement 'Never Again!' When people who can't afford to run a car, or to travel abroad, pay good money for a train journey to the seaside, they are entitled to expect something better. More than most people, I sympathize with them, because I can remember a time when it was so very different.

When I was a small boy, our father would take me to watch Derby County on a Saturday afternoon. Later my mother and sister came too. I remember the carriages we sat in, on that relatively short journey – old non-corridor stock with no facilities, and hard seats. Sometimes that old stock was used for the evening excursions from Derby, to places like Belle Vue, Manchester, the 'Playground of the North' it was known as. A Saturday night excursion ran there and back for half a crown (2*s.* 6*d.*). Now that was value for money, even if you did have to cross your legs on the journey.

I never did go on one of those excursions to Belle Vue, but I and three of my mates were there on the last Saturday in August 1939. We had all been working on the Saturday morning. It was the last journey ever, when passed cleaners from Derby were sent away to work a Saturday at another depot. I had been sent on several trips like that in the summer of 1939. As the junior passed cleaner, I was first on the list for such jobs when we were on the day shift. 'Old hands' (that's our seniors) couldn't be spared. I daresay they wouldn't have minded travelling as a passenger on Friday, working Saturday, and back to Derby on Sunday. Although we only got paid the cleaning rate, it was two shifts in one week when we were paid to travel by train. Oh happy days!

It would have been considered a crime to have people standing in carriages back then. At all the principal stations there were carriage sidings and locomotive depots, and men available to work trains at short notice. This is how railway work was done then.

The LMS ran long journeys through Derby; London to Manchester or Sheffield; and Bristol to Leeds or Newcastle, with 10 or 11 coaches. Now let us suppose it's Friday afternoon, and people are travelling from London and points north to Manchester. At Leicester, the platform inspector sees around 100 people waiting to join the train. Some people will get off there, so there may just be a few people left searching for seats, but he knows that there will be a similar number waiting at Derby. The moment the train leaves, he is on the telephone to the platform inspector at Derby. 'Can you strengthen the 6.40 Manchester train, please?' The train will be at Derby in around 25 minutes – it is not a problem. The message is relayed to the foreman at Etches Park sidings. The shunter with his engine, picks up two coaches which are standing in the siding, ready for anything. In around 10 minutes the two coaches are in front of the engine, standing at the signal.

As soon as the Manchester train has cleared the signals, the extra coaches get the signal for their journey to the station. Meanwhile, the waiting passengers at Derby have been advised that seats will be available at the rear of the train. The shunting engine propels those extra coaches into the station at around 15 mph, slowing down as they near the train. The carriage shunter couples up the extra coaches, doors open, and the waiting passengers fill the empty coaches.

Five minutes have elapsed for 'station duties' - which means parcels and goods being loaded and unloaded from the guard's van. The wheeltapper, with his long-handled hammer, has been checking the wheels. If they ring like a bell, no problem, but sometimes, there is a dull thud. Unless it is very serious, that coach will be 'red-carded'. That means it will be taken out of service at Manchester. If on very rare occasions the fault is considered dangerous, the carriage will be taken out of service there and then. The train leaves, the passengers settle down. For us, job done, no fuss. Back to the sidings, time for a cup of tea.

Sometimes strengthening the train means it is overloaded for the class of engine at the front end. The solution to this problem is to ask for an assisting engine. Derby No. 4 shed will have a standby engine and crew available. All the possibilities will have been considered in advance. At each end of Derby station, north and west, there will be a class '2' passenger engine, shunting coaches as required. The enginemen will have road knowledge: at a minimum they can go to Leicester to the south, Birmingham to the west, and Manchester or Sheffield northwards. Many's the time, as a fireman, I have been on one of those three passenger shunting engines, north end, west end and Park sidings, and seen such operations carried out. Twenty years later, as a driver, I have been on a standby engine. Just once, standing at the north end of the station, ready to assist a train to Manchester or Sheffield, but I was not required all day. Mostly you were knocking about around the shed, doing something else, but you were there if the need for an assisting engine, or even a special train, arose.

In wartime, the steam crane at Derby, with its complement of breakdown vans, would be available. A set of men were booked on at 9.00 pm every night. 'BD Vans' was the name of the job, they were there just in case bombing raids caused a major disaster. No-one else was kept in reserve. The crane driver and the fitting staff would be doing their normal work in the shed. (Though it was not unknown for off-duty fitters to be called out, when a major incident requiring the steam crane arose.) That a steam crane was available is another example of the way that the railway in those days was equipped for all eventualities, all geared to making the operation run smoothly for its customers, whether freight or passenger. The crane was required for lifting heavy weights, usually in an emergency, when disaster struck. It may involve lifting an engine which is on its side, or several coaches piled on top of one another. Not very nice work, to do or even to write about.

I remember another job for the steam crane, with no passenger vehicles or casualties involved. In the first week of August 1964 I signed on one day at 7.20

am. This was to take the steam crane to Hugglescote colliery, near Coalville. There had been a runaway of loaded wagons; they had all been derailed, and there was coal lying around. One of those accidents caused when someone releases wagon brakes, and away they go. I played a small part in the clean-up operation.

I required a conductor driver from Coalville, because Hugglescote, although nearby, was on a route we didn't normally use. On arrival there, he left us. It was a simple matter then of placing the steam crane in the best position for lifting, and stabling the vans. The crane came with all the necessary equipment needed by the fitters. It would have been possible to send the engine back to Coalville then, but that wasn't done. Probably nobody expected the job to last as long as it did.

The morning passed, and afternoon came. We found that we were quite near to the road to Coalville, which had a handy public telephone box. That meant that I and the fireman, David Sillance, were able to tell our wives that it looked like being a long job. Luckily for us there was also a fish and chip shop nearby, so we fetched our evening meal, and waited for the time when another train crew would arrive and take over. That happened soon after midnight. The railway motorbus which brought them from Coalville took us back to Derby. I signed off duty at 2.20 am, a total of 19 hours on duty. But it was the easiest overtime payment I ever earned. As always, we took the smooth with the rough.

I began this chapter with the upset suffered by passengers hoping to have a nice day out at Skegness, and continued with the details of how in the 'old days' people hardly ever had to stand up on a train journey – the outbreak of war changed all that. On the railway, as elsewhere, resources became stretched to the limit. If we were going as passengers to Birmingham to work a train back to Chaddesden, the train we caught would be crowded with service men, and women. The only possible seat for us would be in the guard's brakevan. Often sitting on parcels, and sometimes joined by others seeking relief from the crowded corridors. Tired people slept wherever they could lie down, or just stretch their legs out. That was wartime - travel in the 21st century should not mean standing up all the way, or very late arrival at your destination. It is simply a matter of having the resources required. In the case of the Skegness train, that would be a few spare diesel-multiple-units (dmus), so that six cars, instead of three can be provided for a summer Saturday train. On many other journeys, passengers today are still standing.

In Scotland, they had to cope with very severe weather in wintertime, which meant using snowploughs. Another resource that was there when the need arose. We had several in the wintertime at Derby to cope with similar conditions between Rowsley and Peak Forest, on the Manchester line. In the very severe winter of February to April 1947, trains actually got stuck on that line. Even then, railwaymen carried on working. Nobody froze to death, because steam heating to the coaches was provided.

The key words here are resources and adaptability. It's all about how to cope when the going gets tough – and the tough get going. There is another key word I have not used yet in this chapter – *safety*. In all journeys by public transport, that is the major requirement. Punctuality, comfort and speed are second, third and fourth. Later I will give safety in railway operations the attention it deserves, by telling how and why it can be achieved.

Chapter Fourteen

Blacker than Night

In wartime on the railway, blackout conditions were imposed on engines moving in the dark. A heavy sheet had to be fixed between engine and tender. Secured by ropes, the aim of the sheet was to prevent light from open firehole doors penetrating the darkness. The possibility of enemy air raids against transport of goods by rail was very much to the forefront of managerial strategy. The workers' strategy was just get on with the job.

As it turned out, the areas of Derby's railway system which were damaged by enemy action were few. The one raid which did affect Derby station did entail loss of life and traffic disruption for a short time, but that was the only local problem that I remember.

Train crews were issued with a better gas mask than the general public. We carried our gas masks for a while until it became apparent that we were never going to need them. Some people took to air raid shelters when the sirens sounded and I spent just one part of one night in a shelter. I then decided that I might as well go to bed because if there was a bomb with my name on it that was it, anyway. In any case, I was often at work when it was dark.

Having a blackout sheet on the engines was a real bonus for us in bad weather. The class '1' freight engines were proper open air jobs, with a skimpy little roof overhead. They were designed with a short wheelbase so that they would go round sharp curves in shunting yards. The wind blew in to the cab, with nothing to stop it. And when it rained, we got very wet. Rain was far worse than snow. It made a big difference when you could put the blackout sheets up - which you were allowed to do in daytime as well. That improved conditions no end.

And so we move on to 1941. In June of that year, I became a registered fireman. In other times, that might have been a cause for celebration, but our minds were on other things. For those of us left at home were always deeply conscious of the war. Even on home soil, our personal safety was always at risk. Although the anticipated invasion of Britain by the German Army did not happen, bombing raids were a fact of life (and death) night after night. Derby was lucky to escape what happened to Coventry, Birmingham, Liverpool and London and many other cities as well. Those who remember those times, have remarked on the fact that Derby did not suffer proportionately. Perhaps the fog over the Trent valley made it difficult to locate. There were also decoys built, put up to divert attention from possible targets such as Rolls Royce.

On the night of 15th January, 1941, though, the railway station was hit and I was no more than half a mile away at the time. One of my mates, Arthur Wharam, was still unattached and we had been to the 'Green Dragon' for the evening. That particular hostelry ceased to exist quite a long time ago. John Scotton, the landlord, and his wife, took a shine to the three young engine cleaners who, from 1937, used to go in and play darts when they were on the day shift together. We were always well-behaved, of course, and no-one ever asked us why we were not away in the armed forces.

In any case, we had an answer ready. Like all the other young men, we had stood in the queue to be registered and given a medical of sorts. I was working on the Saturday that I was supposed to register so I simply turned up at the first suitable Saturday after that. Taking one day at a time. I was given a card to carry around with me but I don't remember anyone ever asking to see it.

To return to the bombing of Derby station. Arthur Wharam and I were standing close to Trinity church on London Road, about to go our separate ways. He heard the sound of an aeroplane, and so did I, but he realized it was indeed a 'Jerry'. So he pushed me to the ground and dropped down beside me. When the crunch came and nothing near us was disturbed we got to our feet and bade each other goodnight. I continued walking along London Road, passing Midland Road without any idea that the station had been hit. Around two o'clock, the caller-up came knocking and I was on duty at 3 am. Walking over the Hulland Street bridge, I could see that a large part of the main roof had collapsed. A porter and a railway policeman had been killed. It seems that about half the bombs dropped on the station failed to explode. I don't think we turned a wheel that day.

Mention of the 'Green Dragon' brings back memories of something that gave me a very small worry which was quickly resolved. Mr and Mrs Scotton enjoyed our company and would ask us to stay on a while after closing time for a final whisky and milk. Licensing hours were very strict, of course, and you could be arrested for drinking as little as 10 minutes after closing time. So, with the four of us chatting away one night, I froze solid when a police sergeant and constable walked in. 'Hello boys', said John Scotton. 'What are you having?' Two convivial glasses of beer later, they walked out through a back door left unlocked for the purpose. Panic over.

I also remember going out to work at three o'clock one morning in the blackout. Walking down a street near London Road, Derby, a voice came from the entry which served three or four houses. 'Now then, my lad, where are you going?' I realized that the voice belonged to the borough policeman, who didn't recognize the footsteps of the new kid on the block. 'I'm going to work', said the kid. 'And where might that be then?' In a tone which gave no doubt that he did not believe me. 'No. 4 shed, LMS Railway', I replied. 'Off you go then' said the constable grudgingly. Now, if only we had the same standards of vigilance today. The next morning, I went down the street at the same time and past the same entry. I know perfectly well that the constable is there. But he didn't say anything. Nor did I. If I had challenged him, I might have ended up at the station - police not railway!

That policeman would be used to the footsteps of the regular drivers and firemen, coming and going to No. 4 shed at all hours of the night. He would see the caller-ups going on their rounds. Every man on duty after midnight and before six o'clock had to be called. The regular drivers would be up and about when the call came. Because they had gone to bed in the early evening, it was how they conducted themselves. A life mainly devoted to bed and work for 51 weeks of the year.

Working bank holidays was also accepted as normal. There were two days in the year which led to a day off in lieu if you worked them - Christmas Day

Rowsley-based Midland '2P' 4-4-0 No. 40499 with a local train at Derby. Notice the bomb damage to the train shed roof, the roof was removed during rebuilding of the station in the 1950s. *H. C. Casserley*

A view of Derby station in early BR days with the damage to the station roof having caused it to be removed. *P.J. Lynch/Kidderminster Railway Museum*

and Good Friday. If you worked on the others, it was just hard luck. I also remember that football matches were played on Christmas Day and Boxing Day. The year 1938 comes to mind because Derby County went to Goodison to play Everton on Christmas Day and Everton were lucky to get a draw - or so the papers said. Next day, there was a return fixture at the Baseball Ground. County won and went to the top of the old First Division. About two weeks later, the same two teams played in the third round of the FA Cup, Derby lost and their league form also deserted them.

I'm not too sure about the rate of pay for bank holidays but Sunday rate then was only time and a half. The best rate of pay was if you booked on at, say, 1.30 pm and hadn't finished by 10 pm. The driver would look at his watch and say, 'We're doing well now, mate, every penny's three-ha'pence'.

Sometime during the war, the drivers who reached 65 were allowed to carry on working if they wished. I remember one man who stayed on for a while was Bill Gamble, ASLEF's Derby branch Chairman. Some people, who didn't approve of that called him 'the old weasel'. But this was a man who had done a lot of work in the trade union movement when being a union official was a risky business. He had been involved with unions since 1913, at a time when service records which said 'left the service' often meant 'dismissed for being a union member', so it was unfair to call him a 'weasel'.

In June 1941, the big move up, sanctioned at an open meeting, was operated. The drivers in the spare link, moved out into the main goods links, well 22 of them did. Those in the control relief and preparing links moved up into the spare link. And that's where I was placed. It was at that time, with a train working to Rowsley and return that I made the longest day in my working life. It was the winter of 1941 and my driver was Jack Ashley. We were on duty for 21½ hours. I also remember that it was his last week in railway service. He would be in his early 40s and was one of the first people to take a job in a different industry – change all around. But there had been a lot of promotion that year and I was one of the ones who took a great leap forward. We certainly didn't know that after the big move up of 1941, there would not be the same sort of promotion ever again. For me, it would prove to be a long wait to get to the top of the ladder.

Chapter Fifteen

The Class of '41

In December 1941, after six months in the spare link, I was moved up to a position in the London goods link. Seventy years later, I still remember '41 as a momentous year for me. My years as a passed cleaner had been the first steps in a life as a footplateman. We could not see then all the changes that would overtake us just a few short years later.

For almost four months - December 1941 until March 1942 - I would not have a regular driver. My booked mate, Charlie Archer, was off sick for all of the 11 weeks before my next move. Drivers from the spare link, or passed firemen, would be filling in for him. Which was exactly how work was covered - day by day, week by week.

We didn't lodge at London any more because of bombing raids on the capital. So we lodged roughly halfway at Wellingborough. The train was taken on to London by another set of men. It would get there, the job went on. There must have been many nights at Cricklewood sidings near London when nothing moved for hours at a time. It was years afterwards, as fireman, and later as driver, that I actually lodged at Cricklewood and also at Kentish Town.

The barracks at Wellingborough was a very busy place in 1941. Trainmen from London lodged there, when working to the North of England and to Scotland. And many like us, whose journey to 'The Smoke' had been interrupted by the bombing raids.

There wasn't any point in making plans. We lived in the hands of the Almighty and the fortunes of war. Compared to many men and women of my generation, I was having an easy time. So many had fought and died in France. The evacuation from Dunkirk and the 'Battle of Britain' had come and gone. The survivors of those perilous times tell of shared hardships. But I wasn't a conscientious objector or anything like that. Just a regular guy, taking life and death as he found it.

Bus services at the time were a lot better than they are now. I was able to get home for some of the time in every weekend, to parents eager to see me, to my mother who, having lost her young man in France in World War I, was particularly anxious to know how I was faring. My sister, Ida, who started work in service at Langley Priory after I left, was also away from home. That's how it was for young women who worked as housemaids or kitchen maids in the big houses. They have their own stories of service or servility to the so-called landed gentry; like everything else in life, good, bad or indifferent.

So many changes in train workings were happening at that time. That period of 11 weeks was soon over, and then it was time for another move. On the first Monday in March 1942, I was placed in one of the three North Road goods links with Bill Beardsley who was getting on for retirement age. Like me, Bill was a countryman – from Holbrook outside Derby. At a time when a lot of men were given nicknames, he was known as 'Wittling Bill'.

Most of our trains served the collieries, then the dominant feature of the landscape between Derby and Leeds, there were pitheads and slagheaps in abundance. Bill told me that, pre-war, they had lodged at Normanton and Stourton, large marshalling and interchange sidings on the way to Leeds, places where a transfer of wagons between LMS and LNER took place.

In the North of England, there was a real hotchpotch of lines running into different towns. Take Chesterfield, a town where they had three passenger stations at one time. Three companies competing for passengers, Great Central, Lancashire, Derbyshire & East Coast and Midland railways. There is a classic picture of three trains at Horns Bridge, Chesterfield: a goods train on the Midland Railway, a passenger train on the line below and another one on the bridge above. Maybe the photographer didn't have to sit all that long to get his shot. At that time, around 100 years ago, it was truly the age of the railway.

We didn't work beyond Rotherham Masborough in 1942, and we lodged at Canklow, a nearby depot. Only 36 miles from Derby but, when I describe the journey, you will see how many calls we made on this relatively short stretch. A typical day would see us sign on duty at 9.35 pm, we would prepare our own engine, and leave the shed at 10.20 for Chaddesden sidings with departure at 11.05.

Our first call was the down sidings at Ambergate; some wagons to detach and some to pick up; take on water for the engine. After one or two fast trains had gone, we were turned on to the main line. There were several colliery sidings between Ambergate and Clay Cross but no goods line so we didn't have another stop till just after Clay Cross, at Avenue sidings where they dealt with a lot of colliery wagons for the Erewash Valley line. That was a route where you could bypass Derby on a journey from Nottingham to Chesterfield. So there would be wagons to put down and pick up there. Then it was a short journey down the goods line to Hasland where there was a locomotive depot, I believe it still opens as a railway museum, it was the same procedure here. Horns Bridge at Chesterfield was next. We would fill our water tank again at a small siding near the passenger station.

On we went, over the Old Road, the first railway from Leeds to Derby, famous for several reasons. It was surveyed and built by George Stephenson and over which trains ran from Sheffield to Derby until a more direct route, involving a tunnel at Dronfield, was opened. We would pass Tapton House, on a hillside overlooking the valley. George Stephenson lived here for a time so it's almost hallowed ground. Our next call was Staveley Works in the district of Barrow Hill. There were a large number of sidings, but you couldn't see much of them in the dark. They had a passenger station but the station names had been removed. There was a real fear of German paratroopers at the time so anything which might help them had been taken away. Our blackout sheets cut down the glare of light when the firebox was opened. If an enemy aircraft had spotted a moving light, they would have a fair idea it was a train.

Even when we left Staveley Works sidings, there were still several other places to call. At Beighton interchange sidings we detached wagons for the LNER and picked up our own. Next call would be Treeton, then Eckington and finally Woodhouse Mill with the journey's end at Masborough sidings.

All this was possible because there were no fast trains running over the Old Road. And everywhere we had called there were collieries with loads to be picked up and they had to be supplied with empties. It was quite different to train workings to the south, east and west of Derby.

Having detached our train, we then went 'light engine' to Canklow shed. It was now about 6.00 am and it had taken seven hours to cover 36 miles. Tired, and in need of a wash, we walked to the private lodgings in one of the grimy streets surrounding the shed. It was a way of earning your living that had been going on for a very long time.

Like many a house at the time, there was no bathroom. You washed at the kitchen sink. The couple who lived here got up and went to work. We went to bed, and shared the same bed, because there was only one in the room. So many of those houses had just two bedrooms and two rooms - kitchen and parlour - downstairs. I remember that in the wintertime we had Yorkshire's very own version of the hot water bottle. A clay brick warmed up in the oven overnight and wrapped in a flannel. It would give out a steady heat for several hours.

We got up again at lunchtime and walked down to the Canklow Hotel. They sold beer brewed by Bentley's of Rotherham – two kinds, bitter and strong. Strong ale was stronger than any draught beer served nowadays. The workers in the steel industry had to have their liquid refreshment, so there was never any shortage of beer in Sheffield. There were certainly shortages in other parts of the country. People queued for all manner of things. Basic foodstuffs were rationed. You had to produce coupons to get items of clothing. I remember the utility mark CC41. It was good quality clothing.

Sunday evening, I remember one when I was at home and wanted to find a pub that was open. We had three in Breedon at the time. I was out on my mother's old pushbike so I went to Breedon for a start. None of them open, not at the front anyway and I was a bit too shy to try round the back. So I rode through a procession of villages, all of which featured pubs with no beer. I got out quite a way from home to a pub called the 'Forest Rock', which is still there, near to the monastery, beyond Coalville. The front door was open but there were so many people trying to get in that I gave up and went home.

As I remember, Derby never had a beer shortage. Like Sheffield, there was a lot of work to be done that was vital for the war effort. We were doing some of it, no doubt about that. So someone, somewhere, made sure that workingmen could always get their beer. There were a lot more pubs in Derby then than there are now.

The guard on our trip to Canklow, who was also lodging, came with us for this lunchtime drink. There were very few customers, apart from railway workers on night shift, in the pubs at lunchtime. Then it was back to our lodging house for the meal which we had brought with us. After that, we just went back to bed. There wasn't anywhere else to go. Canklow, in wartime, was a drab and dingy place, I expect it is quite different now. The pitheads, the locomotive depot, the miles of sidings, all those have gone now. It was never as attractive as the apple orchards I had seen on the way to Gloucester or the green fields of Leicestershire and Rutland en route to Wellingborough.

Sometime after the people who lived there came in from work, we rose again to prepare for our return journey. It was quite different on the way home. No more than one or two sidings to call in, including Chesterfield. And we would end up at Derby, once again at about six o'clock in the morning.

That autumn of 1941/1942 also saw the first time I was given the chance to drive a passenger train, from Wirksworth to Derby. 'You'll be all right', said my mate, Harry Pritchard, and I was. Now, as regular fireman in 1942, I was to experience a routine of a different turn every 10 weeks but with the regularity of a time on duty virtually unchanged from Monday to Saturday. So that would be one week with something constant. And six days working with the same driver on the same job. Yet every day something would be different.

Some jobs in the North Road link were better than others and some took you into conditions which apply when traffic is worked in two directions on a single line. Single lines of railway could be found all over England, Scotland and Wales. I can only write about what happened on the LMS but something similar must have taken place all over the country. Always to be borne in mind in any discussion of safety is the tendency of human beings to make mistakes. One regulation for working on single lines at least had the benefit of simplicity. It was called 'One engine in steam'.

Integral to all forms of single line working is the instruction, 'A driver must never enter a section of line without the basic authority in his possession'. Our authority to work over the single line was the 'Staff'. A simple metal bar, about a foot long, square-shaped, with a rounded end for a person to handle. This was inscribed with the message 'Shirland Colliery Sidings'. It was kept in the signal box of that name.

The staff was handed to the fireman by the signalman when the train of empty wagons entered the single line. It will be kept on the engine in a safe place but visible at all times. When we leave with the loaded wagons, en route to Ambergate, I, the fireman, will hand the branch staff back to the signalman. Because the driver of the next train, be that today or tomorrow, will not enter the section without it. There are no exceptions to this. If an engine breaks down for any reason, the staff will be conveyed back to the signal box so that the driver of any assisting engine, or a breakdown van train, can take possession of it: a safe system.

There is one other thing to remember. At Wingfield station, we would have picked up the 'branchman'. He was a simply a travelling shunter whose duty it was to help the guard deal with the train. A complex operation as you will discover. The rest of the branchman's duties consist of liaising with the staff responsible for wagons leaving Wingfield Colliery. We also work empties in and loaded wagons out of the sidings there, on a different turn of duty. If he has any spare time, that will be taken up with assisting the work at Wingfield passenger station. The shunters at Ambergate sidings, where trains from Shirland and Wingfield were shunted, and marshalled into trains for other marshalling yards to deal with, also had other duties. This applied where a siding had no dedicated shunting engine. The staff, head shunter and his assistant, the under shunter, cannot work without an engine. But they were not allowed to sit in the cabin, waiting for the trip engine. The LMS didn't believe in shunters having no useful work. So they walked a short distance to the passenger station and helped out with other station duties. If there wasn't a passenger station nearby, the shunter would be utilized as a 'branchman'.

We had two weeks work to Shirland Colliery which was about halfway between Ambergate and Clay Cross. There was a special way of working here which did not happen at any of the other collieries in our area. Nowhere else did we have to go through a tunnel to get to a colliery siding and there wasn't another tunnel like that one. At just 220 yds long, you wouldn't think there was that much to worry about. But it wasn't easy, because it was only built to take nothing bigger than our class '2' goods engine. And there was very little clearance for them, so you wouldn't put your head out of the cabside in case you lost it.

The layout of the lines at the colliery had been arranged with absolute economy as the guiding principle. There were no facilities for a train engine to pull 24 wagons up to the colliery, then return down an empty siding to take out the loaded wagons. So how was the job done?

Where you can't pull, you push. And when you have brought 48 empty wagons to the sidings and only 24 can be taken up at a time, that means two trips through the tunnel. It was on a rising gradient so there was no chance of coasting through the tunnel which rapidly fills with acrid choking smoke. Because the tunnel was always damp, sanding gear must be in good working order and the sandboxes must be full when you left the shed. There was another problem - curvature of the line, so this reduced your speed still more.

With all these restrictions, there was only one way to do the job. Like this. We had to get clear of the main running lines as quickly as possible. First off, we would detach the first 24 wagons, place them in the siding, in the shunting neck. All these movements were controlled by Shirland Sidings signal box. Back out to the main line, pick up the other 24 wagons plus the guard's brake van. These we drew up into one of the two running lines and run round them. Now the brake van would be next to the engine.

In winter time, while we would be waiting to draw out onto the main line, I had to do something else. To reduce the risk of slipping, ever-present when the rails are wet, I would take several handfuls of sand from the boxes, carefully held in a sponge cloth or even a handkerchief and, shaping this like a funnel, I would trickle sand out onto the rails where the line curved and adhesion was so important.

When the main line was clear, the signalman would let us out. We had to draw the train out in order to take a run at the rising gradient. I would build up a good fire because the driver was going to give this raft of wagons a good thrashing in order to get up some speed.

We then start the propelling movement that will hopefully take us all the way up to the colliery. Regulator would be right across, and the wagons squealing as they went around the curve. Due to the rails being sanded by hand, we were going well. As we reached the tunnel, the driver shut off and coasted a little way, then opened the regulator about half-way. This was just enough to take us through the tunnel. When you saw daylight, it was a big relief because the cab was full of smoke. Some of the drivers and firemen had been known to dip their sponge cloth in a bucket of water and hold it over their mouth. I never tried that, I just held my breath. There wasn't any other way of doing the job, sanding the rails and getting a good speed up before entering the tunnels were the keys to getting through.

So what happens if you start slipping in the tunnel? There is only one thing to do. Shut off steam, the wagons will push you back out of the tunnel very quickly. Just as well, because trying to continue forward would put us in grave danger of suffocation. No 'ifs' or 'buts' about that.

Having failed in one attempt which happened to me once in that year, you wouldn't give up. You would go back to the signal, tell the signalman that you will have another go. The fire would be built up again and at the second attempt you would get through, partly because there would still be some sand on the rails inside the tunnel. As the fireman, I would have been using the lever which is on the engine for sanding while we were running.

There were, of course, another 24 wagons waiting for us in the shunting neck. We then draw those up and run round them, still with the brake van attached. As before there was a residue of sand outside and inside the tunnel. The same procedure for them, go as hard as you can. Having got through the tunnel, we arrived at the colliery sidings, left the brake van at the end of one siding and picked up the loaded wagons. I can't remember how many loads we took but the miners were turning a lot of coal out in 1942.

On the way back to the main line, it was all downhill as far as Wingfield. At Shirland, the guard took his handbrake off, when we had the required number of loaded wagons on the running line, and rolled quietly on to the train. We started away gently, it was now a matter of stopping when we reached the signal. The journey through the tunnel was not a problem going back, the weather often was, there wasn't much protection for the crew on class '2' engines. If it was snowing, you'll stand with your back to the fire, the flakes will hit your front, but that was all in a day's work. You would be, of course, running tender-first all the way back to Ambergate.

There would be more shunting to do when you got there, some of the wagons would be destined for Chaddesden, others for Rowsley and beyond and a few for the line which went towards Butterley, where trains are now operated from the Midland Railway Centre. But the only coal they will deal with now is what they need for their own engines.

That was one branch line we worked out of Derby. There were three more to collieries, Ripley, New Lount and Wingfield. Wirksworth also had a passenger service until 1947. Ripley, and the Ashby branch line, lost their passenger services in September 1930.

On each of these lines, the working practices were different to Shirland. They were worked by the Electric Token Block regulations, because there were several signal boxes on those branches. But that is another story.

Chapter Sixteen

All Change

Every young fireman at Derby looked forward with hope to the first Monday in March every year. Having served 12 months with one driver in a link of 10-week turns, each one was different. Then it was all change. If the year about to end had been a good one, you were hoping for more of the same. Supposing that you had been subjected to a rather indifferent year, then you were looking forward to something better.

We were now 3½ years into the war and a possible invasion of Britain by Germany had receded into the far distance. Our daily newspapers told us of the struggle taking place around Stalingrad and other Russian cities. The might of a great military machine was exhausting itself on the frozen steppes of the Soviet Union.

In our main line goods links, the increase from eight drivers and fireman to ten had caused rapid promotion in 1941. Now we were settled into a routine, for a year at a time. Having finished a good year with Bill Beardsley on the North Road, what would happen to me in 1943?

For me, in fact, it was my best year in all my time as a fireman. I was firing for Billy Kirkman. He was the first of the younger drivers I would be firing for, over several years. It was the events of the so-called 'Great War' which caused Bill Kirkman to become a driver while still a relatively young man. This is how it happened. Like many another young man at that time, he volunteered to join the armed forces. Although under age, the army turned a blind eye and Billy found himself in France. There wasn't much 'greatness' about the Great War over there.

If being wounded instead of being killed can be described as lucky, then that is the way of it. He was shot up around the waistline and when the army realised he was under age, he was invalided out and sent back to England. So I think it was in 1916 he started work as an engine cleaner, at around 16 years of age. Which meant that his promotion to fireman was much quicker than was the case for hundreds of men who entered railway service from 1919 onwards.

Billy was left with two consequences of his military service. He blinked his eyes a good deal due to shell shock and he wore a heavy wide belt around his waist for the rest of his life. I never saw it and it was only mentioned once. But this little man had the heart of a lion.

No-one would expect a driver to take his turn with the shovel on long distance train workings. Shunting and local trip work, yes, many of us got driving experience while still a fireman. It was how you learned your trade. I had been firing for Billy Kirkman for five or six weeks before our first trip together to Wellingborough. I had my share of the driving to Ripley and other local turns. In 1943, we worked the afternoon turn; St Mary's No. 9 shunt engine. This is very boring work for a young fireman.

Our morning turn to Wellingborough was a much more interesting trip. We signed on for this turn at 3.40 am and left Chaddesden sidings at 4.52. Our return working was to sign for duty at 11.00 pm and leave Wellingborough for Chaddesden at 12.12 am. The week before, Bill asked me if I knew much about the road to Wellingborough. As a passed cleaner between May 1939 and June 1941, I had been there several times when the 4.52 had required a pilot engine, a regular feature on that and other lines at the time. And I had also lodged there on a few occasions. 'All right' said Bill. 'I will work both trains on our first trip, just to show you how we go on, after that you can work the return train to Chadd', and so it was that from the second trip that week, I worked the 12.12 to Derby.

Our other working was around 6.20 pm from Chaddesden and involved working to Wellingborough with empty wagons. These were taken forward to Islip, a siding where iron ore was produced, by another set of men. We then lodged on Monday, Wednesday and Friday. Our return working, on Tuesday, Thursday and Saturday, ran to this schedule: Sign on at 2.50 pm, leave Wellingborough shed at 3.10 and run light engine to the sidings at Islip. Those empty wagons had by now been loaded up with iron ore, known to us as 'monkey muck' because of its colour. This train went all the way to Glazebrook near Manchester. The processing of iron ore was very important in wartime.

We had to marshal our own train at Islip and then run tender-first with it down to Wellingborough (London Road), fill up with water there, run round the train again and, after that, set off for home. There was some weight in that train, I can tell you, around about 1,000 tons. It would be around four o'clock in the morning when we arrived at Chaddesden where we would be relieved. Of course, Bill always did the driving on that part of the trip, which worked out very well for me because I drove the two light trains and he drove the heavy ones. It was quite an experience for me, at 23 years of age, to be driving trains to and from Wellingborough.

On some of our day turns, we used to meet up in the Rutland Arms at night for a drinking session. Bill taught me how to play crib. That was a time when darts, dominoes, crib and solo whist were all pub games. There was no television, and eating out was not yet in fashion. There was still a war on and it was essential to keep the pubs well stocked with beer. Working men and women didn't have a lot else by way of enjoyment. I do remember going to the Grand Theatre and the pictures in the early war years. It isn't surprising that we lived from day to day in 1943.

Working goods trains to and from Wellingborough called for good train management, because of the varying gradients we encountered. There was an instruction in force that goods trains could not run more than 40 miles without the wagons being checked for axle lubrication. Oilers and greasers, the men who did this were called. A lot of mineral wagons, that is those that convey coal, coke and other minerals, had axles lubricated by grease. So the examiners carried a tub of grease. Into this, they put a metal bar, took out a lump of grease and put it into the little box above the axle of the wagon. This inspection took place on a goods line just beyond Melton Mowbray.

Even with this attention, there were still occasions when the axle boxes ran hot on the journey. Sometimes you could look back while running and see a shower of sparks coming from one of the wagons. This meant that the wagon

Beyer Garratt 2-6-6-2T No. 4994 at Cricklewood shed in 1935. We rarely got Garratts at Derby in my time. Most of them worked from Toton to Wellingborough or London. The coal bunker is circular, and can be partially revolved, to bring coal forward. *W. Potter/Kidderminster Railway Museum*

had to be detached at the first convenient siding. I think quite a lot of the wagons with grease boxes had been used on short distance workings by 1943, but we still ran down the goods line at Melton, to wait while early morning passenger trains passed us on the main line. The greasers were no longer there.

It was only when we left Brentingby that the gradients became really interesting. First, there was the steady climb up to Ashwell. A few hundred yards beyond the station, there was a bridge carrying a road over the railway. 'That's called Saviours Bridge', said Bill. 'Because Toton men with their long trains pulled by Garratts reckon if they can manage the long climb up there, they can get all the way to London'. The Beyer-Garratts, articulated locomotives, could manage the heaviest trains from Toton to Wellingborough or London.

On odd occasions, we would get a Garratt on one of our trains. It happened to me twice in 1943. I remember we got one on the night empties one day. So I said to Bill, 'I had better do the firing tonight'. These engines had a very deep firebox. 'No, it's all right', he said. 'We will take turns to fill the firebox'. So it was five minutes shovelling in turn. I think it took us about 20 minutes.

Soon after leaving Oakham, the railway became something like a switchback. Falling gradients to Manton were followed by the line running level, after which it rose again to the signal box at Wing. That's where engine and train management had to be of the highest quality. There is, of course, no substitute for experience, which, if you are not driving yourself, you gain from watching your driver. I think I was the only one of 10 men passed for driving in 1955 who could say, 'I will be entirely capable of working passenger or goods trains, loaded or empty, over the routes to Wellingborough, Manchester or Crewe'.

Leaving Wing, you soon entered Glaston tunnel and emerged after 1 mile 82 yards. Then there was a very short tunnel at Seaton, just 206 yards. Then we cross the great viaduct, the longest one I ever worked over. It has 82 arches and it crosses the Welland valley. It is a marvellous experience when you got to the far end at Harringworth to look over the side down at what appears to be a miniature village. Some years ago, and again very recently, I have taken a car journey to Seaton and Harringworth to see that viaduct. When I was driving a train, our practice was to go as hard as we reasonably could, getting as much speed up as possible. Hopefully you would be at Gretton, getting on for half-way up the hill, before you felt the full weight of the train.

Gretton doesn't get a mention now but it was very much there in 1943. I can well remember working the 12.12 ex-Wellingborough in the other direction coming down the incline from Corby. You kept the train under control with the brake until you passed Gretton and saw the distant signal for Harringworth. That meant an almost clear run to Wing. Release the brake, pick the train up gradually. We had all loose-coupled wagons so there was a skill in getting all those couplings, around 40 of them, at full stretch. Then again, go as hard as you can, to get the train racing across the great viaduct. On the odd occasion, the distant signal would be at 'caution' which meant you must stop at Harringworth. So you continued braking and all the impetus was lost.

Outwards again, another long tunnel at Corby, then we were soon at Stewart & Lloyds, which was the great steelworks near Corby. A very busy place in

1943. We used to run full trains of coal to keep the fires burning. And that was the most testing part of the journey, from Oakham to Corby or vice-versa. A gentle down gradient to Kettering and then a fairly level run to Wellingborough.

It would be about 12 o'clock when we arrived there. We would leave the engine on the shed and walk to the barracks where you would be allocated a single room each, driver, fireman and guard. Wash and brush up then walk to the nearest pub, called the Chequers, I think. After about three pints it was then back to the barracks. Sleeping wasn't always easy because trains were running all day and night in the cutting below the barracks. Another hazard was that some of the older men made a lot of noise with their snoring, sometimes punctuated with a sort of whistling sound. However, when you have been awake since 2.30 and have worked a full shift, it would be about 9.30 in the evening before I woke up.

There is something else to say about the return journey. There were four sets of catch points in around 19 miles between Glendon and Oakham. Catch points were provided when there were heavy gradients just in case a coupling broke and part of the train started to run back down the hill. If that happened, the wagons would simply come off the road at the catch points. There might then be one almighty pile-up but there would be no danger of a collision with the next train coming up the hill.

There wasn't anything comparable on the lines from Derby to Birmingham or Rotherham. And, while there were similar gradients to Manchester or Sheffield, it was rather more straightforward, either as a steady climb up or a continuous roll down. It was quite an interesting trip from Wellingborough to London as well but those Garratts were known as 'fireman killers'. I daresay the Toton firemen would be fed up after one year on those engines. So, 1943 was the best year I ever worked as a fireman though there were some others which were almost as good. We worked hard on duty and enjoyed ourselves as much as was possible, always remembering that this was in the heart of the war years.

The Midland Railway was incorporated into the LMS in 1923. But, just as I had always cleaned engines to Midland standards, so I was trained by Billy Kirkman 20 years later to work trains on the same principles and to the same standards.

Chapter Seventeen

Life with the Lubricator

When people now wish to describe a very poor year in their personal lives, they use the term *annus horribilis*. The old engine drivers, speaking of a bad time following a good one, were very blunt: 'After the Lord Mayor's show comes the donkey cart'. In modern terms, the refuse disposal vehicle!

As far as my working life was concerned, 1944 would be just as bad as 1943 had been good. The link that I would now move to was on the West Road, Birmingham, only, for about eight weeks in every ten. It didn't help that, by March 1944, the war was 4½ years old. The civilian population was tired of nights spent in air-raid shelters.

It had always been the case at Derby, indeed all over the railway system, that most of the goods trains ran in the evenings and early mornings. So, if you were not at work when the air-raid warnings sounded, you would probably be coming home from work after the 'all-clear'. Everyone, whether in the armed forces or in civilian life, was feeling the strain of the war effort.

From the first Monday in March 1944 I was booked with a driver who I will only call by his nickname - 'Lubricator Pete'. This is because I don't want to upset any of his descendants and I don't think there will be many people around who remember that nickname. He had started work in the footplate grade at Stockingford, a small depot in the Midlands. At many of the sub-depots, supervision during the night hours was minimal. But it didn't escape the notice of Pete's colleagues that he went to sleep with his head up against the drop lubricator on the class '2' goods engines. And that's where he got his nickname.

Like many men in the 1920s, he was moved to Derby when Stockingford shed, among others, was closed, together with other men who, in the main, were older than him. Because he had started work around 1916, he became a driver at Derby while he was still relatively young. That was something he never talked about, his cleaning and firing days. He didn't talk about much else either. We had very little conversation did Pete and I, only what was necessary in the course of our duties. In fact, I found out quite early in the year what it would be like working with this bloke. Working a train to Birmingham around one o'clock in the morning, after we left Chaddesden, there would be several parts of the journey when we would be on the main line. Pete would be sitting on the seat in the class '4' goods engine. Eyes closed - that is not a misprint - eyes closed, except when we were getting near a distant signal. Then he would open them for long enough to see the signal aspect and, if it was clear, promptly close them again.

I had never, never met anything like it. I knew he wasn't actually asleep. But I also knew he certainly wasn't alert. So, of course, I made sure that, in between periods of firing the engine, I was always watching out for the signals myself. The main motivation for this was self-preservation. Only once did he have to ask me, 'Hey, was that back signal off?' We called the distant 'the back one'. Around three-quarters of a mile ahead we reached the home signal. I was able to answer, 'Yes', so that satisfied him and it was eyes-closed time again.

He wasn't a bad engineman as such, for I never saw him in trouble stopping a train. It isn't actually a crime to be bone-idle, which he certainly was. We would run onto the goods line at Water Orton, behind other trains waiting to enter Washwood Heath sidings. There could be five or six trains in front of us. Naturally, as soon as we came to a stop, it would be time for him to settle down to sleep. And I would also be tired by then, having had to watch for all the signals as well as doing my own work. Rightly or wrongly, I thought, 'Right, if you can go about with your eyes shut while we are on the main line, I will do the same when we are standing still'. I have never done anything like that before or since.

One of the very few times that I did have what you might call a conversation with Pete, he told me about something that had happened to him a year or two before, which had resulted in the sack for two firemen and two shunters. Because of the blackout, there were always opportunities for pilfering. A few people saw the chance and were prepared to take the risk. The prime mover in this was the West End passenger shunter on one shift. His job was to marshal vehicles on two lines to the west end of Derby station, West End dock, front and back roads. Because these lines were a little way beyond No. 1 platform, he saw the opportunity one night to tamper with a loaded van. Open the van doors, get inside, close the doors tight behind him and then use his handlamp to see what articles he could steal. I don't know how long this went on but there came a time when there were enough complaints to mean that it had to be stopped. So, of course, the railway police set a trap. The shunter and two young firemen were caught and, of course, that meant instant dismissal. Lubricator Pete told me that his fireman was implicated and therefore Pete himself was questioned at length as to whether he knew anything about it. Pete insisted that he had never seen any stolen goods and when his fireman disappeared from time to time, he just assumed he was going to the toilet.

Ex-MR class '2F' 0-6-0 No. 58110 at Nottingham Road, Derby on 12th June, 1949. Notice the springs, outside and above the foot framing. *H.C. Casserley*

The other place where pilfering took place for a time was St Mary's goods yard. Part of the yard was occupied by the bond stores, spirits and such like, goods subject to customs and excise duties. I have been firing on the shunting engine which serviced the sidings leading to the bond stores but I don't remember ever seeing inside the building. But if someone realises that a vanload of whisky is standing in a dark siding, well away from the inspector's office, well, there's temptation for you. Again, eventually, the trap was set. And one very unfortunate driver, Joe D, who knew nothing about the operation, was caught in the trap. I don't mind giving an indication of his name because I am sure he was innocent. He was unlucky, though. If the shunter in possession of the stolen goods had simply secreted them until it was time to go home, Joe would have been in the clear. Instead, the shunter climbed onto the engine and said, 'How about this, driver?' Before Joe had time to say, 'Take it away, nothing to do with me', the detective had followed the shunter up the engine steps. Those of us who knew Joe realised that he was innocent. But the law didn't look at it that way. So he was charged with receiving. Same ending, instant dismissal. I daresay there were some other people, in some other places, who didn't get caught. At the time, everyone knew the consequences. There we are, wartime, rationing, shortages. Temptation. It's all about human nature

With allied armies preparing for the invasion of Europe, there were signs everywhere that the war years were finally coming to an end. And there was hope for the future for all of us who had been through the terrible years when so many - both in the armed forces and civilians - had suffered injury and death.

Sixty years on, we are still hearing of things which happened to people in concentration camps. Like some other periods in history, another example of man's inhumanity to man. My personal liberation came in March 1945. No more 'Lubricator Pete', Whoever I was going to be rostered with as the war drew to a close, it could only be an improvement.

Ex-LMS class '2F' 0-6-0 No. 58207 passes Engine Sidings signal box on 11th June, 1949.
H.C. Casserley

Chapter Eighteen

Fit for Heroes?

This was the year of liberation for the continent of Europe. Thousands of men and women who had been involved in the war effort could now return to civilian life. The major cities of Britain were liberated from the threat of massive bombing raids. Equally, there were many in Germany who could think of peace again. It wasn't all over. There was still a theatre of war in the Far East. That was finally concluded by the dropping of atomic bombs on the Japanese cities of Hiroshima and Nagasaki. Historians will argue that it might have been avoided but that is always the privilege for those who look back with hindsight.

But what about the transport system in Britain, which was something I was part of? Having seen how the LMS railway operated in peacetime, with all its good points and its bad ones, I knew it could never be the same again.

As a young railway fireman, I could still be rostered to work with drivers who had started their railway careers before and during World War I. Many of them had been used to working a 10- or 12-hour day. Some had even taken part in the footplatemen's strike of 1911 which led to the recognition of their right to belong to a trade union. Previous attempts to negotiate working conditions and rates of pay had always been smashed by a united front of railway companies.

The key to success for a railway trade union was having enough money to help members if they were unfairly punished. A system of fines for various misdemeanours was operated by the Midland Railway at Derby. This was in place from 1900 to about 1925. ASLEF's Derby No. 1 branch would hear members' complaints about harsh treatment and, if they agreed, the fine would be re-imbursed. This was a practical, common and demonstrable way of showing that a union really worked.

Of course, there were many drivers and firemen who never normally went to trade union branch meetings. Most of them would turn up at special open meetings when major changes to working practices were being proposed, but the normal monthly meetings would attract only 12 to 20 members.

Whether members attended branch meetings or not, everybody was bound by the same wage levels. As the unions pressed for wage increases, so the level of interest grew, especially after the Labour Government was returned in 1945. That was the very first election at which I was entitled to vote. I was over 25 but there had been no elections during the war years.

On election day, I was at work on a shed turn and that gave us a chance to listen to the results on the radio as the canteen had a set. Neither canteen nor radio would have been allowed before the war but times had already changed. I went to work at 10 o'clock at night after the polling booths had closed. Around 1.30 am, the time for our meal break, the first results were coming through. The announcer, in his BBC matter-of-fact voice, gave out the figures for each constituency. There were hardly any fringe candidates, just Conservative, Labour and Liberal. At that time of the morning, a lot of results were coming through from the great English cities - London, Manchester, Birmingham - and the industrial towns. Seat after seat was announced as, 'Labour elected, Labour gain from Conservative'. While most people were in bed, we knew the result before we went home.

As a child and a very young man before the war, I had only known Conservative governments. The village of Tonge had probably only about 30 voters in 1929. Can you imagine a candidate turning up now to canvass that number of voters? Well, Breedon Parish then was in the Loughborough constituency. And, in that last but one election before the war, Mr Winterton, the Conservative candidate, addressed a small group of us on Tonge village green. That was my first political meeting and I have been to very few since. Having a keen interest in politics at that time, I was certainly prepared to believe politicians. I haven't lost interest - just the belief. However, that may be, Mr Winterton was elected. Members of his family are still in Parliament, 70-odd years later. It must be a way of life for them.

My father believed in the Liberal Party. That isn't surprising because it was a Liberal Chancellor, David Lloyd George, who introduced a national retirement pension scheme. And Dad drew his 10*s*. a week for a number of years. Having a retirement pension helped to remove the fear of the work-house in old age.

So - back to that 1945 election. It's safe to say that Loughborough, a fairly rural constituency, had never elected a Labour MP. Well, we did in 1945. What has all this got to do with me as a footplate man and the railway in general? Quite a lot, in fact, but we'll get there later. Way back then, there was a sense of anticipation that things would change and, hopefully, for the better. Perhaps they did. But slowly, of course. For the railwayman, all too slowly.

The railway system was not in very good shape in 1945 (even though it was a lot better than it is now). The permanent way had suffered from a lack of maintenance. The steam engines were suffering from stretching the maintenance intervals as well. And the workforce had suffered, too. Long hours of duty became the rule rather than the exception. Pre-war, if any footplateman was on duty for more than 11 hours, there was a special report into the circumstances. All that had gone. Some things were the same, though. Passenger trains ran on time and every member of staff was dedicated to looking after the needs of the travelling public.

In 1945, I was working on the Crewe link with a mix of goods and passenger traffic. Passenger trains stopped at many stations which are no longer open and an unusual feature was that Derby Midland was an open station. This meant that tickets were not collected at the barrier. Express trains running into Derby had travelling ticket collectors. For local services, the station staff, at Tutbury, went through each coach collecting tickets. Six minutes was allowed for this so you can see we had a fair few passengers.

That six minute break became a challenge. I was told that the fireman of the previous year, George Weston (no relation) had used the time for a special purpose. George Weston became a Jehovah's Witness in later life. Well, he certainly wasn't one in 1944. He would race across to the pub and use four of his six minutes for downing a pint of beer. Well, of course, I had to accept the challenge. Stupid, of course. But it was a good pint and you're only young once.

The man who told me about George was my driver at this time, Ezra Owen. There were more biblical names then and I well remember Abner Cowley and Enos Fisher. But Ezra was simply known as 'Ezzy' and he was my little mate … and little

Uttoxeter station on 17th August, 1955, the year I spent in the Crewe link. A Stanier 'Black Five' class 4-6-0 No. 45148 stands in the station with a Derby to Stoke-on-Trent passenger train. Neither the Churnet Valley line, or the locomotive shed are visible in this picture.

H.F. Wheeller/Kidderminster Railway Museum

My ASLEF credential card. *Author*

Associated Society of
Locomotive Engineers, Firemen, Cleaners & Motormen

No.......... *Scale*........ 1

Name and Address of Member J.W. Weston

285 Brighton Rd

Name and Address of Secretary F.A. Robinson

58 Marlboro Rd

Branch Meetings will be held on 2nd Sunday in Month

Commence at 10:30am Close at 12/30

The Price of this Card is 1d.

he certainly was. He told me the story of how he started work at Coventry on the London & North Western Railway (LNWR) around 1918. He was 5 ft 4½ in. tall and he was given another six months to grow another inch and a half. For four months he struggled with stretching exercises which made no difference at all. So he was resigned to the fact that his railway career was over. Then, suddenly, the minimum height requirement was lowered to 5 ft 4 in. Salvation for Ezzy.

Together we worked the Derby-Crewe line. After the first five miles, to Stenson Junction, it was all the former North Staffordshire Railway. They had built their own small depot at Derby as had the London & North Western. For years, working goods trains from Chaddesden to Crewe, we went out on the main line at the LNWR junction. Actually, the LNWR had been quite bold in the early railway days. With their own locomotive depot, they also ran through to St Andrew's goods yard and they had built a very big warehouse right outside Derby station. Obviously they were challenging the Midland Railway for goods traffic but, without access to any of the collieries in South Derbyshire, they were never going to win. It was the carriage of coal for which early railways were built and it continued to be the main earner on most of the system for years .

When the LNWR discovered that they couldn't beat the Midland at Derby, they upped sticks and concentrated on Crewe. There, in a town virtually built by the railway, they had a great engineering works, miles and miles of goods sidings and two locomotive sheds.

The North shed at Crewe was one of the great depots. I believe it had some of the longest mileage turns in Britain. One of their links went to Perth in Scotland and the men lodged there. There were passenger workings, of course, with those marvellous 'Royal Scot' and, later 'Coronation Scot', locomotives which were classed as being too heavy for some of the underbridges in our area. So the biggest engines we worked from Derby were known as 'Baby Scots'. Some baby ... still, pound for pound, our Midland Compound was second to none and those engines did great work over the LMS system. Provided you knew how to handle them.

The North Staffordshire Railway, affectionately known as 'The Notty', kept its little depot at Derby open for a considerable time. One or two of our old drivers remembered that shed closing and the few drivers transferring to No. 4 shed. Bob Tomlinson and Jimmy North, I think, were old 'Notty' men.

It's a long time ago. But some things stick in your mind better than others. How many people still alive remember the staff toilets at Stoke station pre-war? A long, narrow, building, just east of the station, with about 12 cubicles each divided by a side partition. No doors. No privacy. No flushes. The toilet seat was a great oak beam that ran from one end to the other. For a country boy like me, there was no great culture shock but today they would be regarded as outrageously primitive. If the station inspector was looking for a porter or shunter, there was no hiding place.

I enjoyed my year in the Crewe link, despite all the hours of shunting at Tutbury and Uttoxeter. Sometime in the future, there would be a bigger challenge, which I would also accept. The prospect of working a heavy train down Stoke Bank. That, of course, would be subject to me staying the course on footplate work and ultimately becoming a driver. That would only take another 10 years.

Chapter Nineteen

Cold Comfort

And so on to our first war-free year. On the first Monday in March 1946, I was booked into the Bristol link with Albert Watson. Albert was another Midland man nearing retirement age. He was well over six feet tall and well built. For his time he was a very cultured man, with a precise way of speaking. He never used four-letter words, although he did say to me, when we were working a stopping train to Birmingham, 'Put a bloody good one on, John, and sit down'. By which he meant to fill the firebox before we started the journey and have a rest because there wouldn't be much chance of taking it easy later on.

It is said that opposites attract. Albert had a friend of the same age, Archie Clark. He was a real rough diamond, was Archie and more than a bit uncouth. They didn't socialize a great deal but the story was always told of how they went to one dinner together. Anxious to show his friend how to behave, Albert sat down and said, 'Archie, will you have a serviette?' To which Archie replied, 'Yes, Albert, I can eat one of the buggers if you can'.

We had a lodging turn at Bristol when we were working a train around 8.30 am from Derby. For some time, we relieved a set of men who worked the train in from Nottingham and we took it forward the rest of the way.

Albert Watson was a top engineman. At a time when the standard at Derby was particularly high, I can't remember anyone that I fired for over the years who was better than him. As with Billy Kirkman in 1943, I was the second young fireman to be booked with him. At the age of 25-30, you are just about at your best physically and we needed to be to cope with what was arguably the most demanding job in the link for the fireman, the 8.29 am Derby to Bristol and the 1.30 am return on the mail train.

It wasn't a difficult start when the train came in from Nottingham. The fire was already built up, nobody on these turns would hand over to the next man with a run-down fire. So we set off from Derby, calling at Burton and Tamworth. We always used the water scoop to pick up water over Wigginton troughs, just before Tamworth. It didn't matter how you set the water scoop, it wasn't possible to get the tank exactly full. The gauge would show almost full. Albert would then always stop at the small parachute tank at Tamworth and I would climb up to get the extra three or four inches. It was his one failing - a complete phobia about running out of water. So he was known to some of his mates as 'Water Watson'. He had probably done all his firing on smaller engines but the 'Patriot' class '5XP' engines had a 4,000 gallon tank.

Our next stop was New Street, Birmingham, one of the busiest stations on the system. There were no water facilities there. Midway between Birmingham and Gloucester, Albert would always turn and stare at the gauge, worrying about how much water was left. In fact, we would always have more than a 1,000 gallons left when we got to Gloucester, where we had to fill up again even though it was only another 35 miles to Bristol. It was on arrival at the small LMS shed there that life got tough for the fireman. I had been working at full stretch for over four hours - just when I needed a break, though, I had to carry out the disposing duties, clean the fire, smokebox and ashpan. Then I could sign off and make my way to private lodgings.

All the express trains were heavily loaded at the time. None more so than our return working - the night mail train. Starting from Bristol at 1.30 am with 14 coaches, it picked three more up at Gloucester, so it was 17 all the way up to Derby. The train ran right through from Bristol to Newcastle, the major movement of Post Office traffic between those two cities. I wonder how many aircraft or road vehicles it would take to move that lot. I think we had around 20 minutes at New Street, while all the interchange of mailbags was going on. So that was a little break for a very hard-working fireman. And it was fairly easy running from there to Derby.

Before that, we had stopped at Bromsgrove, where the usual business of taking on water and station duties took place. Here you face the mighty Lickey incline - a gradient of 1 in 37.7, the steepest main line climb in the British Isles, I think. At the time, all express trains had assistance in the rear. Either from 'Big Bertha', the purpose-built banking engine or from one, two or even three tank engines. On the night mail, always three, of course. The exchange of engine whistles took place before we started. I cannot remember exactly but it may have been two long whistles and a 'crow'. What was this 'crow'? Can you do that on an engine whistle? Yes, of course, you can even on a '5X'. Just string together a 'cock-a-doodle-do'.

As it said in the rule book, until those signals have been given and exchanged, none of the engines must move. Going up the Lickey wasn't any harder than the rest of the journey but rather slower. The three tank engines certainly did their share of the work. It's all very much in the past, of course. Nowadays, the diesel engines storm up the incline without any help. Long gone are the days when wagon brakes had to be applied on goods trains going down the Lickey.

I remember my odd trips on the 'Gloucester goods' as a passed cleaner. As at Gloucester, we only had private lodgings at Bristol. Very much on GWR territory there. Great Western enginemen had a barracks to lodge in; but we were never allowed to share it.

My six months with Albert Watson had been a very good introduction to full-time passenger work from Derby. I have some sad memories of that time, though. Working on the footplate, you are never far from death or injury. As a passed cleaner, firing for George Trotman, we were passing through the old Sawley Junction station (now Long Eaton) on a parcel train from Leicester to Derby. George remarked that something had hit him in the mouth. Some five or six miles later, we were stopped by signals at Spondon Junction. It was just breaking daylight. The signalman told us that our engine had killed a man on the track at Sawley. Examining the front of the engine, below the buffer beam, we found bits of human flesh. George had to go to the subsequent inquest. He assumed that it must have been the man's cap that flew off his head and hit him. There was nothing to say otherwise, nothing in the cab. This kind of thing wasn't uncommon in the blackout of 1940/1941.

The death of an adult is one thing - this is something else. One summer morning, on the Derby-Bristol turn, we had taken on water at Gloucester and

The Lickey banking engine, ex-MR 0-10-0 No. 2290 'Big Bertha', photographed at Derby in 1938. In my opinion, three little tank engines performed better on Lickey banking duties than this single engine. *L.W. Perkins/Kidderminster Railway Museum*

'Jubilee' class 4-6-0 No. 5612 *Jamaica* with a Bristol-Derby-York train at Tramway Junction, Gloucester on 17th May, 1947. *W. Potter/Kidderminster Railway Museum*

station work had been completed. But the signal stayed at danger. After a couple of minutes, I said to Albert, 'Shall I go to the signalman and find out what's wrong?' 'Hang on a bit', he replied and waited two or three minutes before telling me to go ahead. When I got to the signal box, the cause of our delay was explained. A train on the opposite running line, from Bristol, had killed a small child, under two years old.

Until the track had been examined, we could not go on. After a wait of about half an hour, we were allowed to move cautiously forward. Some way up the track a platelayer stood guard at the line side, with a sack covering a small body. Nothing else visible - just the sack. Down through all the years since then, I can still shut my eyes and see that sack.

A happier memory earlier, in the spring, was of seeing all the fruit trees in blossom between Bromsgrove and Gloucester. It was a truly magnificent sight. The trees then had to be about 20 ft high to get a full crop - nowadays they need only be about 8 ft. Obviously, that's progress - but I did love those blossoms.

There's another memory from the Bristol link. Jack Wild, the drinking man's drinking man was known as 'Sludge'. There was a suggestion once in the *Derby Evening Telegraph* that men from other depots used to engage in drinking contests with 'Sludge'. I don't believe it; they wouldn't have stood a chance. In a single session, I could down as many pints as he could. Just as I kept time with Billy Kirkman three years earlier. But there were two huge differences, Billy never drank on duty, and I only drank for one session a day. Jack Wild would always have two - maybe three - sessions a day. Before work, after work and, if at all possible, during work - seven days a week. But only once did I ever see him drunk.

I was a serious drinker in my way but only as a young man and only on isolated occasions. A couple of pints with my driver before coming back from Burton, Sheffield or Rotherham, that was fine. I never really counted the two pints with Billy Kirkman at Wellingborough because the beer isn't so strong south of Leicester.

For all his drinking, 'Sludge' was one of the best mates I ever had. It was with him as driver that I left Birmingham one severely cold day during the terrible winter of 1947. I had a small window in front of me. On one of the high overbridges in the Fiveways area near Birmingham, a hand suddenly appeared over the bridge and threw something at us. Just a snowball - but a snowball with a difference. Something inside it hit the window and took it clean out. I had ducked instinctively so no damage was done to me but it was a very cold journey from there to Worcester.

Came the week of February 1947, my last ever of three trips lodging at Bristol. Go out Monday morning and return Tuesday; repeated on Wednesday and Friday. And weather conditions such as I have never experienced before or since. Indeed, that winter was notorious for unusual stories of frost and snow causing havoc with transport; passengers in the Peak District were stuck in snowdrifts which had previously only happened in Scotland. We had three water cranes on Derby Locomotive depot and there were three more on the passenger station on platforms, one, four and six. As always in severe weather conditions, fires were provided to stop the water freezing.

On one very cold Sunday night, though, no-one had been sent out to keep the braziers topped up. A cold, thin wind took away what little heat the fires were still providing and the water froze in five out of six points. The only one still working was on No. 1 platform where the overhanging roof stopped it from freezing up as well. The train came in from Nottingham, as always on No. 4 platform – no water. So we had to run round to No. 1, fill up with water, re-couple and set off with the engine for Bristol.

Between Tamworth and Birmingham (New Street), we began to struggle with the brakes dragging on the coaches. Keeping 21 inches of vacuum was necessary, particularly on long journeys but the gauge needle was flickering around 19 so the coach brakes were 'rubbing' as we say. We kept going and managed to get up the gradient from Saltley to Proof House signal box (so called because of the way in which the barrels of guns had to be tested or 'proofed' for accuracy).

So we limped into New Street where the problem had to be sorted. We had plenty of steam which, through the large and small ejectors, creates and maintains the necessary vacuum in the train pipe. The pipe runs all the way to the end of the train. Under each coach, a metal pipe runs from one end to the other. Between the engine and the first coach - and between every coach - there has to be flexibility; every passenger engine and every coach also had a composition rubber pipe, about a yard long, on the upright end of the metal train pipe. So, the carriage and wagon examiners have to check every coach for leaks. And, about half an hour later, someone came to tell us what had happened.

Those flexible pipes have a metal ring at the end, with two lugs and a rubber washer. That's the bit you have to get together. On that night everything was frozen but workable. While we were in Derby station, though, under the roof, a partial thaw had set in. Ice had dissolved and small drops of water formed around the train pipe couplings. Between Derby and Tamworth, those droplets had frozen again, gradually forcing apart the two rubber washers. That is the only way that air could be admitted to the train pipe except by the driver or the guard, in the case of the guard in emergencies only. So that, uniquely in my experience, was what had caused the delay.

We left New Street around 45 minutes late. There were no further problems, it was a little warmer in the daytime. The delay meant that we were so late arriving at Bristol that there was no time for disposing of the engine. We had to sign on again for the return working about nine hours later.

I talked earlier of my time with Albert Watson. We parted company when he moved to the local link. A vacancy had arisen there, and he moved over to that link, as often happened when men neared retirement age.

As in 1941, I didn't have a regular mate for the rest of the year. In 1941 it had been because Charlie Archer had been off sick. This time, I should have been working with Fred Archer, but he too was ill. Just a coincidence, they were not related, they just shared the same surname. So I had drivers from the spare link for a full six months. The best of them was 'Sludge' Wild; simply because with him, I did a share of the driving on local trains.

Winter continued into what should have been spring. Snow came, and it was slow to go away. It was one of the coldest winters ever, and it lasted a long time.

A songwriter once wrote, 'Spring will be a little late this year'. It certainly was. The frost fires, the braziers sited against the water cranes to stop them freezing, were kept going for longer than usual.

In the autumn of 1946 I had bought a motorcycle, from a furniture shop, of all places. The shop was Seccombe & Page in Sadler Gate, Derby. It could only have happened in a Britain recovering from wartime restrictions. Rationing was still with us. The motorcycle was an impulse buy, seeing the shiny new motorcycle amongst the chairs and settees, I was hooked. I remember riding home to Tonge for the weekend, and later riding it out almost to Isley Walton, to a bend in the road where there was a good view for miles around. A blanket of snow covered everything, and not a car could be seen anywhere.

March 1947 was the beginning of my second year in the passenger links. I was moved up to No. 2 link, London and Manchester. I was paired with an old LNWR driver, who had been at Derby a considerable time. Harold Blower was a man who didn't make conversation with his fireman. He just got on with his job, and left me to get on with mine. What he was like with a fireman who had no passenger experience, I have no idea. It wasn't difficult for me, but there wasn't any feeling of being together on the footplate. No-one else ever remarked on his way of life, and he never mentioned his wife or children. Truly a man who came to work, did his job, and went home. I didn't have a problem with that. I had been to London and Manchester as a young fireman, and it was my second year on passenger work. So I knew what was expected of me.

On the line taken by the Manchester trains, between Ambergate and Matlock, there were several tunnels. The first was a short one, Lea Wood tunnel. When the engine came out of it, the fireman would be the first to see the distant signal for Cromford. I had been trained to watch for it, and to shout across the cab to the driver, 'Right away' if it was clear, which it almost always was. There was a period of intense shovelling after Ambergate on the express trains. The train would be stopping at Matlock, so I would get a little break at Lea Wood. Every other driver would acknowledge the shout, just by raising his arm. Not Mr Blower. He just ignored me, and carried on. Whether he was the same when other men were his firemen, I never knew. He was a good engineman, but obviously, his fireman never did any driving. We were never a team, he wasn't a team player. Since nothing ever went wrong, it didn't really matter.

Working with Harold Blower, we covered the routes between Derby and Manchester and Derby to London St Pancras. It was always special for Derby enginemen to work into London St Pancras and Manchester Central. Two stations which were at the end of the line. Both of them had the great arched roof, spanning five or six platforms. That is the feature which makes me think of them as railway cathedrals. I have heard that expression used by David Dimbleby, who said that the railwaymen were the priests, I don't agree with that at all.

You can go to other great stations in London, Birmingham, York, Bristol and Leeds, amongst others. To me, none of them have the same majesty as the two great Midland termini. Terminus as distinct from a terminal station – our Midland Division Sectional Appendix listed five of those. They were Derby, Leicester, Birmingham New Street, Sheffield and Nottingham. There was no

'Jubilee' class 4-6-0 No 5572 *Eire* awaits departure from platform 5 at Manchester Central with an up express in April 1946, a time when I was working in the Bristol link. *J.W. Neve*

'2P' class 4-4-0 No. 499 departs Manchester Central with a passenger train on 24th April, 1947. At this time, I was in the London-Manchester link. The class '2P' shown is working an express train, probably to Liverpool. *H.C. Casserley*

explanation in the Sectional Appendix as to why these five were called terminal stations. The answer was something I had to work out for myself.

The stations listed had one common factor, and this gave me the clue. They were all stations where branch lines terminated: several routes in and out. At Leicester for example, at that time, trains came in and went out to Peterborough, Wigston and beyond towards Rugby, and to Burton and Coalville. From these places, and their intermediate stations, Leicester marked the end of the journey. A changeover point if you wanted to travel on further. A terminal station is a completely sensible name for it.

There was a very good reason why I worked this out for myself. The 1937 Rule Book mentioned in one short paragraph what drivers must do when entering platform lines at terminal stations. A quite unusual instruction. They must enter those lines at such a speed that they can stop the train with the engine handbrake, if necessary.

There was a reason for this, which went right back to the time when vacuum brakes had been known to fail. It was a 'belt and braces' approach to train working. Another point is that the local trains I have mentioned often only had four or five coaches. More than one train could be accommodated on one platform line, if necessary. The passengers coming in from say Coalville, could catch another train if they wished to. It was, of course, in my time, part of the instructions to the platform inspectors that they could hold a train back a few minutes in order for a passenger to make a connection. That's something that's hardly ever done on today's railways, where they have to contend with fines for late arrivals.

Railway managers didn't want one train hitting another in a platform line. The signalling system was arranged so that this was very unlikely. This was done by means of calling-on signals. These were positioned below the stop signal controlling the entrance to the platform. This then was the safety procedure, 'the belt'. 'The braces' was the act of making the driver ultimately responsible for controlling the speed of the train. The 'belt and braces' approach is there to ensure that collisions between trains do not happen. This of course was at a time when railways had a very good record for safety. This was only made possible by making safe working an absolute priority. This was achieved, in the case of railway workers, by them following a long period of training. Not in the classroom, but on the job. The instructions for entering a terminus were unwritten and entirely a matter for common sense. Treat the buffer stops as if they were made of glass. Sometimes, mistakes proved that they were, indeed, rather fragile.

Never a problem with steam trains, not for experienced men. Sometimes with diesel-multiple-units (dmus), lightweight as they are, funny things happen. Stopping at Barrow-on-Soar one day, I thought I was making a normal stop. Somehow I finished up with two coaches overshooting the platform, and just one on it. There was no harm done on that occasion. These units did sometimes seem to skate, as though they were on ice. I don't suppose I was the only driver that it ever happened to.

Having mentioned the two stations at the end of the line, I will turn now to the locomotives we worked on the London and Manchester trains, in the steam days. We almost always used the 'Patriot' '5XP' class, on the London and

A general view at Wigston South Junction on 28th June, 1947. Curving away to the left is the line to Birmingham. The engine shed and carriage sidings are in the background. I was working through Wigston regularly around this time. *V.R. Webster/Kidderminster Railway Museum*

Fowler '4F' class 0-6-0 No. 4036 on a down goods train through Trent on 12th July, 1947. This engine was a long-term resident of Canklow shed. The only way to oil the crank axle on a class '4' was from a position lying on your stomach on the foot framing on the fireman's side. *H.C. Casserley*

Manchester express trains. They were hard work for the firemen, but, one day, he will be the driver. Like the 'Black Fives', they were built by a team under Sir William Stanier. He was head-hunted by the LMS Board of Directors. They got tired of the in-fighting between Derby and Crewe, after the Midland and the LNWR became part of the LMS system. They needed a new man at the helm of the motive power department, so they went to the GWR, and approached Stanier, a rising star at Swindon.

It's one of my regrets that I never got to fire on, or drive, a GWR 'Castle' or 'King'. Recently, I have been writing about railway managers being unwilling to learn from locomotive practices in other countries. Over a century ago, George Jackson Churchward, chief mechanical engineer on the GWR, went abroad to study locomotive design in other countries. Norman McKillop, a practical engineman, before and during my working lifetime, and also a writer on technical matters, has this to say about Churchward, 'No locomotiveman would deny that he was a genius. His pioneering work with the long travel valve should almost make him the patron saint of every fireman in Britain' (*see Appendix*).

There was no time for dreaming on the express trains to London and Manchester. As with the Bristol turns in 1946, timings were being accelerated, now that permanent way maintenance was getting back to pre-war standards. Loads were being reduced to compensate, but it was still heavy work for the fireman.

Also, as in 1946, the winter workings of 1947 brought changes in the link workings. No longer were there two links working to Manchester and London. Twenty turns were reduced to 12, and Harold Blower, along with several other drivers, elected to move to the 'old man's link', as they called the link passenger men could progress to before retiring. This link was local working only. I did not go with him, I moved into the No. 1 London link, the No. 2 link ceased to exist.

My new driver was Len Beard, I have no recollection of what happened to his previous fireman, my own future in the link was all that concerned me at the time. As we approached the date when the four Grouping companies would become one, to be known as British Railways, so many changes were being made. We knew that the Transport Act had been passed, and we would all be working for British Railways from January 1948. Len Beard was known to his contemporaries as 'Whiskers'. He was the man who would really set me on the way to finally mastering the rules and regulations which applied to all the staff in general, and to footplatemen in particular. We didn't have time for long discussions. There was one defining moment, which I can recall totally.

It was around 20 minutes past four one weekday afternoon. We were preparing to work the 4.34 pm from Manchester to Derby. A very unusual train, because we had to stop at about 10 stations. Contrast this with the express trains, which made three or four stops, and the slow trains that stopped at every station along the route. My well-worn notebook lists the timings of so many of these. The duration of the journey ranged from around 1¾ hours to 3½, from Derby to Manchester, that's some difference.

I had been building the fire up on the Compound, which we always had on this working. When I took a little breather, Len put a very simple question to

Compound 4-4-0 No. 1016 on shed at Derby on 11th May, 1946. A conveyor belt is being used to coal the engine. *H.C. Casserley*

Fowler class '4' 2-6-4T No. 2361 takes water at Derby station on 13th July, 1947, prior to departing with a stopping train from platform 4. This picture shows the water crane that froze up in extreme weather conditions in early 1947 (*see page 116*). *H.C. Casserley*

me. 'Now Johnny, suppose you are the driver of an engine with seven or eight wagons, setting back into that little yard over there. Riding on the brake van, the guard moves his arm up and down. What would you do?' That didn't seem very difficult. So I gave him what was the obvious answer. I said, 'I would slow down, proceed at caution'. There was a diagram of hand signals in the Rule Book, illustrating exactly that signal. 'Proceed at caution' it was called. 'You would?', he said. 'Yes', I said after a moment's thought. His next remark was like a blow from a heavyweight boxer. 'The inspector would be entitled to fail you for that answer', was all he said. Those words really hit home. I turned my back, and looked out of the cab on my side. Where had I gone wrong? The next 25 minutes passed without a word between us. There wasn't anything I could say, and I wasn't going to ask for an explanation. So I simply got on with the shovelling.

We left Central station, and made our first stop at Stockport Tiviotdale. In the space of the minute before we left, he decided to enlighten me. 'Now then', he said, 'I know that you go to the MI [mutual improvement] classes, and that you read the Rule Book, as and when you have time at work. Next time you look at the hand-signal diagrams, look for a small foot-note at the bottom of the page. It says this. When riding on a vehicle, either arm moved up or down denotes STOP. I have had to spend many hours at home reading Rules. If you are ever going to be as good as me, that's what you will have to do'.

It was a completely sound explanation. And yes, I had read that small footnote myself, more than once. It was just the way he framed the question that caught me out. Hard, but fair. My first answer would have satisfied 999 drivers. And that was how all those drivers would have interpreted that signal, as indeed, so would Len Beard. But he was the odd-man out, the one who wanted the answer by the book. One man in 1,000.

Now, I had a benchmark to aim at. 'If you are ever going to be as good as me'. So, I could be. And when, the best part of 10 years later, I gave my first MI class lecture, 'Protection of Trains', I believe I was. Even if he had come to that class, I would have been completely comfortable with any question he could have asked.

Driven to reach this high level, I too, spent many hours of my own time in study of the Rules and Regulations. When the time came for me to be passed out for driving, Mac Haynes, the inspector, asked me one question about wrong line orders. 'Now Johnny, how many wrong line orders are there?' 'Four', I replied, but I went on to tell him who they were issued by, who they were issued to, and the colour of the paper they were printed on! Mac Haynes' next question had nothing to do with protection of trains, and the use of wrong line orders. Because I would have given him more answers than he could have asked questions.

Like Len Beard in his time, I would have engaged any footplate inspector in a discussion on the rules. I can tell you two stories to give you an idea of the level he had attained. One of these I heard from Mick Watson in 1951. Mick had fired for Len Beard in the Gloucester goods link one year, way back. One of the turns they had in the eight weeks work, pre-war, was the top yard CME works shunt; a change from seven weeks of main line turns. When Mick had time, he studied the Rule Book, and asked Len Beard the hardest questions he could find therein. One day, he seemed to have stumped Len, who was busy shunting wagons, it being his day driving, 'Turn about' as we called it. Len, smoking his pipe, seemed to ignore the question. For something like 10 minutes, he completely ignored Mick. After that time, he turned round and answered the question, correctly of course. It had taken some thinking about.

The other story concerns Len Beard, inspector Smith, and Harry Fowkes, another footplate inspector. Len Beard and Mr Smith were having a minor difference of interpretation about some aspect of the rules. Listening to their conversation, Harry Fowkes said, 'He's got you Smithy'. It would be nice if I could say that, after those golden years of being a top man on Rules and Regulations, giving more MIC lectures than any Derby driver had ever done, I had been able to retain that standard.

When we changed over from steam to diesel, in 1963, everything changed. People didn't attend MIC lectures in their own time any more. Our tutors trained us in classrooms on the mechanics of the diesel locomotives. We were paid to attend as part of our normal duties. We had our own driver instructors, six Derby men. And we were passed out by footplate inspectors, after practical training, most of which was done on the Churnet Valley line.

So, why did I not maintain the high standard of knowledge I had reached. Well, knowledge is a bright jewel, but if not kept polished, it will inevitably tarnish. When single manning of trains came in, there was no-one to talk to, like there was in the days when the driver had a fireman with him. I remember having Jimmy Stanton as my fireman on a London lodging turn, a couple of days before he was going to be passed for driving. We spent part of the evening at Kentish Town barracks on a tutorial. But that was a one-off. The opportunities for instructing firemen on attaining the necessary knowledge became fewer and fewer. Those days were done.

While I was still on the main line, as a passed fireman, and later driver, I had no fears of being faced with a situation that I could not cope with. It is strange that we spent so many hours in discussion of circumstances that we might never encounter in the course of our daily duties. The long period of training, with so many different drivers over 18 years, gave me so much knowledge of what may or may not happen.

With Len Beard, I was able to take my turn driving on all the stopping trains. That's as much as anyone could expect. The most interesting of these was a morning train from Derby to Kettering, by way of Nottingham and Melton. That gave me another bit of road knowledge that complemented the working of goods trains to Wellingborough, which I had gained in 1943.

Before the end of 1947, training of drivers in the London link on the new diesel-electric locomotives began. It was limited to six men only for a start, and Len Beard thought it was going to stay that way. They were given the impression that a small elite group of drivers were going to work six turns only, mainly with Nos. 10000 and 10001. These were the numbers of the new engines built by the Derby works.

Whoever gave them that impression didn't have much idea of what influence the trade union would have. It would not have done for the other six drivers in the link to be excluded from doing the same work as the first six men. So although it started off with just six men being trained, once the turns that these new diesels would do in the link had been worked out, the other six drivers were trained.

In the end, although only Derby men had them for a while, they were later sent to Willesden, to work trains from London to Glasgow. It seems strange that it was another seven or eight years before the Modernisation Plan was announced. So began the gradual run-down of steam engines

The hardest job for the fireman was the 12.05 working to London: hammer and tongs all the way to Hendon. We were relieved at St Pancras, and after a break, another engine was brought down to us to work the 4.25 pm back to Derby. Once we left London, it was a continuous round of shovelling coal into the firebox for about an hour, until we reached Sharnbrook, and had a short descent to Wellingborough. We did put the shovel down just long enough to look after the business of putting water into the boiler. A very demanding job for the fireman, but the fact that we were still on mileage rates of pay made it all worthwhile. The daily journey of 256 miles meant payment for 16 hours instead of eight. That only happened for one week in 12, so the extra money was something I enjoyed only twice in six months.

By March 1948, my two years on passenger work was over. Now back to a steady progression through the goods links. It had been good while it lasted. Looking back, there had been that one defining moment in 1947 which set me out on a mission. Jack must be as good as his master. That doesn't mean that he would ever stop learning.

English Electric/LMS 1,600 hp Co-Co diesel-electric No. 10000 approaches Leicester with a St Pancras to Derby express on 8th May, 1948. *N. Newbold*

Chapter Twenty

Nationalization

Ask a railwayman what the year 1948 means and you will only get one answer - it was the year of nationalization. On 1st January the railways of England, Wales and Scotland went into public ownership. Life would never be the same again. It was then over 10 years since I had first entered railway service as an engine cleaner at No. 4 shed, Derby. I had seen the best and the worst aspects of working for a privately-owned railway company. And I had so many experiences of footplate work during the summer of 1939 that were never going to be seen again. There had been some changes for the better - most of them gained by the unions. We now had a day off every fortnight and although we still had some lodging turns of duty on freight train workings, they would be almost finished by the end of 1948.

Outwardly, railway management would have preferred to have continued as they were. Exactly how they would have raised the money to refurbish and modernize a system badly run down by nearly six years of war I really don't know. Certainly, the railways of Britain had done sterling work for the wartime Government of the country. Running booked and special passenger services for the movement of servicemen and women was just part of the job. Working goods and parcels trains under wartime conditions meant that routine maintenance had been shelved. The lines over which we ran trains had been badly affected by years of neglect.

It seemed to me then - and it still does - that the Government were extremely generous in their settlement arrangements for the shareholders of the four Grouping railway companies, which had been established in 1923. In addition to the LMS, they were the London & North Eastern Railway, the Great Western Railway and the Southern Railway. The arrangements which were concluded with these four companies meant that the taxpayers of Britain would be paying central charges to the shareholders for 40 years. In my view, this was about 32 years longer than they should have been doing so. I think those eight years would have reflected a similar period - during the war and just after it - when the companies had served the country well.

The Grouping companies found that the staff cuts they had made in the pre-World War II could not be repeated. There was too much alternative employment for men to take kindly to being transferred away from home and being made redundant. After the war, it was the time for the younger men employed by the railways to look closely at the virtues and vices which would flow from continuing in the same job. Opportunities for railway service in other countries were opening up. Several passed firemen at Derby opted to become drivers on Rhodesian Railways. I remember Jimmy Mathers and Ivor Roper went over there. Jimmy lived to a great age and he always seemed very happy with his pension from Rhodesia.

Could I have done better for myself at about this time? Perhaps. But bear in mind that, at 28 and with 10 years' service, I was still a boy. Men were not used to being passed for driving until they were 40-45. Although the young men who started in 1934 and 1935 were now passed firemen, they were years away from getting into train links.

The two years from March 1946 to 1948, when I was firing in the passenger links, probably saved me from looking for alternative employment. Most of our passenger trains ran at more reasonable hours than the goods trains. Through the war years, we had become accustomed to long and uncertain hours of duty. Now that the railways were under the control of the British Transport Commission (BTC), perhaps excessive overtime would be a thing of the past. Although our rates of pay were not as attractive as they had once been, there were compensating factors. Qualifying periods to reach the top rate of pay in the footplate grades had been considerably reduced and there would not be many cases in the future when men had to wait until they were nearly 50 before being paid top whack.

A few men were able to leave railway employment and take jobs as colliery enginemen. One young man from my parish got the job of engine driver at the Castle Donington power station. A regular day turn and, presumably, a nice little pension when it was all over. Good luck to him. Before the new power station at Ratcliffe-on-Soar opened, I went to a big group interview held at the Dog & Duck at Shardlow. I wanted to find out whether their pay and conditions were better than those offered by British Railways. That must have been sometime in the late 1950s or early 1960s. What concerned me at the time was that we still did not have a scheme that provided an adequate pension. It had been talked about for many years but not enough pressure was ever applied by rank and file members. The interviews did not lead to a job offer for me. The interviewer told me, 'We shall certainly want to see you again' but it didn't happen. Our improved pension scheme finally came along in 1969, when I was 50. I was one of the very few people who opted to pay my contributions back to age 40. Putting my money where my mouth was, I paid a double contribution until I was 62 and, having left footplate work in 1974, I was able to retire completely in 1981. Having got that off my chest, I'll go back to 1948.

There were many changes. The first was that a lot of West Indian people had come over to Britain. It was said that management went down to Southampton to meet the Sunday evening arrivals with the promise of employment for them on British Railways. It makes sense. Now that the Government – (which means the taxpayer) - was underwriting employment costs in our brave new railway world, empire building could begin. Ironic that the last gasp of the old Empire should co-incide with whole new empires in the railway business. I do know it wasn't just West Indians who were recruited because, before I retired, I worked with many other nationalities - Italian and Polish among them.

So some things changed after the four Grouping companies became one, British Railways. Yet some things remained the same. The annual movement of firemen still took place on the first Monday in March. For me it had been a case of every move had taken me over a different route. North goods, South goods, West goods, Crewe goods and passenger. Then there had been two years on passenger work, the first one Bristol and Leicester, the second London and Manchester. I had now been almost everywhere that Derby men went, so nowhere was entirely new to me. My move in 1948 was to the South goods link for the second time. Just

Ex-MR Johnson '1P' class 0-4-4T No. 1429 in Derby shed on 25th January, 1948. This looks to me like one of the engines that worked the 'Tutbury Jinny'. On that route, the engine pulled just one coach, that had been specially adapted with a brake in the coach, operated by the driver on the return journey (engine following). *A.N.H. Glover/Kidderminster Railway Museum*

Robert Stephenson & Hawthorn No. 7817 of 1954 was employed at Castle Donington power station. It is seen here on 5th March, 1966. The driver of this engine was Lionel Gadsby, like me from Tonge village. *L.W. Perkins/Kidderminster Railway Museum*

like the first, I did the driving three days out of six. My new driver was Reg Hirons, another dependable character, with no apparent vices, but with one very annoying habit. When we were standing waiting for signals he became Reg the drummer. A regular tattoo beat out with his fingertips on the rail of the cab. 'Dum-de-dum-dum, dum-de-dum-dum', repeated time after time, it almost drove me mad. But I didn't tell him so. It only ever happened when he was driving, he didn't do it when he was firing – I wonder why?

As part of our working routine, we had two weeks of lodging turns. One week leaving Chaddesden at about 11.00 am with stone empties going via Leicester and Market Harborough, returning with the same empties loaded up the next morning. The other departed about six in the evening, which ran via Melton. One incident with this train I remember clearly. ASLEF nationally had been pressing for the abolition of lodging turns. I knew this from my attendance at Derby branch meetings, whenever work allowed. This incident happened in either June or July 1948. We went to take the train out from Chaddesden, expecting to leave there as normal, and lodge overnight. However, when we arrived at Chaddesden, there was no guard for the train. How could this have come about? Simply because in a time of full employment men could pick and choose what work they took up, and they were not choosing to take up railway work with its unattractive shift work and irregular hours. We waited for several hours, still no guard. Finally they managed to find one - a Leicester man. He would only go back to Leicester with our train, so it would have to go on from there the next day. We set off, left the train in Humberstone Road sidings and took the engine to the Leicester shed. There we were instructed to catch a passenger train to Wellingborough. After all this messing about we were thoroughly fed up. So we said, 'No, we will go back to Derby'. The running foreman shrugged his shoulders, there was nothing he could do about it. Had it been 1938, we would have been disciplined. We got back to Derby and were told to report the following afternoon, to do something else.

A week or so went by, then Reg was asked for an explanation. I had been a prime mover in the decision not to lodge, so I felt it was now up to me to answer the request. I wrote out in detail what had happened that night, and told Reg to copy it out in his own handwriting, and submit this as his reply. This he did, and we heard nothing more about it. A few months later, BR agreed to ASLEF's request, and we saw the end of lodging turns as a way of life.

In the autumn of 1948, came another one of those occasions when I had a near brush with death. This time, other people's lives were also on the line. We didn't normally work the 'Royal Scot' engines at Derby, because of stress on some bridges due to their weight. In that November we were called on to go speed testing. Not quite the same as Formula One, but on this occasion, a terrifying experience. Reg Hirons and I, with the inspector in charge, were sent on a run from Derby to Trent with this massive engine, No. 46120 *Royal Inniskilling Fusilier* with just a dynamometer car, designed to measure locomotive performance. The instruction we were given was simply to go as fast as we could between Spondon Junction and Sheet Stores, almost seven miles. That doesn't sound very hazardous, but going is one thing, stopping is another.

We set off, and soon I was shovelling coal furiously to keep sufficient steam for a fair test. The engine was bucking and rolling about, lacking the weight of

'Royal Scot' class 4-6-0 No. 46120 *Royal Inniskilling Fusilier* at Derby shed on 13th November, 1949. *L.W.Perkins/Kidderminster Railway Museum*

I am leaning (with both elbows) on the cabside of No. 6120 next to my driver, Reggie Hirons. We were sent on a run with this locomotive and a dynamometer car from Derby to Trent in November 1948. This was to be the the day when there could so nearly have been a fatal accident. Reggie has his 'tapping fingers' in position! *Author's Collection*

a train behind it. A heavy train is always a steadying factor. High speeds with a train are not something to be concerned about, provided you can stop within the specified distance. Track maintenance had suffered during the war, along with many other things. Until today, we have been restricted to 70 mph. But no longer are we working for the LMS, this is British Railways, the dawning of a new era. That's what they told us, anyway.

After five miles, we had worked up a pretty good speed, and it had been a bumpy ride. When Reggie saw the outer distant signal for Sawley Junction was set at caution, he made a move to shut the regulator. The inspector saw this, and said, 'No, no, driver, keep going': a major mistake on his part.

About half a mile further on, the second distant signal came into view. Reggie immediately shut off the steam and applied the brake. It made no difference. The impetus we had worked up, only doing as we had been told, would not be denied. The weight of a full train, three or four hundred tons, is not behind us to slow us down.

The inspector was now getting alarmed. He moved across to apply the handbrake. That made no difference, the brake was already fully applied. With a train of goods wagons, where only the engine and guard's brakes are available, the handbrake would have made a difference. But not today. So we sailed on, the situation was becoming serious.

We raced through Sawley Junction station at about 70 mph in defiance of two home signals set at danger. That was bad enough. The signal box was on my side, and I could see the signalman at the window, holding a red flag. His face was another colour, it was white. To him, we were that awful occurrence, a runaway train.

He had no means of knowing that we had been trying to stop for over a mile. And then an awful thought occurred to me. 'Suppose there is a train going across our route, at the signal box ahead. We shall hit that train. And we won't hit it slowly, but fast. There is only another half mile or so to go'.

That day, we were lucky. We finally came to a stand beyond the Sheet Stores Junction, round towards Trent station. We had passed four stop signals at danger and run right through a block section. Immediately Ferdinand 'Ferdie' Way, the inspector, went back to the signal box to explain what had happened. He had to accept responsibility for the fact that he had ordered the footplatemen to carry on. Ferdie was not a 'Midland' man, he had come to Derby from Templecombe, way down south on the old Somerset & Dorset Railway. Perhaps that explained why he lacked the local knowledge that would lead other inspectors on such a job to go to the signalman at Spondon Junction to ask for a clear run through to Trent, before embarking on the test. The three of us might easily have lost our lives that day, due to his omission.

So I will remember 1948, all those years ago, for many things; my second full year in the Wellingborough link. As in 1943, I did half the driving on our main line goods trains. Working to Wellingborough was much more interesting than to Birmingham or Rotherham Masborough: a variety of gradients that weren't really matched anywhere else that Derby men normally went. There wouldn't be another year like it until I was passed for driving, by which time the barracks at Welllingborough was long gone.

Chapter Twenty-One

Jolly George

The annual movement of firemen to a different link with a different driver had given me a lot of experience in the working of both goods and passenger trains. Every year had been different. The end of lodging turns of duty brought more changes, and some trains that had run previously now no longer ran at all. In 1949 I was moved into another link to work with driver 'Jolly George' Wilson. He didn't get that nickname because of a physical trait, like 'Happy' Frank Smith, who was never known to smile. No, with George Wilson it was his use of the English language that made him stand out.

Amongst drivers, firemen and guards at that time, there were a number of committed Christians. Amongst them I can remember 'Parson Bill' (driver Bill Lewis) and Cyril Toms, a guard at Chaddesden, both well-known characters. George Wilson was the only driver at Derby in the 1940s and 1950s who was a member of the Plymouth Brethren, a religious sect still in existence today. In my lifetime I have also met several people who were Jehovah's Witnesses and Seventh Day Adventists. It is every person's right to have a faith of some kind, or none at all. As a person with a very strong Christian faith myself, I don't mind at all.

George Wilson was a comparatively young man when he became a driver. He was a very good mate to me, in the same way Billy Kirkman had been six years earlier. Coincidentally, neither of them went in for swearing in the conventional way. But George had his own words. Many times, he would use the word 'jolly'. When something wasn't going to plan, he would describe offenders as 'Jolly monkeys'. Another time one of his own particular phrases would crop up would be on occasions when the goods train we were working was switched from the main line to a goods line. There would usually be some delay, resulting in long hours on duty. This could be a regular occurrence in daytime when there were passenger trains about. Other drivers would call it, 'Going down the back', but George would say, 'We are going down the camelling back'. What the 'ship of the desert' had to do with English railway lines, I don't really know, but those were his two favourite words, 'jolly' and 'camelling'.

I cannot remember now whether he worked on a Sunday, but I must have worked with other drivers that year when he was on holiday. The link we were in was known, pre-war, as the Liverpool link, but in the 1950s we didn't go all the way to Liverpool. As a passed cleaner, I did have one turn on the Sunday night Liverpool goods before we lost the turn altogether. Now, we didn't go beyond Gowhole sidings. I remember one goods train we used to work from there, which gave me the valuable experience of working a goods train down Manchester bank. This was a stretch of line between Rowsley and Peak Forest. When going up there were very heavy gradients, the outstanding feature of this stretch of line. Any goods trains with a heavy load had to be assisted from the rear by Rowsley men on the banking engines, as they were called.

One day, when our train was not running for some reason, we were called to give assistance ourselves when a London to Manchester express train required assistance from Derby to Chinley. We were given a class '2' passenger engine, and coupled up at the front, the normal way of assisting passenger trains from Derby. It happened to be my turn to be the driver that day, and George was quite happy to do the firing. We stopped at Matlock, Millers Dale and Chinley. I had often worked the slow trains between Derby and Manchester, but that was my first chance to work an express train, a very valuable experience for me. It's those days that leave you thinking, 'I can do this just as well as anyone else. And one day, I will'.

Another experience that year fell in the 'once in a lifetime' category. Whenever engines were not steaming properly, there was a temptation to run the water level down. For me, that was never to the point where the fusible plug was affected. And so this next event should never have happened. We had a working from Derby to Rotherham of a fast goods train which ran from Birmingham to Leeds. It was called the 'Jubilee', although I have no idea why. Saltley men worked it as far as Derby, where we took over. It was the only goods train that I knew of that was timed to run through Derby passenger station.

This particular afternoon, the Saltley men were having a bad time of it, but they still tried to keep going, which was a big mistake on the driver's part. At Derby, every man on main line work would hand over to the relieving crew 'in good nick', as we say. That means with a good fire in the firebox, and a high water level. This meant the men taking over had a good start. On this day, George and I were waiting in the London Road relief cabin at the usual time. We were advised by the signalman at LNW Junction that the train was approaching, just a little bit late.

We were waiting on the old ticket platform when the train arrived. I stepped onto the engine, to find the fireman looking anxiously at the water gauge glass, with neither confidence nor hope. No water in sight. 'I don't know if we have dropped a plug' he said to me. I knew exactly what to do, even though I had never done it

Rowsley shed in November 1949 with, *from left to right*: Stanier '8F' 2-8-0 No. 8748, and Johnson '2F' 0-6-0s Nos. 3113 and 3043. Rowsley men worked a lot of goods trains towards Manchester, and also the banking engines. *Real Photographs*

before, and there was no stated procedure. Picking up the firing shovel, I thrust the blade into the firehole door. At once, a jet of steam turned it over in my hand.

George was just climbing onto the engine. 'Lead plug gone, George', I said. He got off again. You don't take over in those circumstances. 'I'll get some jolly help', he said. The fireman turned to his driver. 'There', he said, 'I wanted us to whistle for the goods line at Stenson'. The damage was done, but we still had to get the engine and train off the main line. George was soon back. 'This engine must go to the shed [he said] and the carriage shunt engine will take the train forward to St Marys'.

So I stayed with the Saltley men, because taking a light engine through the passenger station and on to No. 4 shed was a move they would never normally make, but it was nothing new to me. Luckily, there was just enough steam left for the engine to limp to the shed.

Now that the train was at St Marys, we had to take another engine off the shed to work the train forward. We would be running pretty late that night. No competent driver should have kept going in that way, with the intention of handing an engine over to another crew in such a shocking condition.

Another year, another route, another driver. That year, 1949, with Jolly George, was one of the best, in the sense that he was one of the men who treated you as an equal. Some of the drivers of his generation acknowledged that they were the lucky ones. Their turn as cleaner and then fireman, before promotion to driver had been shorter than mine. Those of us who had stuck with it now had to accept that promotion would come much more slowly, returning to pre-war conditions. But now we didn't have a better class of work to look forward to. And Derby didn't fare very well in the new allocation of workings. Resentment grew, a gradual process. One that would affect me more than most.

Stanier 'Black Five' class 4-6-0 No. 4981 emerges from Milford tunnel with a Manchester to Derby stopping train *circa* 1949. Everybody's favourite engine, the class '5', as it had no inside crank axle to oil. *F. Carrier/Kidderminster Railway Museum*

Chapter Twenty-Two

It isn't the Money, It's the Principle

The five years from March 1945 to March 1950 were the best in all my 18 as a cleaner and fireman. There had been so much experience gained in these years: one year on the Crewe link, two on passenger work; a good year again in the Wellingborough link, then a year with George Wilson.

The next five years, taking my story up to March 1955, would see a gradual decline in the class of work allocated to footplatemen at Derby. Over the course of those years I would reach the heights, and plumb the depths of my time as a trade union representative and there would be another kind of union, relating to my personal life, the beginning of my time as a family man.

I have mentioned some of the changes in management attitudes after the war. In particular, the relaxation of the harsh disciplinary regime. What did the men at Derby, and at other depots where there were active trade union branches, have to say about these changes? I had always been interested in the trade union movement and saw it as having a significant contribution to make - not just to the railways but to British society as a whole. I can remember the prevailing attitudes in 1948 as still very much a 'them and us' mentality.

From 1948, the British Transport Commission was in overall control of the British railway network (and other modes of transport), and the General Secretary of the National Union of Railwaymen (NUR), Jimmy Benstead, became a member of that body. Under the BTC was the Railway Executive, of which the ASLEF General Secretary, Bill Allen, became a member.

I remember how some members of the union reacted to this appointment. He was even branded a traitor by a few, who couldn't move on from the past. This view was very forcibly expressed at an annual Assembly of Delegates (AAD) in the early 1950s, which I gave up part of my annual holiday to attend, as an observer, not a delegate. I wasn't allowed to speak or vote even though I had spent a good deal of my spare time standing at the bottom of Hulland Street bridge, collecting members' subscriptions on Fridays. It wasn't much compared with all the sacrifices which had been made by the trade unionists of earlier generations.

Those members of ASLEF who were complaining about Bill Allen's position would, I think, have shocked the men who founded the union. If the idea of starting a trade union is to improve working conditions for members, then surely you have to talk to management in your workplace. Starting a union in Victorian times was very difficult, many people tried and failed because their efforts were ruthlessly suppressed. The reason that the men who founded ASLEF succeeded was because they gained enough support from footplatemen to pay benefits to those who were suspended or dismissed by railway management, money talking. Even so, it was not until 1911 that railway managements were prepared to even recognize a trade union. And that was only after a four-day strike.

I had noticed by 1948 - and became even more aware afterwards - that trade union members in general did not necessarily believe some of the things that I thought were important; pension provision being one example. I might not agree but I can understand those who say, 'I want the money now'. But I have always believed that the best interests of everyone should take precedence over questions of procedure.

In March 1950 I was rostered with Bert Winter on the North Road. Bert made it clear to me when we were first paired up that he would not be taking a turn with the firing shovel. 'I'm a sick man, John', he said, and I accepted that I would not be doing any of the driving while I was with him. So began a period of stagnation, and frustration for me, but not just for me, also for many of my contemporaries. The work we did was not interesting enough for me to remember any of the turns that we worked. Not a very good year.

In 1951 I was moved to join Mick Watson. From my time with him, I do remember that we worked two Shirland Colliery turns, and one Wingfield Colliery turn. This I had done before in 1942. I cannot remember any other workings, but I was back to doing 50 per cent of the driving. But life in one respect was no better. The senior drivers wanted a system where the senior men had a better class of work than the juniors. There just wasn't enough of the better train workings in the 11 goods links at the depot.

What the senior drivers wanted were three links set up, in three different groups. The senior men would be allocated No. 1 link, the next men down the No. 2 link, and the most junior men the No. 3 link. For those who didn't get the cream of the jobs, bitterness and frustration would set in. As one who was concerned through my union activities for not just myself, but for all my fellow workers, I could see that there was injustice inherent in the system. And whilst many grumbled in private, they were not prepared to speak out in public.

This photograph was taken *circa* 1948 at Hillside House, Farncombe, Surrey. I was an ASLEF delegate at the summer school, Monday to Friday. There are not just ASLEF men, but five or six other trade unions represented here. I am standing second from right. Two years later I went to a much larger summer school at Beatrice Webb House, Guildford.

Author's Collection

I started the chapter talking about what was happening on a national level. Where did I fit in? My own active participation in local union affairs had begun with my attending ASLEF branch meetings on Sunday mornings in the summer of 1947. Just listening to the proceedings for the first few meetings I attended, I was soon asked for my opinions. Having noted my interest, the local branch arranged for me to attend weekend schools, where I would learn more about union activities in general. That took the form of several two-hour sessions on Saturday afternoons, attending meetings with members of other trade unions to listen to lectures.

In 1948 and 1949, I also attended weekends away, again with members of other trade unions, usually fairly locally. By 1949 to 1951, my interest was such that I went to two week-long trade union gatherings in Surrey. This was taken as unpaid leave, but the union did pay for the costs of the trip.

How was I regarded by my fellow workers back at Derby? Well, I was still young John, because I was not yet a passed fireman, and years away from being a regular driver. All that is in the future. In terms of experience as a fireman, and as a trade union representative, I was well established. I had served my time as a voluntary collector of trade union subscriptions, commonly called union dues. You had to be committed to stand waiting at the table, completely unpaid. There have been times when I have made the round trip of 22 miles on my motorcycle, just for that privilege, and whatever else people think about you, they don't question your commitment.

Other workers' commitment was usually rather less than mine. The regular Sunday morning union meetings were usually only attended by about a dozen people. They knew that the management knew this, so if anything important was to be brought up with management, an open meeting would be called for a Sunday evening. Those meetings were attended by a far greater number of men, often about 150. Decisions reached at those open meetings had to be taken seriously by the management.

By 1952, for the best part of two years I had been the assistant secretary of ASLEF's Derby branch. That year, I was nominated to be one of the Local Departmental Committee (LDC) representatives. Those had been functioning since 1923, raising matters of local interest with the district motive power superintendent (DMPS). The meetings took place four or five times a year, all part of what is called 'the machinery of negotiation', which was well established in the railway industry, particularly for footplatemen, who had many grievances, mostly real, but sometimes just imagined.

At No. 4 shed, being nominated did not necessarily mean being elected. The NUR also had a number of footplate members. They, like ASLEF, nominated three representatives. So there would be an election process to go through. Every footplateman at the depot was entitled to vote and the majority of them did. That was because they needed committed people to represent their interests.

Of the six people nominated, three were elected. Although ASLEF had a majority of members, they didn't always get the most votes. In 1952, when the votes were counted, two ASLEF representatives, Frank Robinson and John Weston and one from the NUR, Charlie Hind, were elected.

BR Standard class '5' 4-6-0 No. 73002 passes Way & Works Sidings signal box as it departs Derby with a St Pancras-bound passenger train on 31st May, 1951. In the background of the picture you can see the spire of St Andrew's church, long since demolished. *R.J. Buckley*

Class '2P' 4-4-0 engines Nos. 404 and 40416 stand next to each other in Derby on 13th August, 1950. The former still carries LMS livery whilst the latter is lined out and bears British Railways colours. No. 3 shed is seen in the background. *Oakwood Collection*

Frank Robinson was the only one of us with previous experience to be chosen. So he was the obvious person to be the Chairman of the staff representatives. What about the Secretary? That would be the other ASLEF member, me. Quite unusual, for a fireman to be elected, let alone made the staff side secretary. Most years it would only be well recognized older members of the footplate grades, active trade unionists over many years, who would take the position. I may not have been the first fireman to do this, because I don't remember, 50 years on, who all my predecessors were. It just seems very likely that I was the first fireman to be LDC secretary.

No worries, the job was there to be done and I would do it. Way back in 1938 when I was following Oswald Sharpe's threshing outfit round the villages, I had been able to represent myself. There had been the little squabbles with Butcher Smith and Sammy Jarrom, who thought they could put down the young man. Fourteen years on, I was quite capable of sticking up for other people.

In a sense, it's like driving the steam engine. The right preparation is essential. To represent other people, you need to listen to those who have been doing the job before you. Having done my share of listening and learning, now I simply had to do the talking. And always remember that learning is a lifelong process. It's our experience of the past that helps us to cope with the present and to equip ourselves to deal with the future.

It wasn't just at work that I was taking on the job of representing others. In our parish of Breedon-on-the-Hill, which includes the villages of Tonge and Wilson, 1952 was the year of parish council elections. These are held every three years, and so I went round and got six people to nominate me. That election looked like being contested, until one of the people nominated suddenly withdrew, so that six of us were declared as elected without any voting being necessary. As it happens, I only served for three years on the parish council at that time, but I was to take it up again over 30 years later.

In the early 1950s, negotiating with railway management at local level had reached a very interesting stage. Before the war, workmen had gone cap in hand to the management, who still had all the power on their side. In later years, in the motor industry particularly, the men gained too much power, wildcat strikes being one example of that. I think of industrial relations being like a pendulum, sometimes on one side, sometimes on the other. There is a part of the stroke where the pendulum is evenly balanced. Looking back, it was like that in my time. And that is just how it felt to me at the time.

Our DMPS then was Bill Bramley, and his assistant, a Mr Creighton. We never did get to know where Mr Bramley came from before Derby, there were so many changes going on in the early days of British Railways administration. He still had sub-depots at Burton, Coalville and Rowsley under his command, which made it difficult to get in to see him, unless I could be there at nine o'clock in the morning, which was no easy matter, owing to the kind of shifts we worked. I always felt sorry for his assistant, who I would ask to see when the need arose.

Mr Creighton was a Scot, he had come to Derby from St Margarets, Edinburgh. I used to call in the time office and ask the chief clerk if I might see Mr Bramley. We didn't just knock on the door and walk in, that wasn't the way to go about it.

'Jubilee' class 4-6-0 No. 45683 *Hogue* passes London Road Junction signal box, with a Sheffield-Gloucester train on 21st July, 1951. *D.J. Powell Collection/Kidderminster Railway Museum*

'Jubilee' class 4-6-0 No. 45656 *Cochrane* passes through Wellingborough (Midland Road) station with a Derby-St Pancras express on 20th August, 1951. I have done some miles firing on this engine! *P.J. Lynch/Kidderminster Railway Museum*

A general view of the south side of London Road Junction, Derby on 28th June, 1952. This junction controlled the up and down passenger and goods lines. Engine Sidings No. 2 signal box, just visible on the right, controlled other lines. *V.R. Webster/Kidderminster Railway Museum*

A double-headed passenger train north of Derby is piloted by '2P' class 4-4-0 No. 40418 on 26th April, 1952. The train engine is Stanier 'Black Five' 4-6-0 No. 44984. My first experience of passenger driving was on a pilot engine. *P.J. Lynch/Kidderminster Railway Museum*

Stanier '8F' class 2-8-0 No. 48331 passes Ambergate South Junction with a mixed freight on 24th May, 1952. *W. Potter/Kidderminster Railway Museum*

Ex-MR '2F' class No. 58158 is seen near Breadsall crossing with a Ripley-Chaddesden goods train *circa* 1952. Usually the return journey from Ripley was run tender-first, as there was no turntable there (the same applied for New Lount and Shirland collieries).
M. Carrier/Kidderminster Railway Museum

When I got the nod to go in, it was often the case that only his assistant would be there and he had to tell me that he didn't even know whether Mr Bramley would be coming back to the depot that day. Which wasn't very helpful to either of us. So when we were asking for a meeting of the full LDC, I would put that in writing. Which was to lead to a very interesting confrontation. This was the way of it.

At the time, we had a number of young men in the shed cleaning engines. Having been approached to join ASLEF, as we were 15 years earlier, they asked about the possibility of being passed out for firing duties. Which they were entitled to, being 16 years of age. The message was passed on to me, so I went to see some of them and check it out. After which I made two verbal requests to Mr Bramley, when I could catch him. The case was fairly straightforward. Many of the regular firemen were working their rest days, so there wasn't any pressure from the foreman's assistants to find some extra firemen. Well, I knew what it was like having a long spell on cleaning duties, at a time when no-one could do anything about it. Now someone could, and would. It was up to me, now.

The DMPS had been noncommittal when dealing with my verbal requests. He said that this was something I must leave to the management, who would deal with it in due course. In other words, don't try pushing us. It was time for me to put my plea in writing, which I did. And took it in to him, along with a request for a meeting of the full LDC, we had enough items for the agenda.

Years of practice at writing letters stood me in good stead. I don't have a copy, but I know that it was a letter which reflected my feelings at being ignored. As Bill Bramley read it, his face reddened. When he had finished, he said, 'You must not write to me like this, it's not the way for staff to approach management. I have been to meetings of the Sectional Council, where it is done differently'.

I heard him out, without any fear at all, and then said, 'Mr Bramley, if you have any complaints about my attitude, it's best that you raise them at the full LDC meeting, for which I have brought you the proposed agenda'. At which he calmed down and reverted to his usual 'leave it to management'. The bolt had reached its target.

So a few weeks later, when we had the meeting, this item, 'Cleaners to be passed for firing duties' was first up for discussion. I sat there, as the staff side secretary, waiting for Bill Bramley to make his complaint. But of course he never mentioned my letter at all and simply agreed that the firing instructor would see these young engine cleaners, with a view to them being passed out for firing duties – which I might have thought was the end of the matter.

Some time later, I had occasion to write a letter to him about something else. I then found out that the severe telling off which I was alleged to have had, never reached me. The office staff seemed to think it had. The young lady typist had actually prepared this letter. Her name was Barbara May, Finding out about the letter which I never received, happened like this. I had taken to Barbara another letter which I had written to Bill Bramley and asked if she would type it out for me. Quite unofficial, but she did it just two or three times. When she had read it, she said, 'You ought to be careful what you put in writing to Mr Bramley. You may get a right telling off, like you did last time'. So I looked at her rather puzzled and said, 'I never got any letter telling me off

'2P' class 4-4-0 No. 40900 at the south end of Derby station with a stopping train on 28th June, 1952, before the station roof was dismantled. Four years after nationalization the locomotive's tender still bears the legend 'LMS'. *V.R. Webster/Kidderminster Railway Museum*

BR Standard class '5' 4-6-0 No. 73014 with a stopping train at Derby Midland station on 28th June, 1952. Unusually, it is passing from the No. 3 to No. 4 platform roads. See the old style footbridge in the picture, the flight of steps serves platforms 2 and 3.
V.R. Webster/Kidderminster Railway Museum

at all'. So I thanked her, but I didn't change the letter I had intended to ask her to type. Realizing that it was best not to ask again, because it could have got her reprimanded, I simply put the letter in, handwritten, as with the one that had caused some exasperation to the boss man the first time.

When I got home, I had another look at the reply I had received from him. And then realized what had happened. We were by now, four years into British Railways running the railways. This letter, with which I had only been concerned as to its content, was different. It was typed out on a piece of LMS note paper, unlike everything else, which was headed 'BR'. Which was not at all remarkable, until you draw together a few missing threads. The first letter which was drafted for the benefit of the office staff, and typed by Barbara May, must have been torn up and thrown into the waste paper basket, because it never reached me.

The only person I ever remember telling about it at the time was Frank Robinson, my colleague. There was no point of making an issue of something I had never seen and certainly nothing to be gained by talking about it. This is the first time I have ever written about it. It only proves that some Jacks are as good as their masters … and better than them at writing letters.

There remain two other stories which tell us something about this particular DMPS. He did not usually work on Saturdays. But for a few Saturday mornings, he turned up at the depot in his car, and had it cleaned by one of the shed staff, Jimmy Boam, who didn't normally work Saturdays either. This got an instant reaction from me on the day I saw it happen. Being on some sort of duty which had us waiting work, in the mess room, I decided to clean my motorcycle. When one driver remarked that it had come to something when a man could clean his own transport in the company's time, I had a reply ready. To the effect that if the boss could employ someone on overtime to clean his car, I could use my own labour to clean my motorcycle. There was no answer to that. It just shows how far standards of discipline can be eroded, if you start at the top. Bear in mind that at 30-odd years of age, I was still regarded as something of a young upstart. That didn't stop me from being elected to the LDC in the following year.

Fifty years on, I can still remember some of the other things which were expected of the LDC Secretary. As some goods train workings were lost to the depot, the senior drivers in the goods links complained that the better class of work ought to be allocated in a different way. Fairly quick promotion to the passenger links would have kept them quiet, but it wasn't happening at the time. Although there was a fair turnover of footplate staff, it was the younger men who were leaving. Those, like me, who had experienced redundancy, even dismissed from the service in 1938, simply soldiered on.

For the senior drivers in the goods links, the prospect of no promotion, because the men in the passenger links were in the same age group, was irksome. So they carried their concerns to the trade union branch meetings and when there was no apparent progress through the trade union movement, they began to consider another course of action. I wish I could remember exactly what the grievance was that led to members of both ASLEF and the NUR footplate grades calling for an unofficial strike at Derby. Probably a general feeling of dissatisfaction.

Fairburn class '4' 2-6-4T No. 42174 at Derby station with a passenger train *circa* 1953. In the background the safety valves are lifting on an unidentifed Stanier 'Black Five' 4-6-0 which is pilot engine on a passenger train. *T.G. Wassell/Kidderminster Railway Museum*

Stanier 'Black Five' 4-6-0 No. 44815 near Whatstandwell with a Derby-Manchester passenger train *circa* 1953. This is a stopping train, as can be seen from the headlight on the chimney, a code meaning a slow train. *T.G. Hepburn/Rail Archive Stephenson*

Years afterwards, I turned up a little receipt from Unity Hall, on the old Normanton Road in Derby. That was where we held branch meetings, in a small room for which we paid. This particular meeting of drivers from both trade union branches working together led to the formation of an unofficial strike committee. In the course of the meeting, someone remarked that the room had to be paid for. A collection was taken and the required sum was raised. I was one of only a few younger men present. When it became apparent that no one else was taking any note of what was being said, I produced pen and paper and summarized the concerns of those present.

It was soon obvious that a majority were in favour of strike action, when due notice to our respective trade unions had been given. A Chairman and Vice-Chairman were elected, with authority to make a statement to the local press. When the meeting was about to break up, I reminded them that I had been taking notes, but no one had called for a Secretary to this committee. So a swift decision was reached that I had better do that job. Reports were soon made to our trade unions at national level. This was no sudden impulse for strike action. It was just a group of footplatemen who were concerned at the apparent lack of progress in meeting their aspirations.

Someone else, somewhere, started a conciliation process. Enough assurances were given to the Chairman and leading members of the group that their grievances would be met. Within a few days, all talk of unofficial action was suspended. It is very unlikely that anyone else who attended that meeting is still alive. Just that one small receipt reminded me of something long since forgotten, but now well remembered.

At this time, in the early 1950s, the trade union movement began to realize that they were indeed in a position of equality with management, or at least with that section of management that was still trying to run a railway in the interests of the paying passengers. There was another section of management who saw a chance to further their own career prospects, now that the taxpayer was footing the bill for all the improvements that had to be made.

Standards of discipline were still high amongst those of us who knew what those standards were. And would remain at a reasonable level for a good few years. Men still went to work when they were not really fit, because it was what we had been used to doing. There were, however, changes in our conditions of service that proved beneficial. It was now recognized that we would be entitled to two weeks annual leave, instead of one, and six bank and public holidays. When I started work in the grade, only Christmas Day and Good Friday were so observed. If you worked any of the other bank holidays, there was no time off in lieu.

Improvements in wages and conditions of service still took longer in negotiation that they ought to have done. When the industry negotiating machinery could not broker an agreement, something else had to be set up. The usual formula for this was a tribunal, with a representative from management and staff and an independent Chairman and all this took a long while, a very frustrating experience.

Grievances at local level usually concerned the allocation of special workings, particularly at weekends. The hard grind of lodging away three times a week had finished, apart from a few passenger trains, mainly on Sundays. A Saturday

Fowler '4F' class 0-6-0 No. 44546 at Ripley station with an excursion train from Skegness on 10th June, 1953. Class '4s' did sterling work on excursions.

Roy F. Burrows/Midland Collection Trust/Kidderminster Railway Museum

'3F' class 0-6-0 No. 43367 at Egleton crossing, near Oakham, with a down train of empty coal wagons, probably from Wellingborough and bound for Chaddesden, on 26th August, 1953.

P.M. Alexander/Kidderminster Railway Museum

or Sunday turn to Blackpool or London would be a big boost for the week's earnings, usually this meant signing on twice in the same day. There were occasions when the running foreman or his assistant had to make a choice between two men, which left one of them aggrieved. That man might well put his case to the foreman. If he could not persuade him, next recourse was to appeal to the LDC Secretary. Sometimes he would not be available, out on his normal duties.

In my time, I would get to hear of these disagreements afterwards. When I was available, it was a case of checking out the reasons why one man had been given the job and the other had not. I would go into the running foreman's office, and either he or his assistant would tell me what the thinking was that led to a particular driver being given the turn. Very often, it was a matter of road knowledge for some part of the workings which was not at first apparent. In those days, there were a variety of ways of getting to a seaside destination and to London. In most cases the allocation was correct.

Sometimes the complainant had said to me, 'It isn't the money, it's the principle of the thing', I would suppress a smile, because these blokes were usually the ones who hadn't been at the front of the queue when principles were being handed out and no one ever complained when the job concerned didn't mean a hefty whack of overtime. Fifty years on, I read that this old chestnut is still being used in some ways. Human nature being what it is, principles are easily discarded when money beckons. Nowadays, the sums involved are much bigger than they were in 1952 and it isn't engine drivers talking about principles. People talk about principles like they do about conscience. Years ago, someone said that conscience is not a big drum, it's a still, small voice. I'm sure that's right and I would say that principle is often the very small print after a big sentence. But that's human nature for you.

One of these claims was genuine enough for me to take it up with Bill Bramley. As usual, it was a lodging turn on a summer Saturday. The running foreman, who had allocated the turn, was Harry Dutton. The man who had been given the job was Ernie Pemberton, who just happened to be a deputy foreman. There was a little bit of favouritism here. That was how it seemed to the man who complained to me. He, a young driver named J.R. Toogood, had come to Derby after the war. He was said to have seen service in the RAF, so he was given the nickname of Flying Officer Kite. So, on Friday morning the Saturday special workings were posted in the notice case and I, the LDC Secretary, was approached by J.R. Toogood with his complaint. Principle wasn't mentioned on this occasion. Just the fact that he thought he had a prior claim to the job.

Having checked the rosters myself, in I went to see Harry Dutton, who wasn't going to discuss the matter with me. Well, I might be the LDC Secretary, but I was still a young upstart. He didn't actually say that, just that he had given Ernie Pemberton the job and that was the end of the matter. It was noticeable that the foreman's assistant took no part in the conversation.

Well, surprise, surprise, not only was I available that Friday morning, but Bill Bramley was in his office as well. So, my next call was to the chief clerk to request an audience. and a few minutes later, I was given this privilege. I, of course, took J.R. Toogood with me, as the actual complainant and Harry Dutton was sent for. It was a fairly short meeting. The driver stated briefly that he had a prior claim to be given the job and equally briefly, the running foreman stated his case for allocating it to Ernie Pemberton. At this stage the DMPS turned to me and said,'Without going round the mountain, who do you think should be given this turn?' So of course, I said that driver Toogood should be the man. And Bill Bramley very quickly said, 'Well that's it then'.

I am sure that Harry Dutton was not best pleased that his decision had been overridden. Certainly the next time he saw me, he just glared at me. But he wasn't vindictive in any way. There are two other things I'm sure of. One, that if I had been 20 years older, he would have discussed his reasons with me. We might even have avoided taking the matter any further. And, if J.R. Toogood had not gone in with me, that the decision would have gone the other way. It's like this. Fifty years on, I still think of myself as Mr Nobody, a person of very little importance. When I am representing someone else, well, that is when I grow considerably in stature, a different individual altogether. Even in 1938, when Alfred White gave me an extra 6*d*. and also gave another local man 6*d*., I asked why all the workmen had not been given the same. To which he answered that it was because we lived in the same village as him. It is for you to judge whether that was fair and equitable.

Having in my working life been both a delegate and a representative, it is best that I explain the difference. A delegate is someone who is appointed to represent other people, but to carry out their expressed wishes and intentions. Even if he does not agree with their views, he is there to argue the case in their way. Or to vote for something in the way that they would vote. A representative has freedom to put his own thoughts into words and to move his own resolutions, if he wishes, and to vote on a proposal however he chooses. In both cases he must be prepared to report back to the organization, person or persons who may have asked him to represent them or who have delegated him to make their case.

In debate, it is very helpful to know the rules of debate. As an active trade union member, I was given a copy of those rules, long since lost, but the basic principles are easily remembered. This doesn't make me any cleverer than anybody else. It's just that in a properly run trade union branch meeting, you will get a better understanding of how and why we debate than in a good many other places. At different times in my life, I have been a Chairman, a Secretary, a Treasurer, even a Trustee. It doesn't really matter that I have never done any of these things in very important places or for very important people. The principle remains the same.

It is time that I mentioned what I was doing as a fireman in 1952. Having been for three years in North Road links, I had gone into the Peterborough link in March and was booked with another long-serving Derby driver, Jack Wagstaff. We didn't really get on well together from the start. Probably because I was the LDC Secretary and very much my own man. As a driver, he was one of the best. But whereas a number of footplatemen agreed with the idea of a young man being the LDC Secretary, there were others who could not see it that way at all. They could not say I was arrogant, or that I was trying to impose my ideas on anybody else. It may have been that I was doing too much too soon.

It got to a stage where without saying anything to me, Jack Wagstaff asked for another mate. Presumably someone who wasn't the LDC Secretary. It was simply put to me that it might be better if I was in another link. So they asked would I be happy to go with Charlie Brooks, and I said yes, without any hesitation. Nobody asked any questions, or suggested there was anything wrong with my attitude. And I had a very good six months with Charlie Brooks.

Rest day working for firemen, and at times for drivers also, was a regular feature for life at Derby No. 4 shed. I cannot now remember exactly when we got the 44 hour week. This meant that we had a nominal day off once a fortnight. That was the only way it could be done for footplatemen. There wasn't any way we could work five shifts of eight hours and one of four hours. And even when the young engine cleaners were passed for firing, it didn't make any difference to firemen working rest days, if they wanted to. Some of them even volunteered for Sunday work on labouring duties, all because there was a large turnover of staff generally, mainly amongst the younger ones, who had job opportunities that had not been open to us before the war. So they didn't have the fear of unemployment which we had experienced.

There were the odd occasions when someone would complain about the lack of Sunday work. One chap wanted me to take up his grievance that he hadn't done very well in the last six weeks. So I went in to examine the record. They were a little surprised in the foreman's office, when I mentioned the man's name and I simply went back further than he wanted me to. Over that longer period, he had done better than most of his colleagues. Another grievance, more imagined than real.

There was a joke going around about one man who had managed to work 53 Sundays in 52 weeks. Not quite true, but if you had several of these lodging turns where you signed on twice in one day, and plenty of late Saturday night turns, because Sunday rate was paid from midnight Saturday to midnight Sunday, well you were knocking on a bit.

This concentration on Sunday working, and also working rest days, did fill some wage packets. It was helping a minority of the men, but it wasn't helping the rest of us to improve our career prospects and the men generally were not pressing management for retirement pensions or better rates of pay for the standard working week.

At local level, we had a branch meeting once a month. I would give my report on everything that had happened in the previous month. With hindsight, I would say my reports lasted too long. It was no problem to me to speak for 45 minutes. The only complaint I got was that some of the other branch business had to be cut short, because the LDC report was taking up too much time. Then someone else would say, 'Well, it's the local happenings that interest me'. Well, it was only once a month, and I was only LDC Secretary for one year. A year when the senior men in the goods links wanted to see the work shared out in a different way, which the junior men resented, because they would lose the best workings in their link. The implementation of these changes did not actually happen until 1953. That was going to be rather more than just another year.

Chapter Twenty-Three

Another Kind of Union

In the 1950s I was living back at the family home in Tonge. No longer was the railway able to dictate that their employees lived within the area served by the caller-up and I had my motorcycle to 'commute' to work. At that time, with no shops in the village, my mother had her weekly grocery order delivered by the Star Supply Stores from their shop in Melbourne by an attractive young lady. Now, I had once asked this girl to go to a dance with me and she had replied that she didn't dance. Anyone with a grain of common sense, of course, would have followed this up by suggesting something else, but it's not all that common, common sense.

June Robey, the girl who came with the groceries, still worked in the shop on Derby Road, Melbourne. And I would stop and look in the window display there. She and her friend, Kath, who was already married, used to wonder when I would come in. Sometimes I would and that was hard enough. Asking her to go out with me was much more difficult. I managed it at last; but things could have gone badly wrong on that first date.

We had arranged to meet in the Market Place at Melbourne and catch a bus from there to a show of some kind. Something or other on ice I think it was. The date was 7th November, 1953. I was going to get to Melbourne on my motorcycle and it wouldn't start. The kick-starter had no kick in it. In the end, I had to ask my brother-in-law to take me on his motorbike. No mobile phones then, of course, so I couldn't ask her to wait. I just had to hope. But wait she did. And we didn't miss any of the show. I think I must have walked home afterwards - only three miles or so. I can be quite sure of the date. There used to be a range of cosmetics - 4-7-11. Like the Star Stores, the cosmetics have long gone but I will always remember 7-11-53.

For something that might have started so badly - indeed never started at all- everything went well. I had carried a key for so long and finally I had found a lock. Soon I was calling on her, in Commerce Street, Melbourne. Sometime around the time my own father died - in 1949 - June had lost her own father. They had been in the market gardening business. Reuben Robey had had a stall in Loughborough market and June carried it on for a time. She had learned to drive a car before her father died so, before long, she was taking me out in the car though I was still getting to Melbourne by motorcycle.

Many people went early to bed in those days and soon somebody at the bottom of Commerce Street complained to June's mother that the noise of a motorcycle was keeping them awake. It wasn't me showing off but some people will complain at very little. Anyway, I solved that problem by freewheeling past the end of the street and starting up again lower down.

Our journeys in the family car were usually to the cinema at Derby, normally the Gaumont or the Regal in this high tide of the motion picture industry. There was almost always a queue and we would often see people we knew from Melbourne when the lights went up.

I told my two colleagues on the LDC that I had started courting and that I wouldn't opt for another year on that body and their reply was simple, 'If you're getting married, you'd better concentrate on that'.

It wasn't long - around seven weeks after that first date - before we were indeed thinking of getting married. Driving back from Derby, June would turn the car into a very quiet little lane and we would kiss the moments away; but we never thought of getting into the back seat to get closer. We had old-fashioned ways, in those days.

It came to Boxing Day, 1953, and we went to the pictures after tea. Into the lane she turned and the time seemed right to me so I blurted it out - 'We seem to get on so well, would you think of marrying me?' 'Oooh, John' was all she said. 'Did that mean Yes?', I said. Indeed it did.

So we went home from there - sworn to secrecy, but it wouldn't surprise me if one or two people knew what was going on. Kath Topliss, who worked with June on the grocery counter, may have picked up the odd sign and I remember my sister, Ida, asked me when we were getting married. We didn't formally announce the engagement until Easter 1954, though, and yes, I did ask June's mother for permission.

June and I were lucky enough to have 43 happy years together. I was almost 10 years older than she was and I rather stupidly assumed that I was going to die first, but man proposes and God disposes. Her father had died of cancer, and, when she mentioned that to the doctors at the City Hospital in Derby, they were interested but non-committal. As they had to be, of course. She came home from the appointment, having gone there with our daughter, and told me. I was non-committal as well; but I had a perception of how it would all end.

So, a few weeks later, I had to tell our two children that their mother was not going to get better. I don't think anyone knows how to cope with that kind of thing. But both my upbringing and my working life had taught me to be honest and straightforward - especially in matters of life and death.

In 1953, though, all that was a lifetime away. The year ended on a high note of happiness for two people. It was a huge change for me. But not the only one ...

This was a year of the utmost significance for my working life as well as my personal one. I couldn't go on being a fireman for ever, even though there were three or four permanent firemen at Derby - but, in each case, there was a medical reason. It had been around two years since anyone had been passed for driving at our depot. So I continued in the Birmingham goods link, firing for Albert Harris, one of the best mates I had over the years.

For me, life was very full. 'Getting to know you' was the theme for me and my future wife. After Reuben Robey died, his widow, May, left with two daughters, gave up the family home in Melbourne and took up the job of housekeeper to a man who had lost his wife, Jack Wardle. It was an arrangement that suited both parties and went on for several years. I think Jack Wardle died in 1954 - he was certainly dead by the time we married. His daughter, Joan, who lived in Buckinghamshire, would have sold us his house. We talked it over and it was my fault that we didn't accept the offer. We were both working and I felt that we ought to save hard and get to a position where we could put down a good deposit. I was too cautious; but I had been brought up to be careful with money and it might have been a fault on the right side.

As doors close, doors open. For May Robey, the opportunity came to go into business on her own when a shop with living accommodation came up for sale on Melbourne Market Place. June and I were to live there with her for the first few years of our married life. May did very well with a toys and stationery business in the Market Place shop right up to the time she decided to retire. By that time she had the first signs of Parkinson's disease which is more easily treated now than it was then. She had a very fine singing voice, a bit like Kathleen Ferrier which she used to excellent effect at the Methodist church.

While I am writing of my late wife's family, I must mention her grandfather, William Henry Frearson, an insurance agent – 'The man from the Pru'. Now my mother had an insurance policy with the Prudential. This was back in the 1920s when people would pay a penny or tuppence a week into a policy which would mature eventually and give them a lump sum. Often, of course, it was designed to cover funeral expenses - people didn't want to die as paupers.

Mr Frearson rode round the district on his 'sit up and beg' bike and included our village in his area. So, when he gave his granddaughter away at her wedding, in September 1954, he had some very pertinent memories of the small boy who had run out to greet him at White House, Tonge - 30 years before.

A very special day for two special people.

Chapter Twenty-Four

Strike!

So towards the end of 1954, we settled down to married life living with June's mother at 32, Market Place, Melbourne. My old 250cc BSA motorcycle, bought from the furniture shop, had been taking me to work and back. That was until I visited the motorcycle show at Earls Court and saw a new machine that I wanted to own. It was a 250cc Panther built by Phelon & Moore at Cleckheaton, in Yorkshire. That was a real cottage industry workshop. They were famous at the time for side-car motorcycles. And I was so fond of travel by motorcycle, that our honeymoon had been spent on a motorcycling holiday to the Isle of Man.

I was working on the West Road goods link, and Albert Harris was a good mate in 1954, but still there was no sign of any firemen being passed for driving at Derby. My personal life was going so well that a set-back on the trade union side didn't seem to matter.

At the annual meeting of ASLEF Derby branch, I had been elected to the position of assistant Branch Secretary, a position I had held before my two years on the LDC. Frank Robinson who was Branch Secretary suddenly died quite unexpectedly, just a day or two before the monthly Branch meeting. I had been used to dealing with some of the correspondence while he had been away at Sectional Council meetings, so perhaps you would think it would be natural for me to step into the job. Well it was up to the Branch Meeting to elect a new Branch Secretary. Two people were nominated, Les Kirk, who had been active in the Branch for a while longer than I had, and myself. The voting resulted in a tie, seven all, and the casting vote of the Chairman, Alan Jarvis, was given to Les, a man he knew well.

I was then nominated to take the post I had been occupying, assistant branch secretary, but I declined to accept the position. Why? Way back in 1944, when I was firing for Lubricator Pete, we had a very early Sunday morning turn, the 12.15 am, West End carriage shunt. Through the year, Vic Rawlins, the driver, and Les Kirk, the fireman, were our booked relief at around eight o'clock in the morning. Well, Les was often a few minutes late, which didn't matter, I was often a few minutes late myself. What rankled was that when Les got on the engine and I said 'Good morning', it was very difficult to get any reply. A simple 'Good morning' were the two words he couldn't articulate. Not to me anyway. He could talk in the branch-room, although I had not seen him do so very much in my time, but I was a lower form of life on the footplate. I knew that we could not work together. Mr Kirk was the right man, in the right place, at the right time. Doors opened for him, and another event in 1955 led to bigger things for him. But that's his story, not mine.

The year 1955 turned out to be a big one, sometimes for the right reasons, and sometimes for the wrong ones. We had seen improvements in our working conditions, but wage increases always took a long while to negotiate. At a time of industrial movement generally, this left footplatemen always playing catch-

A great picture looking towards Derby shed in April 1954. On the left side of the photograph, N1, N2 and N3. On the extreme left, the loco arrival line. At the front of the No. 4 shed buildings are the bike sheds. In the centre, the No. 4 shed arrival and departure lines. The small building behind the bike sheds is the office block, and the small building on the right is the messroom and canteen. This area was normally bustling - could this have been taken on a Sunday?

Roy F. Burrows/Midland Collection Trust/Kidderminster Railway Museum

Lines of dormant engines on the ex-Midland Railway shed at Bristol Barrow Road during the ASLEF strike of 1955. A pair of Fowler '4F' class 0-6-0s are in the foreground.

A. Butler/Kidderminster Railway Museum

up and what we described as the differential was gradually being weakened. The engines we worked with were getting older and dirtier. The hours of duty continued to make any kind of social life difficult. There wasn't any prospect of promotion for the senior firemen at Derby. Like a number of the drivers in the goods links, we were stuck in a time warp.

What we called the differential was important for two reasons. Working trains carried a great deal of responsibility for the driver and also the fireman, who hopes one day to be a driver. Getting out of bed at two o' clock in the morning, to go to work, wasn't everyone's idea of the good life. So, if the difference in rates of pay doesn't seem worth the effort, resentment grows. And a whisper becomes a shout.

We were not like a group of men working in a factory, where a shop steward can influence growing resentment and channel that into strike action. Footplatemen have been known to engage in strike action, but never because a few men convince a large group of workers that it is time to down tools, and never because of political infiltration. Politics doesn't come into it. I have read two histories of my trade union – ASLEF, and I know how our fraternity have never engaged in brinkmanship or hasty industrial action. That is not only a matter of history, it is a matter of fact.

I cannot remember the exact disagreement between management and staff which led to our going on strike in 1955. I could take time in looking it up, but that would not now make any difference to how I felt at the time. The big question is, was it worth it? On the face value of our reward for 17 days out on strike, it certainly wasn't. Afterwards a Committee of Enquiry under the chairmanship of Mr C.W. Guillebaud, gave firemen something like sixpence a week extra pay. Drivers got a bit more than that, but nothing significant. And British Railways lost traffic which never came back to us. So that was a very marked downside to industrial action.

The General Secretary of ASLEF was a man from Tyneside, J.G. Baty. A small man with a very big heart. For me the best General Secretary that we had in my 44 years' membership. The Chairman of the management was Sir Brian Robertson. He had been a general in the British Army. I remember hearing that he wanted to conduct industrial relations in a different way to anything that had happened before.

Once again this is entirely my own recollection. Sir Brian proposed meeting the trade union negotiators as a general would, with sole responsibility for management decisions, which his colleagues would not agree to. I dare say they could anticipate experienced trade union leaders gaining concessions that would benefit staff more than management.

I am not going to dwell on what happened over those 17 days. Some trains ran in some areas, because NUR footplate members did not, as a body, join those of us on strike. Individual members of that union at Derby certainly signed on as members of ASLEF without hesitation. One of the first was my driver from 1949, Reggie Hirons. He knew that I was a man of my word, maybe that had something to do with it. Another one was my colleague on the 1953 LDC Stan Bates. He represented ASLEF for a good number of years afterwards, until his sudden and untimely death, while still a relatively young man.

One driver whose name got into the newspapers was originally a Great Western engineman, Sid Cannon of Swindon. On the late evening before the strike was due to start, he refused to work a train back home from Paddington station. This was on the grounds that soon after he left there, literally minutes, his union would be on strike. Someone in management took a hard line and decided this was a case for instant dismissal.

Came the day when a return to work was being negotiated. No victimization of those who had been on strike was requested and agreed, with various other clauses concerning an orderly resumption of duty, and then Jimmy Baty said, 'What about Sid Cannon of Swindon?' To which Sir Brian Robertson replied, 'Sid Cannon is regarded as having sacked himself, by refusing to continue his rostered duty on the evening before the strike commenced'. To which Jimmy Baty had a swift rejoinder. 'If Sid Cannon is not reinstated, Sir Brian, none of us are going back to work'. 'Very well, Mr Baty, Sid Cannon is reinstated'. I am pretty sure that it was Jimmy Baty who told the story himself. As a General Secretary would, he had to visit a number of areas afterwards to report on the settlement.

Some years before, I had heard Jimmy Baty mount a spirited defence of his predecessor, W.P. Allen. Some dyed in the wool old stagers and some not so old had a grievance against Bill Allen. This happened at the Annual Assembly of Delegates, the yearly meeting of rank and file members of our trade union. I was interested enough to give up a day of my annual holidays, to attend the AAD as a visitor, which any member of the union could do.

I think it may have been 1951. I know the meeting took place at Arkwright Road, Hampstead, which is ASLEF headquarters to this day. So any of the members in the London area could call in for an hour or two, if they wanted to. You had to be really interested to sit there on a beautiful sunny day, which I did.

It still rankled with some people that Bill Allen had taken up a position on the Railway Executive. The former NUR Secretary, James Benstead, had joined the British Transport Commission. 'The very idea', they said, 'that trade union leaders should sit at the same table as the management'.

In general, we, the younger members could see that it would benefit working men. Jimmy Baty had no doubt about it. Although, as he said, he would not touch Billy Allen's job with a bargepole, the man had served his time with ASLEF and there was no reason to debar him from taking other employment, and a majority of the delegates agreed.

In March 1955, I was placed with another driver, Billy Cass; still in the Birmingham link and I wouldn't even get a turn with the regulator. Bill was only second to Lubricator Pete, 11 years before, in not doing any firing. Later on in that year I found out just how it was for his unfortunate wife. Quite by accident, for some reason, the foreman's office asked me to call on him with a message. His wife answered the door. 'Bill's in the bath', she said, 'You will have to wait', and promptly disappeared upstairs. I could see her standing outside the bathroom door. What he required was for her to hand him the hot towels when he got out of the water. Do many men want to be waited on like that., I wonder?

There was some form of compensation for those of us who had been on strike for 17 days – rest day working. Not just for firemen, drivers were asked to work their rest days through the summer. Which put extra money in the wage packet, but it also raises a very interesting question. With firemen at the depot waiting to be passed, should that not be the correct procedure? Of course it should. Who is going to make some progress with that? It should have been the trade union branch. But rest day working kept a lot of people satisfied: lack of principle, actually.

I knew the management would not take the initiative here. Not while W. Bramley was the DMPS. But there wasn't anything to stop an individual making a claim for recompense through the Sectional Council. Other people did it, so I must have a go. It meant I had to do all the work myself, but there was nothing new about that.

Other than telling one or two people I could trust, I kept my own counsel. For weeks on end, I studied the daily alteration sheet to find out two things. First, how many drivers were actually working their rest day, and then how many passed firemen were not actually on driving turns anyway. That way, I could build a case. And although other people could see I was up to something, it didn't bother them at all. Rest day working took care of all that? Yes indeed, who cares about principle? Turned the old saying on its head, haven't they?

I remember getting a bit of help from Herbert Clarke, one of the telephone attendants in the foreman's office and going on Saltley Loco now and then gave me the chance to make contact with Les Briers, a one-time Derby man, now at Saltley and the Sectional Council representative there. I submitted a claim to that body for credit and payment for driving turns, due to drivers working rest days. I was still just a fireman, 'Who does John Weston think he is?' Quite late on, I was told that Saltley depot had submitted a claim for exactly the same thing. Well done to them, I say.

For some weeks , nothing happened. Then we had another trip on to Saltley Loco. On the Tuesday, I made contact with Les Briers, and asked him how my claim was proceeding. 'I have a sub-committee meeting to attend on Friday', he said, '... and I am almost sure that this matter is on our agenda. Can you get anything on paper to support your claim?' He assured me that if I could get the information to the LDC room at the depot by Thursday afternoon, it would go with him to the meeting on Friday. Which left me with just two days to get the claim properly formulated.

I believe that somewhere along the way, I had been told that the claim ought to be submitted through the branch secretary. Failure to do this would later cause me some problems. There are people who believe that procedure takes precedence – they had their day. What I actually did was to work on my assorted bits of paper during the late and early hours over Tuesday and Wednesday evening. Failure to provide the information would have surely meant failure to establish a claim and that was not going to happen, whatever the consequences.

So it was that the required details went to Saltley Loco on the Thursday afternoon, and they were submitted to the sub-committee meeting the next day. It may even have been on the Saturday of the same week, certainly soon afterwards, that I saw Les Briers again. I asked him, 'How have I got on?' 'Well', he said, '... you must not tell anyone of this, because it was only a sub-committee meeting. I expect it will be ratified by the full committee, in due course, but keep this to yourself. Your superintendent will be told that the men concerned are to be passed for driving duties and credit and payment for the turns they have lost will be conceded'.

Over the years since then many things have happened, and many things have been forgotten. That conversation is as clear to me as though it happened yesterday. There is one other comment that Les Briers made, 'Our Chairman was very impressed by the detail you submitted to back up your claim'. 'Well', said I, '... that is simply because I had some very good tutors'. To this day, you will not find me claiming that I have managed to do anything of importance in a long and active life. What I do claim is full marks for trying to be a credit to my parents, and for trying to justify the efforts of those who taught me so much and that, for me, is enough.

Soon afterwards, I made two apparent mistakes. It's that other 'P' word, procedure, which for some people is vitally important. The first mistake was to actually go to a branch meeting. With hindsight, I should have stayed away. They could have said what they liked about me, which they did at a later meeting, anyway. My second mistake was to tell the truth. Someone during the course of the meeting, asked the branch secretary, if he knew anything about a claim that had been submitted, for credit and payment for driving turns to the senior firemen. 'No', he replied, 'I don't, I don't know if John Weston knows anything about this'. Oh for the ability to give a slightly false answer. Instead I came out with the truth. 'Yes, I know about it, but I have given my word to Les Briers that I will not tell anyone else'. A fatal error. Every man in that room, bar one would turn against me. Each would feel that he could be trusted to keep a secret. Well, I knew better. I knew that by Monday morning the word would have spread, and my claim could have been jeopardized.

So it was better for me to castigated as a villain than to be remembered as a fool. It may well have been at the next branch meeting that Rue Carhart, now attending the monthly meetings, accused me of a 'diabolical insult' to the branch secretary. Simply by failing to submit my claim through the branch. Rue Carhart, who had not been a regular attender in my time, but I remember him as a good man, had fired the bullet, but had he actually loaded the gun? I think not. It is very likely that the man who was firing for him during that year had actually planted the words and who would that be then, John? I leave it to you to guess.

At a subsequent branch meeting, when I was not present, my accusers had their pound of flesh. Someone moved a motion of 'no confidence' in me personally. My good old friend Bill Clark, told me about that. In the absence of the defendant, he was only reprieved when someone else moved that 'the matter lie on the table'. Which was the usual formula for leaving matters as they were. Some years afterwards, on a training course for people who were actively working in mutual improvement classes, I was taught that for every 'How', there is a 'Why.' I have described in detail how all this happened. And now I have to say 'why?' Why did a trade union branch leave it to one man to pursue a claim for credit and payment for 12 people?

Having dealt at length with the downside, what about the upside? It is all in the Sectional Council minutes for the London Midland Region of British

Railways. It may have taken two meetings to ratify the particular claim. Sometimes, the word 'deferred' is used, to denote that the position requires further consideration. The Minute I saw which settled the matter said credit and payment for driving turns, Derby motive power depot – passed fireman J.A. Weston and 11 others. *That the application be conceded.* They held it back until November 1955, when I was passed. If any of us had failed, they would not have paid that individual.

It was a long time before I went to another trade union branch meeting. I didn't have any confidence in those who had no confidence in me. When the words I have quoted from Sectional Council minutes appeared, I made enquiries, as best I could, as to how many turns had actually been granted, I was pleasantly surprised. As near as I could get to finding out, it was 328. Shared out in different proportions, between 12 people. Only one person, Val Hughes, approached me with the question, how had he been credited and paid for driving turns, at a time when he was still a fireman?

Val asked his father-in-law, Fred Shaw, first. Fred was one of the three foreman's assistants. He said, 'I don't know, see John Weston'. So I told him the bit he needed to know and Val was generous enough to thank me for what I had done. No one else did, probably they were lacking in confidence. I had all the reward I needed. It is said that knowledge is power. If you know that what you are doing is right, you will be given the power to do it.

I don't regret the hours that I put in, working in one way or another in the trade union movement. Being sent to two trade union summer schools gave me the opportunity to meet other trade unionists. Attending local classes of the National Council of Labour Colleges and Saturday afternoon lectures, was all going to improve my education. I had met some very good people and others who were different. We didn't have a wireless set in the house until after I left school. For years after that, my store of knowledge was gradually accumulating. Now we have the Open University. I haven't actually taken any courses there myself, but I can see the opportunities that now exist for people to learn. One day in the House of Commons, 70-odd years ago, has been supplemented by what I have seen in recent years on television. I have heard a few wise words, from some of the people I have listened to.

Very few of them are politicians, but those few stand out. I could appreciate what the late Barbara Castle said to Martin Bell, some time ago, 'Never be afraid to stand alone'. In my own small way, I have done that too.

Chapter Twenty-Five

The Driving Test

The time eventually came when the next group of firemen at Derby were to be passed for driving duties. In my case on 11th and 13th November, 1955. Mac Haynes turned up on the first morning with his bowler hat in 'back gear', as we used to say. Which means that he had it tilted towards the back of his head.

Of course being me, I had to get some part of the first question wrong. Putting his hand on the piece of the tender buffer beam that we call the pad, he said, 'What's the name of this, Johnny?' 'Left-hand tender trailing buffer beam pad', says I. 'I'll kick your bloody arse', says Mac, 'Which side of the engine are we standing on?' 'The right side', was my reply. 'What is it then?' 'Right-hand tender trailing buffer beam pad', which was the correct answer.

You may think that I had got off on the wrong foot or out of bed on the wrong side. For me, it couldn't have been better. He would have to have found some fault sometime during the day. That was now out of the way and the rest of the morning went very well. Mac's main subject when giving lectures was the steam locomotive. Charlie Brown and Ernie Barber usually dealt with various aspects of the rules and regulations. We had a good discussion up until lunch-time on valves and pistons, failures and remedies and so on. I had brought along a few worsted trimmings, as making up trimmings had once been required as part of the test. There had also been a time when taking down and making a disabled engine fit to travel, had to be done as a practical test. The bigger engines made this impossible, due to the weight of the various parts. So it was more theory than practice, as far as taking down was concerned. We didn't have access to the tools required, anyway.

After lunch we sat down for a session on rules and regulations – question and answer, just rolling along. Eventually we came to the section, protection of trains and the use of wrong line orders, rules 178 to 188, in the old LMS rule book. The first question was, 'How many wrong line orders are there, Johnny?' 'Four', said I, and I went on to tell him who they were issued by, who to, and the colour of the paper they were printed on. Had he asked, I could have told him who might be required to countersign these orders. 'A', 'B', 'C', and 'D' those four orders were called. I had gone through the alphabet with one answer. The next question was on a different subject. Once again I have to say knowledge is power. I hadn't fired for somebody as good as Len Beard without gaining the knowledge and the confidence to know when I was right.

After a while we came to the question, 'At what speed can a passenger train be worked down a goods line?' 'Twenty-five miles an hour', I said. 'Are you sure?', said Mac. A moment's hesitation, then I said, 'Yes'. 'Well, look it up then.' I had the General and Sectional Appendices with me, as required, and soon found the relevant instruction. It was, of course, 25 mph. 'Ah well', said Mac, 'you will find occasions where you are authorized to travel at 45 miles per hour. 'Yes', I said, 'on the goods lines between Wellingborough and London.'

We both knew that if I had said 45 mph in the first place, he would have accepted it. A little more thought is required. If the relevant speed for passenger trains on goods lines is 45 mph, there is no need to amend it in the weekly notices, which is where the goods lines beyond Wellingborough are mentioned. These lines were in better condition than those in many other areas.

A few days afterwards, I was with Bill Wall for a day. He, of course wanted to know how I had got on. So I told him about my little mistake and the afternoon question that I had to confirm in the appendix. 'Yes', said Bill, 'you had him there, all right'. Bill himself was a master of brief answers. How many types of lubrication are there? He didn't wait for me to answer, just rattled them off. As a question for experts only, I have left one out. We need five for oil and one for grease. So, splash, wipe, capillary, mechanical, for oil. What have I left out? One specific type of lubrication with oil. See the end of this chapter for the answer.

With a few exceptions, footplate inspectors had all served their time as fireman and driver. So they could be treated as equals, but only by those who had the ability. Surprisingly, some of these men who had been waiting a long time to be passed were not always as ready as they ought to have been, and sometimes, when things were not going very well, the inspector would say, 'Is it this bowler hat that's frightening you? If it is, I'll throw it in the firebox'. Just to settle the man down.

So first day for me had gone very well. Two days after that I went out with Mac Haynes on the second day of my test. This meant working a passenger train out to Rowsley and a goods train back again. With the normal train crew in attendance, the passenger train was going on to Manchester. It's just as well that I had worked plenty of slow trains as we called them, stopping at every station in some cases, because I had not done any driving in the last nine months. We got to Rowsley without any problems. In the afternoon, there was a very heavy goods train to work back from there to Chaddesden. So it was a good all round test for me.

We were the last group of firemen at Derby to be passed on the points system. In theory, 90 points was possible. That meant getting 10 points on each of nine subjects – it wasn't possible in practice. The top pass was reckoned to be 81. There would, naturally be one man, years before, who would claim to have got 82 points. This chap, Ernie Hunt, was never seen at MIC meetings and he didn't volunteer to give lectures. I never fired for him, so I never had the chance to find out if he was as good as he said he was.

I don't think he was in the same league as Len Beard, who said to me, 'If you are ever going to be as good as me, you will have to spend the time at home studying rules and regulations. You will never do it all at work'. I took that lesson to heart, and put the time in, like he said I would have to.

In due course, after the examination, I was called in to see Bill Bramley, like everyone else, and Bill said to me, 'You've done very well, Weston, you've got about as many marks as it's possible to get'. 'How many would that be, Sir?, I asked. 'Eighty-one', he said. So that was good enough for me.

I must mention now the benefits that came to us after the strike in 1955, which would not be appreciated by everyone. For some years afterwards, wage negotiations were settled relatively smoothly and quickly, compared to how it had been before. I never came across a footplateman who was happy to engage in strike action, either before or afterwards, but everyone knew that if our representatives talked of withdrawing their labour, it wasn't empty words.

'2P' class 4-4-0 No. 40411 passes Derby Station South signal box as it departs Derby with a semi-fast passenger train bound for Nottingham on 25th August, 1956.
P.J. Lynch/Kidderminster Railway Museum

Years afterwards, when there were some differences between our LDC and the manager of the locomotive works at Derby, he put it this way, in reply to Harold Hawkes, 'I know that you mean what you say'. With George Radford and myself, Harold was a mainstay of the MIC movement at Derby. We had each of us given up our time over the years to attend these voluntary meetings.

When steam was replaced by diesel traction, the idea of entirely voluntary tutelage of others was shelved, how to handle the new machines was entrusted to paid instructors, and getting to know the theory side of them took place in the classroom. There is still some MIC activity on some of our heritage railways, which are, of course, dependent on volunteers for many of the jobs connected with the operational side, and where some otherwise retired enginemen have been able to continue doing a job they love.

The other benefit that came to me before the end of 1955 was the actual payment for driving turns while I was still a fireman. In my case somewhere around 30 turns. It wasn't a big sum of money for those times, but it meant I got on to a higher rate of pay much quicker than I would have done, and so did 11 other firemen. We all gained something from one man's efforts.

So it was that we came to the end of a very important year, with me now a happily married man and looking forward to another year where I would sometimes be in charge, as the driver of the locomotives I had first cleaned in the autumn of the year 1937.

The missing word is in Bill Wall's term, *displacement*. Hydrostatic displacement, as used in the drop lubricator on class '2' goods engines, for which a special can of oil was issued from the locomotive stores. For many years, that was the only class of engine used on the Shirland branch and I had two years firing in the link which went there. I filled a few drop lubricators in my time. A drop of oil, rising through water on a journey to part of the engine which could not be reached in any other way.

Chapter Twenty-Six

From Fireman to Driver

Following my tests on 11th and 13th November, 1955, I was passed out for driving duties. Reg Haynes, the inspector, told me that I could make out a route card. Every driver and every passed fireman, except those permanently confined to shed work, has a route card. All these are kept in a box in the running foreman's office. When a special working, which may be over lines not normally used by Derby men, is programmed to run on a certain date, the foreman or his assistant will check who is available to drive this special train.

When making out a route card, the prospective driver states that he is competent to work trains over those sections of lines which he has initialled and that he has knowledge of the signals and gradients on those routes. The certificate of competence signed by the inspector for each driver, passed fireman and guard, was sent by the clerical staff from the area manager, Derby, to the divisional manager, Nottingham. I have no means of knowing which set of clerical officers took over six weeks to file my certificate. It should have been back to Derby by 20th November if only someone had applied their mind to it. Christmas must have come early that year because the certificate was actually dated December 28th, 1955.

I have no doubt whatsoever that a clerical officer's certificate of promotion would not have been held up so long. But clever management had managed to save 6*d*. or 1*s*. on what I would have been paid for Christmas Day and Boxing Day of 1955.

There was nothing new in the business of delaying footplatemen's wage increases by any device possible. As young firemen, we were always told by the older men to keep a record of all our firing turns. They knew exactly how the clerical staff operated. Very much 'us and them' at the time.

Your career as a spare driver, of course, was heavily influenced by what kind of route card you had made out. It wasn't easy for any of us who were passed in October and November 1955 to have extensive road knowledge. All of us had done three straight years on the west road. So most of my colleagues who, of course, had been firemen as long as I had, only signed for short distance workings.

I had made my own decision that my road card would include as many as possible of the roads which I had fired on over the previous 18 years: on the principle that whatever I had done as fireman I would also do as a driver. In one sense, this made a rod for my own back. Because, when you have a varied and comprehensive road card, and 12-hour availability, your times on duty on one week could be very haphazard indeed. Take one example from 1956. I was on 6 am coal weigh, firing for Joe Toone, my rostered turn, a very easy job. Just taking loaded wagons to the coal stage and taking empties away to a nearby siding, with a few wagons of clinker from the ashpit to move around as well. Around 11.30 on Friday morning, someone came up from the foreman's office to tell me that I must sign off at 1 p.m. I was needed as driver on the Saturday

'4F' 0-6-0 No. 44262 emerges from Dove Holes tunnel, between Peak Forest and Chinley, showing a 'white feather' on 30th March, 1957. I have been through Dove Holes tunnel hundreds of times. *T. Lewis*

'2P' class 4-4-0 No. 40411 passes Way & Works Siding signal box as it leaves Derby with a stopping train for Nottingham on 30th April, 1957. This was a favourite spot for R.J. Buckley (*see front cover*). *R.J. Buckley*

morning, on duty at 1 am to work the Burton-Leicester parcels. So, all week, I had been getting up at 5 o'clock in the morning. Then, on Saturday, it was get up at midnight for a 1 am start. Nothing nice about that but you take the rough with the smooth.

Was there ever any smooth? A year or two went by and the pubs in the Burton area had a special outing to Blackpool, starting at Woodville, a branch on the Burton to Leicester line. I worked from there, up the Churnet Valley to Macclesfield, then on to Blackpool and lodge. I would sign on again on Saturday night for the return working, bringing the train all the way back to Woodville, then Burton. This was a big money job, two turns of duty on the Saturday, Sunday rate of pay from midnight Saturday. One of the senior drivers who was spare that day complained that he ought to have the job. But when the foreman's assistant said, 'Do you sign for the Burton-Leicester line?' he had to say, 'No'. So that was the end of the matter. They did tell me about it and also said that he was just trying to muscle in. Well, it didn't work. Of course, I needed a conductor driver all the way from Uttoxeter to Blackpool and all the way back. Not only did I sign for the Burton to Leicester line, I also signed for the North Stafford.

They were two of the lines which were on my road card that no other passed fireman on my shift would look at. They all had the same firing experience, so it's a personal thing. You either want to get your first 313 turns quickly (*see below*) or you go with the flow.

The drivers' pay structure went like this (these are the 1939 figures because I remember them better) fireman's top rate of pay, after 10 years in the grade was 72*s*. The first year driving rate was 78*s*. After 313 turns (there we are), 78*s*. became your rate whether driving or firing. After another 626 turns your rate became 84*s*. a week, and still another 626 brought you to the top driving rate of pay - 90*s*. a week, £234 a year. It seemed pretty good then.

It was in 1958 that I reached the top rate of pay for a driver. On February 8th of that year, I recorded 501 driving turns. And on April 30th, I reached top whack. After 20½ years in the railway service, and after the qualifying period as stated above had been reduced.

Just over a year later - in the autumn of 1959 - another huge change came in. Derby men started working London and Manchester turns with diesel locomotives. In the last week of September, I was training on Metro-Vickers diesels on the Churnet Valley line. There it was relatively quiet and you could run up and down without interfering with other trains too much.

On Saturday 10th October, 1959, I recorded my first driving turn with diesels: No. D5701 it was, one way to Manchester, Nos. D5710 and D5712 on the way back. Four days later, I reached my 40th birthday.

This was not supposed to happen. A passed fireman, trained on diesels even before most of the spare link drivers? Scandalous. So how and why had this come about? This is how and why. In the spare link, the smart thing is to sign for London or Bristol, or both. Working mileage turns, was how to make big money. So most of the passed fireman - bar one - didn't want to go to Crewe, Burton to Leicester, or Manchester. Hard work, awkward hours of duty, no extra money - that's how and why.

Ex-LMS 'Crab' class 2-6-0 No. 42709 leaves Derby with a Blackpool-Leicester via Burton-on-Trent on 3rd August, 1957. If memory serves me right, this is a train that called at Woodville and Swadlincote. I was working on this line on that same day (but not on that engine).

P.J. Lynch/Kidderminster Railway Museum

Ex-Midland Railway '1F' class 0-6-0T No. 41804 stands by the coaling stage at Derby on 22nd June, 1958. This is the 6 o'clock coal weigh turn. The engine has a wagon attached at the back, just visible behind the coal stage. There is a lot of spillage here. Note the short cab roof on this shunting engine. *J. Wood/Kidderminster Railway Museum*

Metropolitan-Vickers type '2' Co-Bo diesel No. D5709 on Derby shed on 1st November, 1959. A month before this picture was taken, I was training on the Metro-Vickers class on the Churnet Valley line. On 10th October, 1959, I recorded my first diesel turn.
L.W. Perkins/Kidderminster Railway Museum

Well, I had the bottle to take this on. Up until then my bottle had been mostly skimmed milk, now I was getting some cream. By the end of that year,1959, I had a week of classroom training on diesel locomotives. Our new instructors there had obviously been specially trained in the workings of the diesel; quite different to steam, of course.

The managers were a different breed, too. It is more than possible that the managers of 1959 encouraged these instructors to believe that diesel meant different as regards footplatemen. That, from then on, it would be the technical people doing the driving with the drivers standing behind them just in case. If they thought that, then they were just plain wrong - and they didn't know a great deal about footplatemen.

In steam days, it had always been accepted - and it continued to be - that the man who knew the road would do the driving; with the man who knew the engine there to offer advice if necessary. That was a basic principle, and we were not about to see it compromised. I can imagine the technical people thinking what a great idea it was. It was an easy enough life for them while training was going on, running out at 8 am every day. The reality of timetables was, of course, quite different.

They were very soon told where they stood by our other instructors. Men who had served their time out on the lines, of course. We carried on as we had always done. There would be some easy days that winter, like the week when I was the instructor myself on the Metro-Vickers diesels, and some hard work as well, like the 2.02 am parcels to Manchester. You went to bed in the early evening and got up at a quarter to one in the morning. Signed on at 1.42 am, relieved a parcels train from London and worked it on to Manchester. Then it was down to the Trafford Park shed. If you had a big diesel, the 'Peak' class, that engine would work the 7.25 am from Manchester to London. Our next job was to take the two Metro-Vickers diesels and work the 7.30 am stopping train from Manchester to Derby, and stop it certainly did - it seemed like hundreds of times between the two cities. And you finished work just before 10 in the morning. I have spent a lot of my life grabbing sleep when I could and if I could and I learnt how to cope with it. But I was a bit more than washed up after that shift.

Oh happy days, speeding through Kettering. The double-headed 12.25 pm St Pancras-Manchester train, headed by 'Royal Scot' class 4-6-0 No. 46110 *Grenadier Guardsman* and 'Black Five' 4-6-0 No. 44775 passes Kettering South Junction in October 1957.

P.J. Lynch/Kidderminster Railway Museum

Crosti-boilered BR Standard class '9F' 2-10-0 No. 92025 enters Derby station with an up passenger train on 9th August, 1958. The '9Fs' did a fair bit of passenger work and were well suited to it. *V.R. Webster/Kidderminster Railway Museum*

Ex-MR '3F' class 0-6-0 No. 43205 emerges from Manton tunnel, south of Oakham, with a southbound goods train. This is probably a train from one of the Nottingham depots, running from Derby we usually had bigger trains pulled by bigger engines.

P.M. Alexander/Kidderminster Railway Museum

The 8.40 am goods from Chaddesden to New Lount waiting for the 'right away' at Melbourne on a line I know so well. *Roy F. Burrows/Midland Collection Trust/Kidderminster Railway Museum*

'4F' 0-6-0 No. 44310 is seen on the west goods line as it approaches Derby station. The train is made up of empty mineral wagons on 4th September, 1959. *John Hodge*

Stanier 'Black Five' 4-6-0 No. 45272, one of my all-time favourite engines, prepares to descend the Lickey Incline with a stopping train. This is the engine Ronnie Capstick and I had for a trip to Rhyl in 1955. *J. Tarrant/Kidderminster Railway Museum*

Yes, 1959 was the year of transition. The year when steam started to give way to diesel. But it didn't happen right away and a look at my diaries for that year show the reality

January to September	
To Manchester	48 turns of duty
To Sheffield	47
To Stoke or Crewe	19
To Wellingborough	8
To Birmingham	8
Burton-Leicester line	8

That is a total of 138 main line turns, all with steam locomotives, unless I was conducting a diesel.

Firing turns 10
Driving on shed turns 14
Driving on local workings (including working to Leicester, Nottingham, Burton and New Lount) 88

A total of 112, plus the 138 above equals 250 turns; from 10th October - 18 main line diesel workings; add 10 days being trained on diesels and four days instructing Trafford Park men.

I have noted down a few highpoints from 1959. I had one trip to York - on 4th July, for which I required a conductor from Sheffield. Ten days later, I conducted diesel No. D5706 to Manchester and return. This is while diesels were still being assessed for train workings, one trip to Shirland Colliery, two days road reviewing and one day, 23rd August, conducting to Chester. Going to Shirland Colliery was more of a low point, in fact. It only happened because I had had two years firing when we worked there. It comes back to my intention that what I had done as fireman I would also do as a driver.

Chester is in a different category altogether and I have many happy memories of trains and engines worked to Chester. My involvement with that very special station began on 25th July, 1955. It was on that date that I went on a passenger special to Rhyl, via Crewe and Chester. Signed on at 9.35 am, off at 6.05 pm with No. 45272 one of our marvellous Stanier 'Black Fives'. My driver was a passed fireman, Ronnie Capstick, sometime secretary of the Derby MIC, later head running office inspector at Crewe. Well, of course, Ronnie had to have a conductor from Crewe, which gave him the opportunity to discuss the route with me, in between keeping the engine up for steam and water.

'You know, John', he said, 'If I could just get to learn the signals at Chester, I think I could sign for Rhyl'. Easy said, but learning the signals through Chester General station was a very challenging task, as I was to find out. So, the seed was sown in 1955 but it was three years later before I got my chance to sign for that road myself. The way I did it was a bit mischievous, I suppose, but it was in everyone's interest - including management.

First of all, I asked if I could have two days reviewing the road to Crewe. That was because I had not worked to the passenger station for some time.

Compound 4-4-0 No. 41157 waits to leave Birmingham New Street station with the 6.25 pm to Derby on 22nd July, 1959. *J. Wood/Kidderminster Railway Museum*

Hughes/Fowler 'Crab' 2-6-0 No. 42897 leaves Basford North with a Burton-on-Trent to Skegness excursion train on 6th September, 1959. *P.J. Lynch/Kidderminster Railway Museum*

Reviewing the road meant just that - a refresher course over a certain stretch of line, but it was an unusual request from a passed fireman. Anyway, I went to see Teddy Mumford (the running foreman) and Stan Bates (LDC secretary), the two men who would make the decision and put it to them. 'I don't see why you should', said Teddy. Not a good start, but then Stan Bates said, 'As far as I am concerned, a passed fireman has just as much right to do this as a driver'. That carried the argument and I was given the two days. Although my real reason was to learn Chester station, I didn't need to tell anyone about that. Management were going to get full value from me, that was certain.

So when the train I rode on arrived at Crewe, I had a quick look round the station there and then hopped on the next train to Chester. Nothing particularly complicated about the signals from Crewe to Chester - until you arrived at the home signal for Chester No. 1. In front of you there was a big gantry with five or six stop signals. A little way off to the right stood another big gantry with the same number of signals. In the signal box, I found a helpful signalman. He told me that between No. 1 at the Crewe end and No. 6 at the Holyhead end, there were three more signal boxes as well, I realized that there was a lot to learn.

But I began to make something of this forest of signals. I could see some light between the trees - there was a pattern. The big gantry at No. 1 Chester from Crewe was explained to me and the other one, from Warrington, where the signals read exactly the same. At the other end, No. 6, there were two more big gantries. Again, the set of signals approached from the Holyhead direction was repeated from the Birkenhead line. Chester station must have been quite unusual in that respect, two main lines coming in at each end. We could approach Derby from the south and the west but the signals for these two lines were nowhere near each other, not so at Chester.

That wasn't the end of the problem. Between those two signal boxes, there were the three more I must mention, Nos. 2, 3a and 4. If there was a No. 5, it was probably in the goods yard. I don't think there was another passenger station anywhere with so many signal boxes concentrated in such a small area. I certainly never came across another one like it.

Another well-known - indeed, infamous - aspect of the Crewe line was the real reason why so few passed firemen or drivers in the spare link would sign up for Stoke - let alone Crewe. This was the five or six miles of railway between Caverswall and Stoke Junction - the Stoke Bank. This was a real switchback of a line, two moderate little rises, all the rest severe downhill. The letters 'AWB' in the sectional appendix indicated that wagon brakes must be applied on loose-coupled goods trains. When the only other braking power is in the hands of the driver and the guard, it is absolutely vital that some wagon brakes must be pinned down on all heavy goods trains.

The dangers were mentioned to me by Ronnie Capstick who said to me, 'If you sign for Stoke Bank, sooner or later you will have a runaway. I have had mine'. It's at that stage that you think - 'Not me, mate' but you keep it to yourself. The other hazard was being too cautious. One Derby driver suffered from over-caution and would never talk about his experiences on Stoke Bank. But his regular fireman told me all about it. 'I pinned brakes down at the top of the bank', he said. 'I picked them up on the bank. I pinned them down on the bank. I picked them up on the bank (second time that was). I pinned them down on the bank and I picked them up at the bottom'. Oh, dear!!

So this is how I remember Stoke Bank and my own way of dealing with it. Leaving the top of the incline, the line drops quite sharply through the not very long tunnel and continues to fall quite sharply until you come to Normacot station. There is no signal box there but a short rise to Bridgewood sidings. The only reminder of that now is a public house 'The Signalman'. The competent driver, master of his trade, will have three or four wagon brakes down and the guard will have his brake applied constantly. I would apply the engine handbrake on leaving the summit. On a few occasions, I have had to take the handbrake off and even give a short burst of steam to avoid coming to a standstill, just after Normacot. That is the only concession you have to make. Re-apply the hand brake - there is still a very steep incline to come - and carry on. Next you pass Longton station – still there, but there is no signal box.

Then on to Foley crossing, a vital point on the journey where an overly-cautious driver will come to a stop again. The signalman at Foley will always be watching you closely, in case you look like a runaway, and I always used to raise my hand to let him know that I was rolling nicely.

A few yards beyond his box, the incline drops sharply again. If you are not in control now, you will not stop at Glebe Colliery sidings if his signals are on. And if you can't stop there, you are officially deemed a runaway. The message will go down to Stoke Junction, 'Train running away'. There are two other routes there, one a branch line, the other the main line to Stafford. I have never heard of any accidents there, the road levels out and even the runaway, you will be glad to hear, stops before reaching Stoke station.

On the return journey, before Glebe Colliery siding, you pass Fenton station. I have stopped there several times with passenger trains going to Derby. It was always a real job to get started again because of the steep incline. What it meant was that you couldn't set back more than a yard or so and, as that was the usual way of getting a train started on inclines, it was a real problem.

I mentioned the tunnel between Caverswall and Meir. Only a few yards outside, on the Stoke side, was another set of catch points where, if you started slipping and rolling back, you would soon deposit some wagons onto English soil. There was a whistle code if you needed help in the shape of an assisting engine. However, where would you get an assisting engine in Stoke on a Saturday night? Not a practical proposition. I didn't want the huge delay which this would have engendered so I carried on regardless. Even if there were no assisting engines available, you would always get the same question at the end – 'Now, driver, why didn't you send for an assisting engine?'

Always when you reached that tunnel on the return journey, you were moving slowly. It was a very heavy train, once I was only going at about walking pace, but we didn't slip (the tunnel was usually dry) and I didn't panic. Then, about halfway through the tunnel, we began to pick up pace. For which I was extremely grateful. I always heeded one of the first pieces of advice I was given about Stoke bank. With a brake van at each end, screw the brake down hard on the front van and with four or five wagon brakes down hard as well, you won't have any trouble. I thought that was a good idea and it worked well for me.

I mentioned never having a runaway. Well, I didn't, but there's one interesting entry in my diary, 'Break loose at Caverswall' it states. The appendix instructions about AWB lines were that the guard, unless special staff were provided, should apply the wagon brakes while the train was being drawn slowly onto the incline. When the driver was satisfied that he had enough braking power, he whistled up and the guard rejoined the train. Bear that in mind, while I tell my Caverswall story.

We normally applied the brakes on the leading wagons ourselves, using the coal pick to apply some leverage. Normally the guard was quite happy to leave that to us. On this particular trip, our guard was Billy Unsworth. We talked it through before leaving Chaddesden and I said I would pin the brakes down. 'Why should you do that?' he said. 'That's my job'. Well, I couldn't argue the point because, according to the book, he was in the right. So, at Caverswall, I am drawing slowly onto the incline. I look back and he is on the ground, applying brakes. Instead of ignoring him, I stop the train, trying to make his job easier. Shortly afterwards, he signalled, 'Ready to go'. I tried to start but the train wouldn't budge. He had applied the brakes before there were enough wagons over the incline. I set back once, and give them a yank. Nothing happened. I set back again, and gave them a bit more. Well, most of the train came with me but a coupling broke and four or five of the wagons plus the guard's van were left behind. We managed to couple up again and take some brakes off the wagons. Then we carried on to Grange sidings without further trouble. But it was a very subdued Mr Unsworth for the rest of the journey.

In due course, I had to explain what had happened in a special report form. No doubt he did too, but that was it. No further questions were asked, no further explanations given. It wasn't the only way of working down Stoke bank. One day, on another train, we were stopped at Tutbury so that a Stoke engine could be coupled up to our train. I told the driver how many wagons we had on and would he wish me to pin wagon brakes down. 'No', he said, 'that won't be necessary'.

Standard practice, when there are two engines working a train, was that the driver of the leading engine should control the braking power of the train. We were, of course, fully coupled up so that the vacuum-controlled steam brake on my engine was being controlled by the Stoke driver. I watched the pressure gauge with interest, because it made it obvious what he was doing. All the way down, the train was just kept under control by a 'brake-on, brake-off' technique which was fine for lightly-loaded trains but was certainly not fine for our job. The trouble was that Stoke men had no experience of handling anything like our 2.48 am Grange or the ironstone trains which ran over their lines for a time – horses for courses.

So the Stoke bank played a major part of my memories of the period around 1959. I was still in the prime of life then, but the years were beginning to whirl around faster than they used to and I had some big decisions ahead of me. For the time being, though, let's spend a little longer on the main line of my life (family always excepted): the life of a footplateman. I think the best way would be to take you in some detail (not too much, I hope) through some actual journeys as I remember them.

Stanier 'Black Five' No. 45277 at Hooton, north of Chester, with a parcels train in the 1960s. This is the locomotive we worked to St Pancras on 15th January, 1956.

P. Riley/Kidderminster Railway Museum

Stanier 'Jubilee' class 4-6-0 No. 45626 *Seychelles*, a Derby engine, departs from St Pancras with an express for Manchester. *Revd J. Algar/Kidderminster Railway Museum*

Chapter Twenty-Seven

Going to Town

So back we go to 15th January, 1956. The train we are working is the 3.35 pm from Derby Midland to London St Pancras. Our driver and fireman will take the train as far as Kettering where another crew will take over. Today it is Sunday so you will not see the same trains as during a weekday; because there are far fewer goods trains and the mix of people using the service is different – more social, less work. But work looms large as always because many of those travelling by train are going back to the metropolis. Wives and sweethearts are on the platform waving them goodbye. Today *you* will be riding on the engine.

Now, let's take a look behind the scenes. Our train is in the sidings, where it will have been cleaned, serviced and examined. How many of you remember the wheeltapper and the ring of his hammer on the wheels?

It's time to join our driver and fireman who are busy with the preparation of the engine which is a 'Black Five' No. 45277. A total of 842 of these locomotives were built and they are still held in particular affection by footplatemen. Even today, you can see a number of them working on the private steam lines.

You can see our fireman, Ken, checking the level of water in the boiler and in the tank. Follow the driver, John, on a tour of inspection. He is drawing the corks on connecting rods, and all the outside motions, filling the oil wells and replacing the corks. He will be checking the brake gear, the springs and the great driving wheels. Nothing will be left to chance. The safety of passengers is always the first consideration. Even today, those who are left to remember them, talk with pride of the standards of the Midland Railway, which were carried on in the LMS as it became.

When everything is ready, we still have one requirement. Yes, a cup of tea, so it's off to the messroom to mash. Now we can get out to the shed signal and ring off. The code on the bell tells the signalman that we are going to the passenger station. By now, a shunting engine will have positioned the train in the platform. Our engine is coupled up by the carriage shunter and we open a valve to supply steam heating to the coaches.

All is hustle and bustle on the platform, as the time for departure draws near. The clock shows 3.35, whistles blow and the green flag is waved. Driver John checks that the signal is clear, opens the regulator and we are off. As we move around the south curve and gather speed, you think how wonderful it all is.

A few miles down the line and there is a whole new meaning to 'Rock & Roll'. Rolling from side to side is constant and is punctuated by sudden bangs and lurches. Gritting your teeth you hang on for dear life. Ken is rhythmically shovelling coal into the firebox. John assures you that everything is normal and, as we run into Nottingham, the first stop, everything is happy again, and you are now enjoying the ride.

A few minutes there, while passengers join the train, and we are off again. Back in 1956, it was to Melton Mowbray over a route we called 'The Alps'. Enjoy it while you can, in a few more years, this line will be no more and it will only be possible to go via Leicester.

Class '2P' 4-4-0 No. 404072 leaves Derby with a stopping train for Sheffield on 22nd May, 1956.
D.J. Powell Collection/Kidderminster Raiilway Museum

Caprotti valve-gear fitted 'Black Five' 4-6-0 No. 44745 arrives at Derby with an express for Bristol on 16th September, 1954. In my opinion, the Caprotti engines were not as good as the standard Walschaerts valve-geared 'Black Fives'.
P.H. Wells

We are climbing steadily and soon it will be dark. Suddenly, we are going through a tunnel and then another one, gathering speed all the time. Then rounding a curve, we run into the small station of Melton.

Leaving there, you will see Ken winding down a big handle, like a screw. We are picking up water from a trough between the rails. Wind it up now, our tank is almost full again. Soon we shall arrive at Oakham, then a swift descent, followed by a short tunnel then a long one. Out of that we come and very soon, if it were daylight, you would see a valley below. We are crossing the great viaduct at Harringworth (just as spectacular and emotive as Ribblehead, and even longer), then another long hill to climb and yet another tunnel, the last one before Kettering. As we reach the brow of the hill, the great steelworks of Stewart and Lloyds appears on our left.

There are miles of railway sidings here and hundreds of wagons. It's all downhill now to Kettering. When we arrive, the platform clock shows 5.42 and we are bang on time. For the passengers, another pleasant ride, warm, comfortable and punctual. For you, a truly wonderful experience, and you are surprised to learn that it is John's first official driving turn.

****

Now for another journey. It's five minutes to seven on a balmy evening. You are standing on No. 1 platform of the Derby Midland station. You are looking forward to the journey to Manchester as you will be riding on the front end with the driver, John, and his fireman. You remember the first journey you made back in January 1956 and how you took some getting used to the rocking and rolling motion. Gradually, panic had subsided as you realized that the great monster in whose claws you were was not going to leave the rails.

My mate and I climb on to the footplate. The driver I am taking over from looks at me. A bit quizzically, I think. 'She's a good 'un mate', he says. I know what he is thinking. He's around 60, a driver in the top link. Is this kid of 37 up to the job, he is wondering. None of his business, think I to myself. Off he goes and I have a quiet smile. It's likely that I have packed more experience into my first 37 years than he did. His firing turns would mostly have been on small engines. My time has been served on all sorts over many routes from Derby. Age isn't important, I have no worries.

You join me on the footplate and we watch the station duties being completed. Whistles blow, doors are slammed, the green flag waves. Checking that the departure signal is clear, I open the regulator and give a quick toot on the whistle. We are on the move.

Once again, you notice that we start without much wheel-slip. Too much slipping can lead to permanent damage. As we pass over the River Derwent, I am adjusting the cut-off, up to 55, then 45. Over the Nottingham road bridge, open the regulator a bit more and we are moving well. So pull her up to 30 then 25. Marks on the reversing lever sector plate indicate this. We pass the busy goods sidings at St Mary's and very soon we are in open country. Next we pass over the road crossing at Breadsall and shortly Duffield station with the Chevin golf course on our left.

The big hill over Milford tunnel looms before us, suddenly we are in the dark but soon out again. We pass through Belper station with several bridges carrying roads over the railway. Over the river again and, soon after Broadholme, I close the regulator, wind the gear down and prepare to apply the brake for the curve at Ambergate. This is a very unusual station, built in the form of a triangle. We pass through at the regulation 25 mph and open up again. We left Derby at two minutes past seven and we are due in Matlock at 7.25. There are quite a number of curves, embankments and two small tunnels, Lea Wood and Cromford, between Ambergate and Matlock.

En route, the guard will have been walking through the train, asking passengers in the rear to move up to the front if they are alighting at Matlock. The platforms here are quite small and only the first three or four coaches will actually be standing on the platform when we stop. Three minutes only is our allocated time and we will be leaving at the booked time - 7.28 pm.

After a couple of miles fairly straight, I shut off again for the curve at Rowsley. On our left we pass the locomotive depot and the big sidings where up and down goods trains are dealt with. (From Derby, the line is described as 'up' to London and 'down' to Manchester.) It's almost all uphill, for quite a while now. The beat of the exhaust gets much louder, as I open up again and wind up to 45, working hard now.

You will get a marvellous view of the Peak District from the footplate, this is one of the most scenic routes in all England, and it was a marvellous feat of engineering, with tunnels driven through solid rock, particularly at Headstone Head.

We pass through Bakewell, Great Longstone and Monsal Dale where you will see the road to Litton Mill far below on your right. Just here, there's a sheer drop but the railway itself is built on bedrock. Soon we are at Miller's Dale. A three minute stop here and off we go again. We are climbing up to Peak Forest now and the scenery gets rugged. Just about an hour since we left Derby and we are at the summit. The fireman can take it easy for a bit.

Now we enter one of the longest tunnels on this route - Doveholes at 2,984 yards - not much short of two miles. The railway line from Buxton to Stockport actually passes over Doveholes tunnel. Even the most experienced of drivers is always a bit relieved to see daylight again.

As we emerge from the tunnel and coast down towards Chinley, you will see several viaducts, one of which carries the line from Manchester to Sheffield and Chesterfield. This line will stay open - but the one we have just described will suffer the unkindest cut of all.

Leaving Chinley, we have just 28 minutes left to get to Manchester Central, including a very short stop at Didsbury. Like many other large towns, all the worst features of Manchester can be seen from the footplate.

We pass the quaintly named signal box, Throstle's Nest, and it's slightly uphill again, into Central station. Our return journey will be made in the dark but you have had the chance to witness - from the footplate - the glorious scenery of the Peak District. No-one will ever work a train into the Central station at Manchester again. It's an exhibition centre now.

Chapter Twenty-Eight

The Tracks of My Years

Having taken you on some typical journeys from my time as a driver, I ought to pay tribute to the work of those who were to provide the bedrock of all my years on the tracks, the gangers, and all the other men (and women) who worked backstage, so to speak, on the thousands of miles of track we covered, in my days as passed cleaner, fireman and driver.

Who were these people? Well, to begin with, the ganger, who reported to the permanent way inspector, who in turn was the agent of the district engineer, the person in charge of the maintenance and construction of tracks, bridges and viaducts. There may have been other persons in that chain of command, but the ones I will describe are the men we would encounter in our day to day travels up and down the country.

Every weekday, the ganger would walk the stretch of line that he was responsible for. In the days of wooden sleepers, iron rails and chairs and wooden keys, the ganger would carry a little bag containing these small blocks of wood we called 'keys'. He also carried a hammer, with which to hammer the keys into the gaps between the chairs and the old bull-head rails.

So when the ganger had walked from one end of his section to the other, checking everything to do with the safety of the line, he would hitch a lift back on the 'trip engine', which serviced the sidings at all the little country stations. Nobody hitched lifts on the engines of express trains, except for the footplate inspectors, who were there to check on the ability of the train crew.

On occasions, we were stopped at signal boxes and asked to convey a permanent way inspector, for the purpose of examining the line. This would happen when a driver had reported something unusual, perhaps no more than feeling a bump, which would cause him to stop at the next signal box and report to the signalman. The procedure then was that the next train travelling in the opposite direction would be stopped and advised to travel through the section at 'caution', in case there was a landslide or something unusual. The preferred option was to send an engine through 'light', that means without a train attached. Even a passenger train could be used to examine the line, if no other means was available at the time.

When the district engineer and his staff went out to look at the permanent way, it was in a special saloon coach, with an engine just to ferry them around. No guard was provided on these trips, one of the engineer's staff who was passed out on the rules applicable to all trains on the running lines would carry out the guard's duties. We used to refer to him as the 'flunkey'. He would convey the engineer's instructions to the driver, stating which particular lineside structure we were to stop at. Sometimes we would cover a good many miles a day with these officers, but always there would be a break for lunch. For this we would stand in a siding, taking care not to make excessive noise with the engine. On occasions, there would be a bonus. The saloon was equipped with one or more cases of beer, and the flunkey would deliver two bottles,

BR Standard '9F' class 2-10-0s at shed at Cricklewood shed on 4th October, 1959. The locomotive nearest the camera is No. 92132, to the right is the coaling plant. I had one or two lodging trips to Cricklewood, but more often to Kentish Town. *W. Potter/Kidderminster Railway Museum*

'3F' 0-6-0 No. 43340 with a lengthy rake of wagons, possibly bound for Chaddesden, seen at Burton-on-Trent on 4th June, 1960. *M. Mensing*

carefully concealed, along with the message concerning the departure time. The empty bottles would find their way back in due course.

All this attention to the maintenance of the track meant that trains could run with safety at the prescribed line speeds. In my time on the footplate that increased from 75 mph to 90 mph. Very few of the pre-war steam engines had speedometers fitted, but they did become more common after nationalization. Those of us who worked express trains on a regular basis could work to the time book without even using a watch.

Back in the 1950s, we would work out wagon loads of pre-fabricated track to the site of repairs. If the up main line was being relaid, the down main line would be utilized for the pre-fab train. A travelling crane would pull up the old track and sleepers, a 22 yard stretch at a time. One wagon would be unloaded and reloaded, old track picked up and new track laid down. By Monday morning, trains would be running again over a mile or more of new track, all skillfully laid by professional railwaymen.

This next event happened to me only once in all my time as a footplateman. One Sunday afternoon, I worked the 3.35 pm Derby to London train, which ran over the route from Nottingham via Melton Mowbray and Oakham, the journey described in the previous chapter. This occurred some time early on in my time as a driver.

Rounding the curve near the old Upper Broughton station, the engine exploded a detonator. I passed a platelayer waving a yellow flag from side to side. I knew at once what to expect. About half a mile on, the train exploded another detonator, and another railwayman stood there, with the yellow flag held steady. Another quarter of a mile, and a man stood waving a green flag from side to side, but here there is no detonator. What was happening on the Sunday afternoon, and what action did the rules state I should take?

My actions, all as covered in the Rule Book, were as follows: Shut the regulator, and reduce speed by applying the brake. I knew that I must proceed at 15 mph. And the cause of the disruption? A broken rail had been found, and in those days, the line would not need to be shut for the rail to be replaced, you simply needed another length of rail, enough men to lift it (that would be around seven or eight), and enough time between trains to finish the work. Hence the operation was carried out on a Sunday.

It would probably take less than an hour, once men and rail had arrived at the scene, removed the keys, loosened the bolts, and lifted up the two sections of broken rail. 'Altogether now', lift up the new length of rail, bolt it to the sleepers, put the keys back, and inspect the job. Stability will be established when I, the driver of the next train over that stretch, take my train over the new length of rail, at about 15 mph. No looking at the speedometer was required, just judgement and experience.

So the gangers and the platelayers played their part in the safe working of the railway. So too did signalmen, guards and many other members of staff. What else contributed to the high standards of safety we enjoyed on my time on the railway?

Systems and procedures played their part. How for example was it arranged that two trains could not collide on the same stretch of single track? By ensuring

'3F' class 0-6-0 No. 43254 at Derby North Junction with a Chaddesden-St Mary's trip freight in June 1962. By this time I had been through Links 7A & 7 (local work) and was back on the main line. *P.J. Lynch/Kidderminster Railway Museum*

'4F' class 0-6-0 No. 43955 leaves Derby with a transfer goods bound for Chaddesden yard in June 1962. *P.J. Lynch/Kidderminster Railway Museum*

that an engine did not enter a section until the driver was in possession of a token. This was known as the Electric Token Block System. Usually this token (or tablet as it could also be called) was handed by the signalman to the fireman. On a very few lines the token could be picked up by a mechanical device. This tablet catching device was fitted to a few of our class '4' goods engines, which worked over the Bourne branch. That particular line could be very busy on Saturdays, during the summer season.

I only ever used that apparatus once, late in my time as a fireman, on a Saturday special to Great Yarmouth. My driver, Frank Ryley, had a conductor driver over this line, and he showed me how it was done. It was designed to save time, getting rid of the time spent slowing down as you would have in the normal manner.

If you failed to pick up the token, the driver had to stop the train as quickly as he could. Then the fireman had to walk back to the signal box to collect it. Why? Because big problems arise at the end of the section, if you don't have the token in your possession. Nothing can move until the token has been put in the machine at the arrival end. If somehow you have travelled without it, someone will have to either walk or go by bicycle all the way back to the other section to pick it up. At best there will be a lot of delay, and a lot of explaining to do at the subsequent enquiry. At worst, a collision, and possible loss of life.

In L.T.C. Rolt's book *Red for Danger*, which deals with accidents on railways, there is a chapter devoted to the Abermule disaster. The terrible consequences of having two passenger trains coming together on the same line and colliding, is graphically explained. Driver Jones and his fireman, on one of the engines, were killed, and 15 passengers also lost their lives on 26th January, 1921. Abermule was a small country station on the Cambrian Railways. The story of how the accident came about is complicated, and I shall not recount it here, but four members of staff at this station are mentioned as bearing some of the responsibility.

In a book called *Railway Records*, I came across the following information about driver Jones. In January 1921, driver Jones was well over 67 years of age. Why this man was still working, after the 1919 agreement on hours of duty had been reached, and major recruitment had taken place, we shall never know. Abermule was just one of the failures on the part of railway staff that had the most terrible consequences.

On my very first trip over the Wirksworth branch line, as a young fireman, the driver said to me, 'Have you got the tablet, mate?' 'Yes', I said. 'Where is it then?' asks the driver, because the cane handle has to be hung somewhere it won't fall off the engine. 'It is over the handbrake, there', I replied, '... and is it the right tablet for this section, then?' is the next question. This is only answered by opening the leather pouch fixed to the cane, which has a strap and buckle. Reading the inscription on the tablet, I say, 'Duffield Junction to Idridgehay'. 'That's right, well done', says the driver. Always after that, I made it a practice to satisfy myself that I had that authority to travel over a section of single line. It only takes a few seconds to check. So track maintenance and safe working practices all play their part. But so too does proper maintenance of the equipment, the tools of our trade.

'Royal Scot' class 4-6-0 No. 46143 *The South Staffordshire Regiment* waits to depart from Manchester Central on 21st September, 1962. By the time this photograph was taken we had been using diesels for three years, but the 'Scots' were still doing great work.

J. Marshall/Kidderminster Railway Museum

Stanier class '8' 'Princess Royal' 4-6-2 No. 46212 *Duchess of Kent* at Crewe Works in 1948. Alongside is Derby-allocated 'Black Five' class 4-6-0 No. 44839. This 'Black Five' is familiar to me, but we didn't have the Stanier Pacifics stabled at Derby.

W. Potter/Kidderminster Railway Museum

The highly-skilled engineman knew all about the maintenance of his engine. Bigger jobs of course were in the hands of the fitters, but any engineman worth his salt would know how to go about the lubrication of the engine, and part of that process was taking the trimmings out. These are found in a small box containing oil. They regulate the flow of oil to certain parts of the engine.

There were several types of worsted trimmings, or plug trimmings. I even made one up myself, for my test in 1955. I remember one occasion as a young fireman when my driver said, 'Take the trimmings out, mate'. I knew where they were, and it was easy to take them out. But what did I have to do then? I took all six of them back to the driver on the footplate. He smiled, 'No', he said, 'You leave them in the box'. He realized that he hadn't made that clear. So I took them back, and laid them upright in the box. It was, of course, absolutely vital that they were put back in the tubes before the engine went out again.

Wherever you have bearing surfaces, you must have lubrication. Driver Bill Wall, the master of brevity once asked me the question, 'How many types of lubrication on a steam engine'. He didn't wait for me to answer, instead he rattled them off like this, 'Splash, wipe, capillary, mechanical, displacement, grease'. You can't get any shorter than that.

Some years later, when I went to the Crewe North depot with an engine, I had the chance to look underneath the class '8' passenger engine, one of several stabled there. Known officially as the 'Princess' class, unofficially to some of the Crewe men as the 'Lizzies', they had two outside and two inside cylinders. I wanted to know how oiling two inside cylinders compared to our 'Patriot' class '5XPs', which had two outside and one inside cylinder. So my fireman and I descended into the pit over which the giant stood. I was astonished to find nearly every bearing was lubricated by grease. That made it much easier than our '5XPs' to prepare. Not for them the bother of setting the engine with the left-hand crank just beyond bottom dead centre. This was done to ensure that the inside little end would be inclined slightly downwards. You would draw the one cork, and fill the vessel with oil. That's after you have climbed up the back of the crank axle, to draw three corks there. Wedged up against the great crank webs, hot firebox front plate warming your back. If the engine were to move now, you would be dead. It was always a relief to come out from underneath, having also drawn the four small corks to the bogie wheels. To fill up these vessels we used the small bogie feeder.

Even worse were the class '4' passenger tank engines, which needed you to oil the inside cylinder and bogie. It was an improvement when the modern BR Standard class engines were introduced with rocking firegrates, self-cleaning smokeboxes and hopper ashpans and with no inside cylinders to oil.

Our steam engines were so well built that breakdowns, as distinct from accidents, just didn't happen. I have travelled thousands of miles on them without ever having a broken siderod or crank axle. In my early years, I could truly say they were well made, and well maintained, but not so in the later years.

But it doesn't stop there. The rest of the train may also require attention. Wagon wheels, joined by axles and the axleboxes had to be lubricated. So at one time it was directed that a goods train could not run between Derby and Wellingborough, only 60-odd miles, without a stop for examination. This took place just beyond Melton Mowbray. There our goods train would be turned down the goods line which ran for about three miles to the signal box at Brentingby. Here the oilers and greasers carried out their routine duties.

Greasing was a simple operation, a pot of grease in one hand, a metal bar with a chisel end at the other. Lift the lid of the small box attached to the wagon axle, put in a chunk of grease, and close the lid again. A simple operation, typical of a labour intensive railway system. Yet it could happen that a common user wagon had not been properly greased for several days, or even weeks, if it had been running in places where examination was not carried out on a regular basis. Then you might get a 'hot box', where the wagon axlebox starts to heat up. Usually the first indication would be a shower of sparks. If this went unnoticed, and unrectified, it would lead to axle failure, and derailment of the wagon, with serious consequences.

Part of the signalman's duties was to take a look at all the trains passing his signal box, and to take action if he saw anything amiss. So if he saw a shower of sparks from the axle of a wagon going by, he would notify the signalman at the next box down the line by the telegraph bell code: 'Stop and examine train'. If a train was running under clear signals, and suddenly the signal ahead was placed to danger, the train crew would have a good idea of what was happening.

Sometimes, the guard may have noticed that the axlebox was running hot. His action then would be to apply the hand brake in his van, then release and reapply it. Doing this several times would cause a jolting at the front of the train, attracting the attention of the driver and fireman. Even if they couldn't see anything while the train was moving, the obvious reaction would be to stop and find out the cause. Usually that meant proceeding to the next signal box, and telling the signalman that you had to stop and examine the train. A wagon with an overheated axlebox would have to be detached from the train. Back then, the great majority of the signal boxes had one or more sidings (or 'lay-bys') under their control. A lay-by was a siding that would accommodate a complete train. It was used for that purpose where there was a stretch of line with no adjoining goods lines. This applied on several stretches of the line between Burton and Birmingham. When a passenger train was due along the line, a goods train could be set aside to clear the line, under the instruction 'Back Inside' from the signalman. And when was that most likely to happen? When the train in front of you was delayed by something like a hot box. While the wagon was detatched and stabled in a siding, considerable delays could ensue. But this process ensured the safe working of the railway.

After my long years spent learning 'on the job', I had now reached the place I wanted to be, as driver in my own right. With that right came the responsibility for the safety of the passengers, and the rest of the staff of the railway that I came across on a daily basis. Of course, I was trained to the standards of the Midland Railway, over the course of a long apprenticeship. After the war, the high standards we knew then slowly went downhill, due to a lack of investment and a shortage of staff. And so we find ourselves with modern railway disasters such as those at Hatfield, Ladbroke Grove and Potters Bar.

Chapter Twenty-Nine

'Can I Cab it Mister?'

Trainspotting has been a popular hobby amongst small (and not-so-small) boys for many years. As work (and travel for pleasure) took me up and down the railways of Britain, I would see them poised by the track, mostly equipped with notebooks and pencils taking down engine numbers, later on with cameras too.

When I was young, it was unheard of and maybe I was one of the first. My mother, a town-girl, who had married into country life, would take me to Leicester occasionally. Not an easy journey, especially with a small boy in tow. There was a walk of three-quarters of a mile to the bus stop, and then a change of bus when we got to Ashby. Arriving at Leicester we would walk to Friars Causeway, a small street near to the then Great Central Railway station. My aunt Edith, she of the booming voice, would give me a penny to go to the station and watch the trains. Nobody else seemed to be watching then, and I certainly didn't have a notebook and pencil.

After a while, I would walk back to Aunt Edith's house. By that time they would have had their heart-to-heart conversation, no doubt my mother would be describing what life was like walking out from your back door when the yard was ankle deep in mud and cow manure. So very different to the paved streets of Leicester.

Later that evening my father would arrive. She would have left him a note telling him where his young wife and son were, and arriving home after a long day's work to an empty house he would have undertaken the same journey, to fetch us back. We would all return together, by bus, arriving home late at night. I never heard any arguments about this, and our normal life in the country continued. People didn't rush to the divorce courts in those days. They were like motor cars, they existed, but they were well out of the reach of ordinary working people.

Back home, with one or two other small boys, I would wait on the railway bridge near our house to see the passenger trains coming up from Tonge and Breedon station on their way to Ashby, and the goods trains going to and from New Lount. We used to wait for the smoke of the approaching train to envelope us on one side, then dash to the other side for more smoke. There was a low metal parapet and someone must have decided that it was dangerous, so a higher stone one was built. It is still there, though the trains have long gone.

What I did do with a notebook and pencil was station spotting. Once a year, the limeworks would run a special excursion train for the families of their employees. Escorted by our mother, my sister and I would try to read the names of all the stations we passed through. That kept us occupied all the way (and it's a good job we didn't want the toilet on our journey, because there wasn't one. Not on the non-corridor stock that the LMS used for excursions at the time).

We knew the local stations from our trips to watch Derby County: Melbourne, Chellaston, Peartree and Normanton, before reaching Derby. If the annual excursion was to Blackpool (as it usually was), then it was a mystery tour for us. Often we never saw Derby, because the train would go off towards the North Staffordshire Railway. Just one of the many ways you could get to Blackpool then.

Less than a mile before Stoke-on-Trent, in the area called Fenton, we would be stopped by signals. The local children would run across to the railway calling, 'Penny down, penny down'. Anyone who had a penny to spare would throw it across the line. Certainly there wouldn't be many pennies from our train.

Was there any trainspotting proper before the war, I wonder? Certainly by 1946 there was a lot of interest. At Tamworth there is an unusual arrangement of high level and low level stations. Down below, trains ran from who knows where to Rugby, Crewe, Manchester and London. Up above, on the high level, I was working as a fireman on trains from Derby to Birmingham, Gloucester and Bristol. Tamworth was a real magnet in 1946 for people taking down engine numbers, so much so that the railway company even built a metal compound for them, near to the water tank on the down line. You may recall I told you that when I was partnered with Albert Watson, he had a phobia of running out of water? Well we would stop at the water tank, although we didn't really need to, so the boys in the compound would see me climb up on the tender to operate the chain which supplied the water to fill the tank.

After 1948, I personally didn't see any trainspotters for a few years, as a great deal of my firing turns were on goods trains, during the hours of darkness, but once I was passed for driving, I would see more of them at Derby station. I was working on the carriage shunting engines, and at either end of the station there would be a gang of boys studying the class '2' passenger engines. Here on occasion, a few of the boys would get lucky.

On one occasion in 1956 I was driving an engine on the carriage shunt, and we were stationary on No. 4 platform, Derby station. On weekdays, we would never allow youngsters to climb on the footplate. It was completely against rules and regulations. But this was a Saturday afternoon, and there were no management people watching. The station supervisors wouldn't mind, it would keep the boys occupied. So when two of them approached the engine, asking 'Can we cab it, Mister?', I replied, 'Alright'.

Well of course more boys appeared from further down the platform. We soon had about a dozen in the cab, staring with rapt attention at the steam pressure and vacuum gauges. They were well behaved, and didn't even ask any questions – that was the magic of steam, they were just spellbound. I can only recall a couple of occasions when I allowed this to happen.

In October 1959, I started work on diesel traction. For the next six years, there is a mix of steam and diesel engines recorded in my own well-thumbed little diaries, in which I recorded the day to day details of my working life. Right up the end of 1965 I was still recording steam engines. By then my days on main line workings were dwindling down.

Diesels too had their devotees. In the spring of 1963, when I was driving a diesel-multiple-unit over the Burton to Leicester line, there were a few schoolchildren on board bound for Desford. Every day, one of the boys would come up to the door which separates the driver from the passengers, and stand with his nose pressed up to the glass, watching the dials that showed our speed between the stations, and the engine rev-counter. Every day, Monday to Friday, he was there. I didn't expect to see him one Saturday, but there he was, when we left Leicester.

It being a quiet Saturday afternoon, there were no passengers on the first-class seats next to the driving cab. So I slid the door between us to one side, and he stood in the doorway, watching everything I did. No words passed between us, and he got off at his usual station. Now, well over 40 years later, I wonder did that young boy seek a career on British Rail? Maybe he is driving a train now himself?

Although I was not the first trainspotter, I have books full of engine numbers. There is one significant difference. They represent the years during which I cleaned, fired and drove the engines that you will find in the trainspotter's notebooks. But I never had to ask, 'Can I cab it, Mister?'

The magic of steam – a crowd of trainspotters are on the bridge over the River Derwent watching, as the double-headed down 'Devonian' leaves Derby Midland station on 5th August, 1958. The train is piloted by '2P' class 4-4-0 No. 40552 and the train engine is 'Black Five' 4-6-0 No. 44813. *P.J. Lynch/Kidderminster Railway Museum*

Railway enthusiasts witness a trial run of the all-first class Midland Pullman diesel service at Derby on 9th June, 1960. The Midland Pullman service was introduced the following month. I did once drive the Midland Pullman from Trent to Derby, conducting Stanley Bagguley.

V.R. Webster/Kidderminster Railway Museum

A view from the footbridge at Derby station of Fairburn class '4' 2-6-4T No. 42174 on west end carriage shunt duty. A diesel-multiple-unit stands in the platform in the background.

P. Riley/Kidderminster Railway Museum

Chapter Thirty

The Beeching Years

I have made mention of the fact that 1955 was a pivotal year for me. Well, not only me, as it turned out: the entire British railway system as well. It was on 25th January of that year that Sir Brian Robertson, Chairman of the British Transport Commission, announced the Modernisation Plan for railways. This would lead to the death sentence for over 18,000 steam locomotives.

Later that year, we had a very damaging industrial dispute. Almost the entire membership of ASLEF were out on strike for 17 days. Never mind the causes, it's the consequences that concern us here. Large numbers of passengers and huge amounts of goods traffic left the railways never to return. That was a very expensive lesson. But it had to be learned - by all of us.

There was also a great debate being carried on as to whether the main passenger routes should be electrified or whether diesel locomotives should take over. Many people were consulted; many people had their say. To the best of my knowledge, the number of working footplatemen who were invited to give their views totalled none. It was my strongly-held opinion at the time, as I saw various classes of diesel locomotives coming out on test, that a lot of unnecessary money was being spent. Nothing new there, then.

If public money had not been available, I just do not believe that we would have had two competing diesel locomotive classes hauling express passenger trains over British Railways' lines. Just one - either our Sulzer engines or the English Electrics of the former Western Division - would have been fine. It's just common sense.

There are two points to make. The first is that steam was phased out far too quickly. It should have been kept going until one company's main line diesels were available in sufficient numbers. The second point is that they had diesel main line locomotives over BR lines from 1947 onwards. I know because they were built in Derby. So the people responsible for the Modernisation Plan (I'm not sure it deserves its capital letters) had already had eight years' experience and should have been able to manage all the passenger and goods services with just two types - one for all heavy trains and one for local passenger services.

What was needed above all was a firm directive from the Ministry of Transport to BR telling them to decide between diesels and electrification and to avoid the hotchpotch of varying designs.

If that wasn't what was needed, then why, in 1958, did Parliament suddenly discover the Modernisation Plan was going to cost a lot of money, and that something must be done to check this runaway expenditure?

They faced up to the problem and came up with a dramatic and completely innovative solution - they appointed another committee. With the proliferation of committees came a matching growth in our old friends - the 'fact-finding missions to other countries' - otherwise known as 'jollies'. Whether those MPs who went on the trips had some working experience of railways I don't know. There have never been enough working men and women in the House of

Mineral and freight trains, as shown here, were the revenue earners for all the main line railway companies. Hughes/Fowler 'Crab' 2-6-0 No. 42798 approaches Derby North Junction with a lengthy freight bound for Chaddesden on 31st March, 1962.

P.J. Lynch/Kidderminster Railway Museum

'3F' class 0-6-0 No. 43254 at Derby South Junction working a trip freight from Chaddesden to St Mary's on 4th June, 1962. The signal box in the distance, controlled movements into Chaddesden sidings. *P.J. Lynch/Kidderminster Railway Museum*

Commons. Some time in the 1950s, there was one general election when the Labour Party made just one gain from the Conservatives. That MP was Archie Manuel, a Scottish engine driver and a member of ASLEF. He wasn't on the union's parliamentary panel like one or two others who weren't elected. So Archie was our only representative in Parliament. Considering that Jack Bromley, ASLEF's General Secretary at the time, became an MP in 1924, it took far too long for footplatemen to recognise that you didn't get far without representation. That delay has cost us dear.

The new committee set up by Parliament was chaired by Sir Ivan Stedeford. I have no idea who most of the members were, but I do remember one. He was called Dr Beeching and he was the research director of ICI. He was reported as impressing the others with his grasp of railway finance. In due course, the report was sent to Parliament. But it was never published.

It soon became known that someone was to take over as Chairman of the BTC with a remit to drastically overhaul British Railways. Alarm bells sounded. For around 18 months before Dr Beeching's appointment, railway managers knew that the new Chairman would ruthlessly cut out railway passengers services which did not make a profit, and - this is the nub - *not* to examine how they might be made profitable.

With this knowledge, the managers behaved in the time-honoured way of managers everywhere. They created a buffer zone by way of a lot of new salaried positions. I could only keep in touch with the vacancy lists open to wages grades. What was happening higher up was anyone's guess. I remember going to Canklow shed at the time and seeing a vacancy list of immense length and complexity. The empire-builders were on the move.

There was nothing new in BR appointing more chiefs. We had seen that happen after nationalization. Around 1959, they just redoubled their efforts. Knowing that the new Chairman would cut out half the salaried grades, they thought that if they doubled the numbers immediately, they would just be back where they were once the cuts were made. Simple and very effective arithmetic. So, there was a lot wrong with the railways. There was a need for a remedy. But Dr Beeching was not the cure, he aggravated the disease.

There were many things which he could not have known about when he was Chairman of the British Railways Board. Like most bosses, he was only as good as the people who fed him information. But he must be judged by one question - did he manage to redefine the fortunes of the railway system? The answer must be 'No'. Because if he did, then why did another Conservative government - 30 years later - decide to privatize the railways. The fact that they made such a mess of it is incidental. The decision to do it betrayed the mistakes of an earlier generation. The winners - of course - were the lawyers and the accountants. They always are.

Dr Beeching had many helpers who gave him the information on which he based his decisions as to which lines to close. The one that I am most concerned with is the passenger service between Burton and Leicester. I was not alone in thinking that there was something wrong about this particular closure. We always suspected some kind of 'dirty tricks' campaign. On and off, over the eight years from 1955 to 1963, I worked many passenger services over the line

Contrasts in motive power in these two views of Derby from 1962. *Above:* English Electric type '4' 1Co-Co-1 No. D221 *Ivernia* is working a St Pancras-Manchester service on 20th July. This train is coming in on the main line from Chaddesden. Crewe was being electrified at this time, so the London to Manchester trains were being diverted through Derby. I did some conducting of these trains. *Below:* On 15th August, 1962 Fowler '4P' class 2-6-4T No. 42314 arrives at Derby with the 5.12 pm service from Buxton. Only a few Derby drivers signed for Buxton. I had a fair few trips over that line. *(Both) P.J. Lynch/Kidderminster Railway Museum*

and I witnessed at first hand its revenue-earning potential. On Whit Monday, 1957 I took 10 coaches from Derby and filled them all with passengers at Gresley and Moira. A little later that morning, Ivan Marlow took another 10 coaches to those two stations and they were also fully loaded. The occasion was a Sunday School day out to Blackpool. The other two stations on the line which could fill special trains were Woodville and Swadlincote. A station master on that line used his initiative to ask for a Saturday football special. He got it and he filled it.

One Sunday morning, I went up to Swadlincote with a special train, loading from there to Skegness. It was fairly late around 11.30 am. There were not all that many people waiting and I remarked on that to a porter. 'Well', he answered, 'You are the third excursion today'. Certainly, in the 1950s, people throughout Derbyshire and Leicestershire were more than willing to travel by train.

Of course, the real test is not the weekend specials but the regular services. Derby men worked the 7.47 am Derby-Burton-Leicester on weekdays and the first morning service the other way – always well filled, those trains were.

The Sunday evening service, 8.50 pm Leicester to Burton was unusual in that a lot of people from Coalville and some other stations had gone to Leicester by bus, there being no train service to get them there, but they all wanted to come back by train even though it was just a single fare, significant, but overlooked of course.

When diesel-multiple-units came to Derby, a great opportunity to increase the Sunday morning service was simply thrown away. Probably because the decision to close the branch on Sundays had already been taken. The advantage of this form of traction is that you can have a quick turn-round at any station where a crossover road from up to down platform lines is available and the unit can be driven from either end. About three weeks after those dmus started regular workings from Derby, the Sunday services were suddenly withdrawn. One service we still worked was the 6.15 pm train Monday to Friday, Leicester-Burton. In the winter of 1962, there were some weeks of pretty severe weather which meant that, on some occasions, steam traction replaced the railcars. My diary entry for the week of 17th-22nd December reads, 'Steam traction on 6.15 pm ex-Leicester, every day except Thursday'. The previous train, the 5.45, did not run at all.

Consider – my 6.15 was always well loaded, as was the 5.45 when it ran. It isn't very comfortable for the passengers for six coaches to be crammed into three, and having to wait half an hour on a freezing platform at Leicester does not encourage people to complain much when they are told that the service is going to finish altogether. They just shrug their shoulders and say, 'Oh, well, they've messed us about, let's just go by car or bus', and these were the very people whose support the railways so badly needed.

It is one thing to recommend line closures for alleged economic reasons - 'This line doesn't pay', but it's quite another when you provide a poor service so that your customers walk away and then you say, 'This line doesn't pay'.

For many years, people wishing to travel betweem Manchester and London had a choice. From Manchester London Road to Euston, the old LNWR route,

Barrow-on-Soar & Quorn station in May 1963, looking north. A diesel-multiple-unit stands in the platform as it is passed by an unidentified Stanier engine on a freight train.

Roy F. Burrows/Midland Collection Trust/Kidderminster Railway Museum

Engines around the turntable at Derby shed on 9th December, 1962. *From left to right*: Ivatt 2-6-0s No. 46497 and 46495 and '3F' class 0-6-0 No. 43647. In that week I was diesel marshalling, but we still had plenty of steam work. *F.G. Wood/Kidderminster Railway Museum*

or from Manchester Central, via Derby and Leicester to St. Pancras, through the Peak National Park. I can just imagine the people hatching these plans. It would have been too obvious to just scrap the Manchester-London via the Peak route. So, to start with, they ran expresses from Manchester Central which terminated at Derby; then they arranged the timetable so that passengers from the north-west would have to wait around at Derby for over an hour if they wanted to carry on to London.

It is a sad, sad story. Jobs have been lost, communities have been annihilated and the people of this country have been deprived of a vital transport (and social) service. Yet, despite all this, people are using the railway system that remains in ever-increasing numbers. If they are ever going to get services comparable to what they deserve - and which are enjoyed by rail travellers in many other countries - many changes will have to be made. Starting at the top. So, as I reached the top of my profession, the railways had started on a slow decline.

So we reach the 'Swinging Sixties'. Within the next few years would come the Beatles, free-love, long hair and hippies. None of which would have much effect on my life. You might think that having reached the pinnacle that I had been striving to attain for almost 20 years, my working life would become easier. More time for leisure perhaps, a time to enjoy the fruits of my labours. You would not be more wrong. Due in part to my extensive road card, and in part to the changes in the links I have already described, my life at work was as hard, if not harder, than it had ever been.

In the late 1950s, June and I finally moved into a home of our own, a small rented terraced house in Melbourne. We were blessed with a son, and then a couple of years later a daughter. Then we took the plunge and bought a house of our own. So family was, as ever, an important part of my life.

But my family life was to prove a little unorthodox. Signing on in the early hours of the morning, or finishing late at night, meant that I was often in bed during the daylight hours. The children grew up to learn to play quietly, as Dad was asleep. Still, there were some small compensations to this strange way of life. Time off during daylight hours meant that I could tend the allotment at a time when others might be at the office or the factory, and there were days when I would walk with the children to and from school when other fathers were at their work.

A bonus available to those working on the railway was the provision of free travel for themselves and their family. So our annual holidays were taken at such far flung places as the Isle of Wight, or Scarborough, when many local families only ventured as far as Skegness.

Did I enjoy the same sort of working relationship with a fireman as I had experienced myself when I had been firing? No, those days were disappearing, as diesels came to be used more and more. The steam locomotives I had worked on since before the war were one by one taken out of service, and in the main, sold for scrap. There were very few far-sighted individuals and organizations that would foresee the popularity in future years of the 'Heritage' steam railways, and preserve locomotives and rolling stock for such use. The footplatemen who had worked them in the main embraced the cleaner working conditions, and better protection from the weather that the new diesels offered.

It is indeed very satisfying in relation to main line working when engine, driver and fireman are working well together. Certainly, the vast majority of my driving turns, until single manning commenced, were like that. Lack of speedy promotion meant that many of the firemen who were paired up with me were experienced men. I was able to get on with my work while they got on with theirs.

Towards the end of 1965 when I came out of the spare link, and soon afterwards was asked to opt either to continue in the main line links, or transfer to a local link. It was less money, but better shifts, so that is what I decided to do. I did write to the superintendent, and to the LDC representatives, expressing concern that anyone should have to make a final decision about their future duties without the option of a review later. I said that I had made my decision, and would have to abide by it. Of course, no-one answered my submission.

My old friend Wilf Ward also opted for the local link, and remained there until retirement. He and Arthur Wharam were the two men left over when redundancy payments finished. I would have been in the same position myself, unable to take redundancy and finish my working life before the normal retirement age, if I had not followed a different path at the end of my railway career, as you will see in the next chapter.

'Jubilee' class 4-6-0 No. 45612 *Jamaica* passes through Water Orton with the 10.10 am Birmingham New Street to Derby Midland service on 1st February, 1964. By this time a lot of passenger trains were diesel-hauled. In this photograph, we see a steam locomotive working a stopping train, probably standing in for a dmu.

J. Wood/Kidderminster Railway Museum

Chapter Thirty-One

End of the Line

Pushing 50, it was a time for taking stock, and with me, the ageing process corresponded with huge changes in the world of the railways. During my years cleaning and firing steam engines, the way ahead always seemed clear. It wasn't like that any more. As motive power depots up and down the land closed or retracted, many train crew workers were affected: What did it all mean for me?

Smaller depots were the first to be affected. Market Harborough, Annesley, St Boswell's in the Scottish border country. That sounds too far away to have any effect but, if you had to move your home anyway, why not come to a big depot in the Midlands or London where redundancy didn't seem inevitable.

What really affected my future on the footplate were the closures nearer home. Derby Friargate, Rowsley and, finally, Burton-on-Trent. From all of these, men came to Derby No. 4 shed, and a number of them had seniority dates earlier than mine; which meant that they would go into the main line links before I did.

There was no resentment against the men who had to move or drop out of railway work altogether. When they had joined the service, no-one could possibly foresee what would happen 30 years down the line. For me, the signposts had all pointed in one direction - for 20 years at least. Now there were other factors to consider. After years in the main line goods links, I knew all about unsocial hours of duty. Most of the goods trains ran late evening or early morning. Main line goods working didn't appeal to me at all. But the chance of getting into the two top passenger links receded with every depot closure and the chance of being a footplate inspector on steam engines had disappeared with the advent of main line diesels.

Changes in working practices can have good effects as well as bad ones. So can changes in health. And it was the latter that finally decided my future. If I was going to have a future at all, and that was thrown into doubt when I was struck by a mystery illness.

One Sunday morning, I had signed on at 8 am. I had already moved into the local link, so I wasn't going out on a main line turn. By 4 o'clock that afternoon, it was obvious to me that something was very seriously amiss. I had joint pains. Something that had never afflicted me before. I reported sick on that Sunday afternoon and by Monday morning I was laid up in bed. I remember the week that followed very well because it involved two doctors and a specialist, and a very awkward patient. My GP at the time actually attained a most unusual distinction for a medical man some years afterwards. He served a six months' sentence in one of Her Majesty's prisons, and came out again to resume his practice because it had all been to do with money - not medicine.

He had managed to lose a couple of patients while he was in Melbourne. Two meanings to 'lose' in this context. One is when a person decided they want another doctor. The other is more ... terminal. I was going to be in one or other of these categories because I knew there was something unusual about my illness. He didn't.

Lying there in bed at home, I had a severe pain in my right knee and, for the rest of the week, I could only get out of bed to hobble as far as the toilet. Having told the doctor exactly how poorly I felt, he gave it as his opinion that I had a touch of 'flu and would soon get better. He then went downstairs and told June the same thing. I had had colds, 'flu and bronchitis a few times in my life and I knew that this was something different, and if he wasn't going to do anything about it, I would have to take action myself. So, when he came back on Tuesday, I was ready for him.

He restated his influenza theory and I made it plain how I felt. From what I could see, I wasn't any good to him and he wasn't any good to me. So I wanted a second opinion. That set him back a bit. 'Well', he said, 'I can get you a second opinion if you want but it might take a month or six weeks'. Keeping my opinion that I might be dead in a month or six weeks strictly to myself, I told him to go ahead. He came again on Wednesday, with a message that perked me up. He had arranged for me to be seen by a Dr Matthews from the Derby Royal Infirmary, who would call two days later. 'Thank you', I replied, 'You couldn't have done better for me'.

Now there was another problem – I no longer had a GP. At which point June made her own decision, 'I'll go and see Dr Boardman' (her doctor), she said, and that proved to be the right approach. 'Good gracious', he said. 'We can't have the chap without a doctor'. It was that easy, just a matter of getting registered and that was the first step on my road to recovery which was just as well as the pain in my joints was now moving at will from right knee to right ankle, to left ankle to left knee. Four places in four days. So what next?

What next was five o'clock on the Friday afternoon; suddenly the pain vanished. I think it must have been because I now had faith that help was on its way. At about a quarter to seven, Dr Matthews showed up and asked a lot of questions about childhood illnesses, and I told him how I used to catch cold by going out in an open-necked shirt.

After about half an hour of this, with me wondering where it was getting us - he suddenly said, 'I can help you [pause] - you have poly-arthritis. It's an allergy arthritis and it goes right back to your childhood illnesses. Who is your doctor? So I told him that my doctor was now Dr Boardman.

'Right', he said. 'I am going to give you an injection of cortisone now', which he did, in my thigh. Then he made out a prescription for cortisone tablets, starting on 10 a day and coming down to one. I was to go and see him again in 10 days time but he assured me that I would be fine. I already knew that. It's a matter of faith. Later, I was to find out that H.L. Matthews was one of the top men in the country on the diagnosis of this kind of illness. He had, in fact, treated my sister for an allergy, which turned out to be dust from poultry feathers. So, off I went to the the Royal Infirmary 10 days later. I had lost half a stone in weight and all the colour had gone from my face, but he was pleased enough with my condition and so was I. I asked him about recurrence. 'Possible', he said. 'But not very likely'. Two years later, when I developed Menieres disease, I would have liked to have seen him again but it wasn't possible because the diagnosis was too straightforward.

As recently as 1997, I had joint pains again but this time it was due to a partially slipped disc. There was no treatment prescribed so I got a book about herbal remedies out of the library and, by the same divine providence which has worked in my favour quite a few times, found a remedy - Kordels celery plus 2000. I mentioned this once on the radio and the switchboard was swamped with enquiries. So I had to put out a health warning the next day saying that no-one should take it without consulting their GP first. It could be dangerous for some people to take tablets on the advice of a layman. Medical ethics, again, but this time, they made sense.

So, it was the combination of a changing world and my own health that led me to opt out of main line work in 1967. The options were either to continue on the shifts which I had worked for nearly 30 years, with a preponderance of unsocial hours work, or take the other chance of going on to local work. I went for the latter. There would be less money because there was no overtime working, but money wasn't the over-riding factor.

For some years, I had been applying for some of the supervisory jobs that were being advertised. I had never got as far as an interview. Maybe my time as a staff representative on the LDC was working against me. It wasn't a job you could do without ruffling a few feathers and I was a skilled ruffler.

There was, however, one other avenue open to me. If I didn't take it now, I could forget all about a salaried position. That was to apply for a job as deputy running foreman. They were the cover for the outside foreman during sickness or holidays. The main man was the running shift foreman. His No. 2 dealt with the allocation of the men to the engines and the engines to the men. The times, they were a-changing. So it was time for me to change direction as well.

Going from the workers' to the management side just wasn't a problem for me. I had seen far too much of 'them and us' attitudes to think that this apparent gulf was a good thing for anyone - for the unions, for the people they represented, for the managers themselves or for the efficient running of the railway. So I stepped across the threshold of my new life with enthusiasm, vigour, fresh ideas; and the confidence of someone who had been there and done it. Of someone who had worked faithfully and well at that most challenging and rewarding of jobs - a footplate man.

Midland Mainline were kind enough to provide a seat in the cab for me on 13th September, 2007, the occasion of the 70th anniversary of my starting work on the railway, as I travelled from Derby to St Pancras. I was treated to a tour of the refurbished station, before travelling back to Derby in the cab of their new Meridian train. What a marvellous day out! *Derby Evening Telegraph*

Epilogue

Safety on the Railway

The most important aspect of safety in railway operations was how every one of us was dependent on others. We, at the front end, had cause every day of our working lives, to be grateful for the efforts of others.

First off, the men who built the great locomotives we worked. In the railway workshops at Derby and Crewe. Their efforts produced machines which ran for millions of miles with remarkably few breakdowns. Then we must thank all the people who kept them working. The fitting staff who, I can remember, used to have their own nameplates on the engines they were working on, and the boiler washers, tube cleaners, shed men – all played their part in keeping the great wheels turning.

The lines over which we worked were maintained by the platelaying gangs. Every weekday, the ganger walked through his section checking for loose keys. They are the wooden blocks that keep the rails fast within the chairs bolted to the sleepers.

On the passenger stations, the carriage and wagon examiners, and the men who looked after them on the railway all played their part in maintaining safety standards.

Goods and passenger guards were the grades most concerned with train movements along with the footplate crews and signalmen. There were others connected with the signalling system, fog-signalmen, signal and telegraph linesmen.

Passenger guards also had responsibilities in the event of an accident involving their trains.

So many pieces in this jigsaw; but they did fit together and the final picture was complete and interlocking and, over-arching everything else, the whole was somehow far greater than the sum of its parts.

So that has been my aim. To show how safe working of trains really meant just that at a time when there were many more miles of track and many more trains running than there are today and when there were two men at the front of the train. Of course, we had to put our trust in a lot of other railway staff. Most of all, driver and fireman trusted each other. In those days as well, the managers knew their responsibilities and understood whether their men were in the right or in the wrong. Accidents were few and far between - but incidents there were aplenty.

Two references were required to even gain employment as an engine cleaner, two men on the footplate, two ways of doing things - right and wrong. Human fallibility is always there. Nobody gets it right all of the time. But there was one rule which everyone understood. The safety of the travelling public must be our paramount concern. At all times in all circumstances. Those are the basic reasons for the claim I made at the beginning of this page. It remains my contention that by 1937, when I joined the LMS the safe working of trains had reached the highest level.

Appendix

The Midland Compounds

We had a lot of experience with the Midland Compounds at Derby. In 1944 there were eight of them allocated to No. 4 shed, and in 1950 there were ten. They were originally designed by S.W. Johnson in the early 20th century, a later batch were designed by R.M. Deeley. Many, but not all, were built at Derby.

Norman McKillop started work on the North British Railway in 1910. He was paid 10s. a week for a 12-hour shift. He doesn't say how old he was when he joined the railway, or when he became a fireman, and later, a driver. I would expect that he became a driver in the 1920s, after ASLEF had won the eight-hour day. He wrote articles about locomotives in ASLEF's monthly journal, under the pen-name 'Toram Beg'. He was the obvious choice to write the union's second history, *The Lighted Flame*, which was published in 1950.

I have brought him into my story, because of what he said about the Midland Compound, 'Probably the best welcome given to the "foreigner" on the new LMS was handed out to the Midland Compounds. It is quite true to say that I have never heard a disparaging word said about this remarkable type. I have marvelled at their smoothness. They ran like greased silk, with unbelievable loads for the size of the engine'.

He mentions the Compound as being a 'foreigner', because in 1923, no less than 125 separate railways were combined into the four Grouping companies. That meant that a lot of drivers were handling engines they were not accustomed to. Some footplatemen didn't handle the Compounds very well when they were first introduced to them. That is because they worked them on what we called the 'Simple Engine'. This meant that only two low pressure cylinders are being used, because they only opened the regulator half-way. That was alright on a lot of locomotives, and I ran thousands of miles as a fireman and driver on the other Midland engines with the regulator not fully open. But the Compound was different. You had to start away on simple engine, with the regulator half open, and as soon

We end as we began, with this great engine – on 13th August, 1959 I worked Compound No. 1000 on its first loaded run after refurbishment at Derby locomotive works. Derby station was busy with onlookers and the BBC programme 'Blue Peter' came to film the occasion. *R.J. Buckley*

Midland Compound 4-4-0 No. 1000 at Knighton (Leicester). I am standing next to the locomotive's cab with Mr Orchard (of the Traffic Department), having worked the train of 12 carriages on 13th May, 1959. We have propelled the train round from the London to the Burton line, and are now facing the right way to return to Derby. *Author's Collection*

as you have some speed, pull the regulator right across. This makes use of the high-pressure cylinder, situated between the main frames. Unlike other types, steam doesn't make its way to exhaust after leaving the high pressure cylinder. Instead, it is diverted to two low pressure cylinders, one on each side of the main frames. It does further work there, before escaping to the atmosphere, via the blast pipe and chimney.

The basic concept of using steam twice, instead of once, made them, I think, the most economical engines ever built. It was done through the regulator valve in the steam dome. Crank settings were at 90º for the two lower pressure cylinders, the high pressure one bisected the obtuse angle. If this class had been given a bigger boiler, it is possible that the class '5' engines designed by William Stanier for passenger work would not have been needed. Stanier was brought in from the Great Western Railway to stop the 'in fighting' between the ex-MR and ex-LNWR men after Grouping in 1923.

Although Norman McKillop was a driver for longer than I was, I had more to do with Compounds than he did. Until the Stanier engines came in, the Compounds, built after 1900, were the biggest engines Derby men worked passenger trains with. Before that, it was the class '2P' and later '3P', which worked to London, Bristol, Manchester, Leeds and other places from Derby. Before most of our Compounds were consigned to the scrapheap, I had a number of trips with them. I remember working one back from Birmingham on a stopping passenger train. I was able to shut off steam, and coast into stations. They ran better than other engines on the level.

We do, of course, still have the Midland Compound (liveried as No. 1000) preserved in the National Railway Museum at York. On 13th August, 1959, I took this particular engine and a train to Leicester and back. That was her first loaded run after being turned out from Derby locomotive works, after a full overhaul and repaint. On the very next trip it took after this, from Birmingham to York, the engine broke down, on the return trip. The cause of this breakdown was very simple. There was a difference between the Midland Compound and the more modern locomotives. The modern engines had mechanical lubricators, this overhauled older engine had no such refinements. As a young fireman, I had seen the old drivers take every opportunity to go round with the oilcan - a classic Midland Railway practice. Of course, this was not part of the modern working procedure by 1959, and the old engine broke down with a hot axlebox at Tamworth, due to lack of lubrication.

I have been to see my old girl several times in the railway museum at York. She sits amongst the other classic early and modern engines, but for me she will always be the star.